MADE E-Z™ GUIDES

Owning a No-Cash-Down Business

Arnold S. Goldstein, J.D., Ph.D.

Made E-Z

Owning a No-Cash-Down-Business Made E-Z™

Printed in the United States of America
MADE E-Z PRODUCTS
384 South Military Trail
Deerfield Beach, FL 33442
Tel. 954-480-8933
Fax 954-480-8906
http://www.MadeE-Z.com

3 4 5 6 7 8 9 10

This publication is designed to provide accurate and authoritative information in regard to subject matter covered. It is sold with the understanding that neither the publisher nor author is engaged in rendering legal, accounting, or other professional services. If legal advice or other expert assistance is required, the services of a competent professional should be sought. From: *A Declaration of Principles jointly adopted by a Committee of the American Bar Association and a Committee of Publishers.*

Owning a No-Cash-Down Business Made E-Z™
Arnold S. Goldstein, J.D., Ph.D.

Limited warranty and disclaimer

Copyright Notice

Table of contents

Introduction to Owning A No-Cash-Down Business Made E-Z™

Within the next year more than 25 million businesses will change ownership, and countless thousands will open their doors for the first time.

You've dreamed about shedding your treadmill job and running your own business, but you may have hesitated because you lacked money. Hesitate no longer!

Becoming a successful operator of your own business does not require capital, personal assets, or a strong credit background. Whether you operate a small retail outlet, a service business, or even a large manufacturing firm, all you need is strong ambition and the know-how this book presents on no-cash-down business takeovers and startups.

You will learn from actual cases the step-by-step process of taking over or starting up any type of business without cash. You can soon be your own boss, expand your wealth, and pyramid even the smallest startup into a multimillion-dollar enterprise. It is easier than you think.

You will profit from numerous real-life examples, such as my friend Walter's experience. For 12 years he worked as a textile salesman. One day while casually reading the classified ads, he noticed a men's clothing store for sale. He had dreamed of running such a business but lacked the cash he thought he needed to buy it. Then he discovered the keys to the no-cash-down takeover. What Walter lacked in cash he made up for in determination and good old-fashioned common sense. Applying the techniques in this book, Walter soon owned his dream business. Since then he has expanded to seven stores with more to come. He now has plenty of cash to spend, but insists he will expand just as he started—with no cash down.

Or take the case of Paula, recently divorced with two children to support. She aspired to being her own boss so she could build an enjoyable lifestyle. Her talent was art. She went to work and opened an art gallery, persuading local artists to display their works on consignment. Knowing the value of no cash down, she talked the landlord into deferring the first month's rent, then she financed the electricity deposit through a small personal loan. Today Paula owns one of the biggest art galleries in her city and has expanded to selling and leasing paintings to corporate clients. Paula is certainly on her way to the wealth she wants.

Yes, Walter and Paula are just two of the many thousands of people who have successfully applied no-cash-down techniques. No cash down is no mere theory or academic possibility, but rather a tried and true game plan I have seen work time and again.

As you go through this book you will see:

- The 4 "key elements" in every no-cash-down deal
- 7 ways a business can generate its own down payment
- 15 methods for turning "hidden business assets" into immediate cash
- 5 little known "takeover" secrets
- 8 sticky situations you want to avoid

Where are the no-cash-down deals? Where do you look for them and how do you approach them? Not only do I answer these questions, I show you practical and proven steps for evaluating the takeover, developing and implementing a purchase strategy, and persuading even the most astute seller. You'll be amazed to learn how you can outfox potential buyers who have money to spend.

Can you afford to wait? Your job won't produce the wealth or financial independence you want. You can only achieve this in your own business. If you had read this book one year ago, how much wealthier might you be today? How many dollars would you have made for yourself instead of for your boss?

When you finish this book you will know:

- How to buy a business for a fraction of its worth and immediately generate wealth
- How to convince others to invest in you
- How the no-cash-down deal can put thousands of dollars in your pocket quickly and with no risk to you
- How to sell the seller your terms
- How to pyramid your first no-cash-down deal into other and more profitable ones

Don't let another year slip away. Invest just a few hours now and you will learn all you need to know to get into any successful business with no-cash-down.

Arnold S. Goldstein, Ph.D.

1

Profitable business for sale: No money down

Chapter 1

Profitable business for sale: No money down

What you'll find in this chapter:

- Creating a no-cash-down offer
- Choosing the right business to buy
- Educating the seller
- Learning to be flexible
- Avoiding procrastination

A sales clerk . . . a personnel manager . . . a retired airline pilot . . . an unemployed schoolteacher . . . an engineer . . . All these people had something in common. They wanted off the treadmill of working for others and dreamed of owning their own businesses—businesses that could generate opportunity, financial independence, and self-satisfaction. But they had something else in common—no cash for a down payment.

The sales clerk now owns a flourishing stationery and office supply store and earns three times his former salary; the personnel manager is still in personnel work but now owns a highly successful franchised personnel agency. The airline pilot is grounded but off and running with a mobile electronic aviation equipment repair shop that services several local airports. Last year his company grossed over $1 million; next year he plans to expand aggressively. Hilda, the unemployed schoolteacher, for 24 years taught for a school system that didn't offer tenure. With tax cutbacks hitting the community, Hilda was one of the first to receive the pink slip. Without missing a beat, Hilda kept on teaching, at her own lucrative speed-reading institute. The engineer, however, stars in this story. Ken was a high-powered electrical engineer earning $100,000 a year, who after 20 years on the job called it quits. Though some of his friends said he suffered a midlife crisis, I knew it was just that his entrepreneurial instincts had gotten the better of him. He had an idea. After developing a line of private label natural cosmetics and opening several cosmetic boutiques in shopping malls, Ken built an empire of 23 cosmetics shops, with 35 more franchised. From engineer to cosmetic king! Like the others, Ken did it with no cash down.

But they never say "No-cash-down"

You're a skeptic. You've read this far but you just don't believe there are good, solid, profitable businesses you can buy with no money down. That's understandable, but I'd like to explode the myth that it takes money to get into business.

First I want you to accept a little challenge. Put down this book for a moment and pick up your local newspaper. That's right, pick up the newspaper from any city and turn to the Business Opportunity section. Scan the listings. There you'll see just about every type of business offered, from accounting franchises to zipper manufacturers. The ads describe the business, its sales, and perhaps even the price. Read carefully. Do you see any that say "no-cash-down"? Of course not. And I bet you never will. Over the past 20 years I have systematically read the Business Opportunity Section of the Sunday edition of the *Boston Globe* and have never seen an ad that said "no cash down." Let's do some quick arithmetic. Since the *Globe* lists about 500 businesses for sale every Sunday, I have read more than 500,000 ads over the past 20 years. Of those 500,000 businesses, not one was advertised on a no-cash-down basis.

No wonder you're skeptical. You should be, because no cash down goes contrary to your experience. You've never heard of a friend, relative, or colleague benefiting from a no-cash-down deal, and even if you have taken a hundred business courses you've heard no professor explain how to get into business without cash. Will you accept another challenge from me? Walk into a business brokerage office and tell them you are looking for a business but have no cash for a down payment. I once conducted that little experiment myself. One morning I discarded my lawyer-like business suit and briefcase for a pair of slacks and sport shirt. Playing the role of a typical business-seeker I walked into five of the leading business brokers in the Boston area. I told them I had just completed a 20-year Army hitch, took early retirement, and wanted a small retail business. I would be interested in just about any type of retail business anywhere in Eastern Massachusetts. My one problem? I had no cash to put down.

The first broker literally laughed me out of his office. The others were somewhat more courteous but nevertheless escorted me to the door after telling me that all their listings required a down payment. And so it goes. Sellers want to sell and buyers want to buy, but few know how to swing the no-cash-down deal.

Don't let this discourage you. Soon you will learn not to take the Business Opportunity ads at face value and you will know how to convert many attractive situations to no-cash-down terms, So what's the catch? If sellers are really willing to accept terms with no cash down, why don't they say so? Simply, sellers follow convention and do not know how to accomplish their own objectives any other way.

> **note**
> The myth that it takes cash to get into business collapses when you show the seller how to accomplish all his or her objectives without parting with a dime.

Down payment required—or, for amateurs only

Try this little test. Let's assume you are anxious to buy a thriving health and beauty aids store in your hometown. You approach the seller and she tells you her price is $60,000 with $15,000 down. She will accept the $45,000 balance over five years. There's one problem: The $15,000 down payment, is $15,000 more than you have. How would you handle it?

Should you take the easy way out? You can tell the seller or the broker that you have no cash, at which point he or she will say, "That's too bad" and show you the door. Or, you can use the techniques in this book.

William V. solved the problem. He asked the seller to estimate his accounts payable due creditors. The seller quoted $7,000 to $8,000, to be paid by the seller at the time of closing. Turning to the broker, William asked him what commission he would make on the deal. The broker replied, "the standard 10 percent or $6,000." Eight thousand dollars to creditors plus a $6,000 commission added up to $14,000, or almost exactly the advertised down payment. Therefore, William reasoned that the seller was willing to walk away from the closing with no cash, but only a $45,000 note. William persuaded the broker to accept a plan whereby he would get his $6,000 over two years, and he persuaded the seller to allow him to assume the accounts payable. Subsequently, the industrious entrepreneur paid both the broker's commission and the accounts payable from the profits of the business.

William had zeroed in on everybody's objectives and devised a simple way to accomplish them without cash.

The seller wanted out and was prepared to accept a deal that included enough cash to pay off his liabilities and the broker's commission.

The broker wanted his commission, but he could get it only if a deal went through.

William wanted the business without digging into his own pockets to buy it.

It worked beautifully. William's store grosses over $300,000 a year with a pre-tax profit of $150,000.

E-Z TIP: Whether you're interested in takeovers or startups, the principles of no-cash-down deals are the same.

I first witnessed a no-cash deal in 1964, when the ink was still wet on my law and MBA degrees. One of my first clients was 21-year-old Steven S., who conceived an idea for "mini" take-out bakery concessions at discount store exits. He had neither cash nor borrowing power, but that didn't stunt his enthusiasm. An effective salesman sells his idea. Steven talked several store owners into deferring for two months security deposits on the leases. Next he approached a company that sold store fixtures and purchased 20 used bakery showcases on credit, persuading the seller to retain title until they were paid for. Then he leased cash registers and coffee urns with no down payment. He also convinced creditors that if his "mini" bakeries worked, he would be back to buy more equipment for his expanding business. Even if he failed, creditors would get their equipment back with little loss of value.

Finally, Steven tackled the problem of bakery supplies. A central bakery supplier accepted Steven's projected income of more than $5,000 a week, and quickly realized what an added $250,000 in sales could do for his own business. So he granted one month's credit at exceptionally low prices.

Without any investment of his own, Steven opened five concessions, produced over $600,000 sales in his first year, and netted a $100,000 profit. At last count he had 16 concessions in three states with combined sales of over $2,500,000 annually. His own income has soared to $200,000 a year.

Steven knew a key point. Sellers will enter deals if you prove to their satisfaction that the probability of gain outweighs any risk. When I taught a management course for the MBA program at a local university a few years ago,

I presented Steven's case and asked the students to discuss its feasibility The results were predictable. They threw around concepts like "net-working capital," "debt to equity ratios," and hundreds of other textbook terms to prove it could never work. Of course they were going by the book and playing by conventional rules, whereas Steven didn't even know conventional rules existed. I doubt if many of those MBA students rivaled Steven's $1 million net worth before age 30!

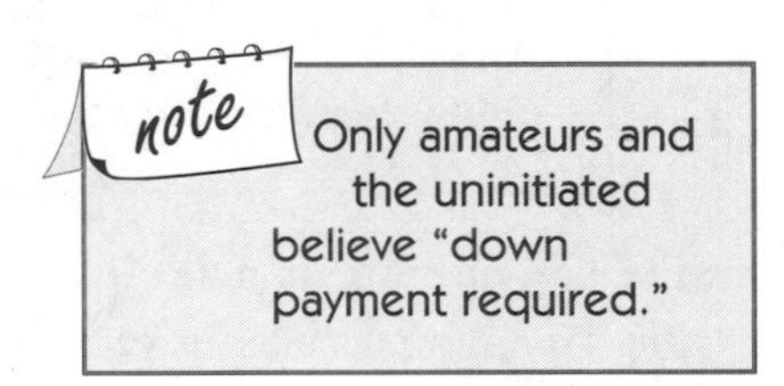

note
Only amateurs and the uninitiated believe "down payment required."

Is Steven's case unique? Thousands of people like him put together deals every year without being hampered or intimidated by the advisers, experts, professors, and conventionalists who follow the book exclusively.

Don't limit yourself with label-itis

I want to talk in terms of you. What type of business do you have in mind?

As you go through this book you will see "no-cash-down" applied to many different businesses. Can it work for yours? Absolutely! That's what makes it exciting. No-cash-down techniques can work for anyone in any type of business anywhere in the country.

I recently conducted a no-cash-down seminar. I said to the audience, "Put me in any city and I'll assemble a no-cash-down deal on any type of business you can name." A member of the audience smirked and slowly raised his hand. "I'm from New York City and I'd like you to get me a cattle ranch." After the laughter subsided I answered, "I may not be able to find cows in Manhattan; would you settle for a worm farm?" Fortunately, most people don't entertain such self-limiting possibilities as a Manhattan cattle ranch. However, this anecdote demonstrates the importance of defining a few simple terms.

First, by *any type of business*, we mean one that's compatible with your experience, aptitude, and interest. This does not imply one precise type of business, but a general range of business endeavors. No person is cut out for only one specific business, because one's aptitudes qualify him/her for a broad spectrum of opportunities. A good merchandiser can successfully promote almost any product. A top-notch automobile salesman can sell more than just cars.

A few years ago I handled a bankruptcy case for a young man, Bob K., who owned a Chevrolet dealership. He was not only broke but psychologically beaten. Bob could not imagine working for another car dealer, but he was worried that he lacked sufficient cash to buy another dealership himself. When I heard of a small but growing boat dealership for sale, I told Bob about it, but he immediately refused, saying, "I'm an automobile man; I know nothing about boats." He had unfairly labeled himself. He walked through life as though "automobile man" were indelibly stamped on his forehead. It took a while to convince Bob that selling boats was not substantially different from selling cars. Although his skills required little modification, his preconceptions required considerable change. Today Bob owns that boat dealership, which he acquired with no-cash-down, and is the enthusiastic commodore of the local yacht club. We jokingly call him "Captain Bob."

Bob's story underscores an important point. Just because you are experienced as a fabric shop manager, should you confine your business search to fabric shops? Why not widen your horizons? What other businesses are available that depend on the skills you possess? Don't be like Bob K.; avoid labeling yourself. Ask yourself some basic questions: What types of businesses would you enjoy owning? What career opportunity would fascinate you?

E-Z TIP

If you want to be in business for yourself, don't limit yourself. Draw up a list of every type of business in which you could excel—then you'll have a road map to guide you in your search.

An acquaintance of mine, Henry C., worked for many years in the burglar alarm field. For five years he looked for an alarm company to acquire, but none was available. With each passing month he grew more and more frustrated. He underwent self-analysis. What he enjoyed most about his job was selling to homeowners and shopkeepers. He liked being on the road rather than being confined to an office, and he was mechanically adept. How many different businesses could satisfy his objectives? Henry soon discovered a large TV installation company for sale for which we arranged no-cash-down terms. Henry bought it, paid the seller from profits, and began clearing $60,000 a year for himself.

HINT

Keep your options open. By expanding the possibilities you'll have your pick of good business opportunities.

Henry didn't suffer from "label-itis." He knew that he could be equally happy in any one of a long list of business situations. Flexibility got him into business and on his way to financial independence.

Know thyself

Many practical business books pitch themselves at so-called "entrepreneurs." Though I have nothing against entrepreneurship, I think the term is greatly overused these days, and, like so many clichés, has lost its precise meaning. When I hear the word I envision a dashing promoter overseeing a vast conglomerate that he started three weeks earlier and will probably bankrupt three weeks later. This book is not for the entrepreneurs but for ordinary people who seek financial independence or security but don't necessarily want to juggle a $6,000,000 cash flow or manage assets in 37 states. When I say, "I want to show you how to get into business with no-cash-down," I have no preconception of what your business will be, how big it will grow, or even how much money you will make. That's for you to determine.

> STRATEGY
> You know better than anyone what it takes to make you happy. Make a list of those things and you will know what you should look for in a business.

Entrepreneurs come in all shapes and sizes. When I was a youngster my mother often sent me to a tiny yarn shop for a skein of yarn. Little more than a local knitting club where nimble-fingered ladies sat around exchanging gossip and making sweaters to keep their grandchildren warm, this yarn shop was hardly a booming business in the traditional sense. I don't know how much the owner, Aunt Bea, made. It was a meager living at best, but the owner was happy. She knew what she wanted and she had it. She wouldn't swap her little shop and the daily exchange of gossip with her friends for all the woolen mills of Scotland.

I remembered this little shop the other day when I met a dynamic young lady, Phyllis C., who was also in the knitting business. She owned a knitting manufacturing firm and two high-powered knit shops in local shopping malls. Phyllis wanted to expand either through franchising or by developing a company-owned chain. Unlike Aunt Bea, Phyllis was excited by graphs and charts, sales and profits, hustle and bustle. Bigger was better.

note

Most people think they have a good idea of what they want from a business. They can define what income would satisfy them and how much effort they are willing to expend, but too often they tend to overshoot their mark. They look for business situations that go well beyond what they can effectively handle and even beyond what it takes to really satisfy them. Jack M., a great guy but a lousy businessman, is a case in point. For years he owned a small convenience store and made a pretty good income, despite the fact that he kept his accounts on the backs of envelopes and his tax records in shoeboxes. He spent most of his time at the dog track, but one day he strode smiling into my office, announced he had just closed his own no-cash-down deal, and asked me to draw up the papers in a hurry. He had agreed to buy a large supermarket in the next town for an exorbitant price fully secured by a mortgage on his own house. I sensed disaster on the horizon. I explained to Jack that he couldn't run a large supermarket the way he ran his little convenience store. He would have to stop his daily jaunts to the dog track and mind the store. Though he was in over his head, Jack didn't heed my warning. It didn't take long for his dream to explode in his face. After the rubble cleared, he had lost his house and original business and was last seen managing a chain store's produce department.

Could Jack have avoided this catastrophe? If he had known what he really wanted, what he was really capable of handling, and what would satisfy him he could have succeeded, but Jack did not know himself.

Unfortunately, for every story like Jack's, there is a story like Marty's. Marty was a young man who worked hard at his own small pharmacy and did a great job with it. With a growing family to support, he admitted he needed the additional money a bigger pharmacy could provide, but Marty suffered a confidence crisis. He sold himself short. Over the past two years I have uncovered two high-volume and profitable drugstores that could supply the income Marty needs, but he has turned them both down. Why? "I don't think I could handle it."

E-Z TIP: When you look for your deal, make certain you know yourself. Ask yourself tough questions. Can you handle it? Will it challenge you enough? Will it satisfy you?

The world is full of Martys and Jacks. The Martys are afraid to make the move, or they sell themselves short when they do, while the Jacks try to walk on water when they can't even swim, and they drown. What type are you? Maybe you're a Marty and need a little shove to see what you can accomplish. Perhaps you're a Jack who needs a little harnessing.

HINT: Be sure you know yourself before you try to zero in on your dream business.

Developing the no-cash-down mentality

After you finish this book you'll know the techniques and strategies, but before you apply them you must develop a no-cash-down mentality. Without it you're the pawn, and the seller and his gang of advisers are the players. It's not just what you know that counts. Whether you call it courage, daring, assertiveness, or aggressiveness, it boils down to one thing: calling the shots. I don't pretend that that's easy or automatic for most people, because such an attitude is not consistent with many personalities. However confidence and experience can work wonders. Business opportunities abound. It may take perseverance to put together your first no-cash deal, but it will happen if you keep trying. You may uncover ten deals that suit your needs and nine may fail to achieve your no-cash-down goal. It's the tenth that counts. Forget the nine "no deals" except for the experience and increased self-confidence they provide.

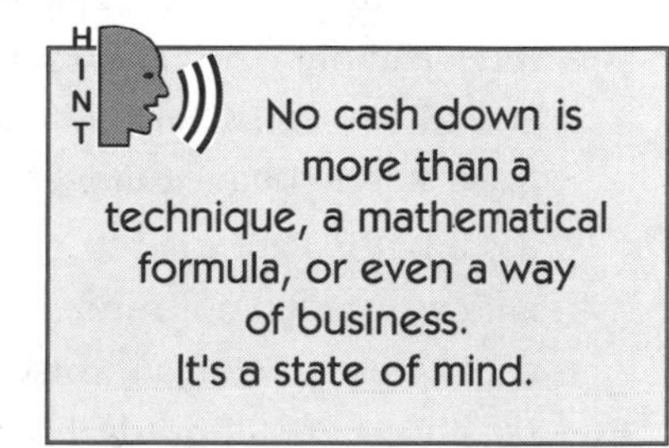

HINT
No cash down is more than a technique, a mathematical formula, or even a way of business. It's a state of mind.

You can't buy every business for no cash down. Many times it's just not in the cards. William V. dug deeper into the seller's motives and his perseverance paid off.

HOT spot

One key is to know when not to accept a down payment demand but to push for your terms. The other is to realize when pushing will simply spin your wheels and waste your time.

However not every case is like William V.'s. In some situations all the logic, financial common sense, and negotiating skill simply won't do the trick. Usually it's obvious from the start, so you know it's time to move on.

Take Paul, for example. He had his eye on a bakery in his hometown that was steadily going downhill. The seller desperately wanted out. Paul was a capable young fellow with lots of experience who wanted to run the business with his family. The bakery was in trouble because it owed the bank over $100,000. Paul reasoned that if the business failed, the bank would only receive about $20,000 through the liquidation of its assets. The seller would not only lose the business but would be liable to the bank for the $80,000 balance. The seller wanted $100,000 cash and would listen to no other terms. For months Paul tried to persuade the seller to let him take over the bakery with a $100,000 note and no cash down. What did the seller have to lose? He could never be in a worse position. Paul offered every type of security possible, but still no deal. The reply was always the same: "I want $100,000 cash."

After months of fruitless discussions, the bakery finally went bankrupt. As predicted, the seller ended up owing the bank a considerable amount of money. Paul's deal did make sense, but he couldn't make the stubborn seller see it. After it was all over I asked the seller why he didn't go along with it. He answered, "I don't understand deals without money." This seller had what I call *seller's block*. He could not see the reality of his situation and consider rational alternatives that would have enabled him to free himself of his liabilities while giving Paul a chance to turn the business around with no cash down.

Paul's story highlights an important point: Many sellers have fixed ideas and cannot be swayed by even the most persuasive arguments. When you encounter such a seller, move out and don't waste your time. Around the next corner lurks a deal with a more reasonable seller.

You can't win them all, but you don't need to. You're not keeping a scorecard. You simply want to get into a business of your own, and one success out of ten tries will put you there. The odds are in your favor.

I know a man who amassed over $2 million in three years. He picked a street at random, knocked on every door, and told the owner he wanted to buy the house, quoting a price 25 percent less than fair market value. Although many doors were slammed in his face, he did buy one out of every two hundred homes he canvassed.

The no-cash mentality requires two key elements:

1) You have to go after every attractive business for sale that would fulfill your needs.

2) You must develop the confidence to propose, negotiate, and push for no-cash-down terms.

Some people think they're cheating somebody if they buy a business on no-money-down terms. Nancy had this problem. She was negotiating for a dress boutique priced at $100,000 with a $30,000 down payment, one-third of which a supplier was willing to lend her. When I urged her to propose splitting the $20,000 balance of the down payment by having the seller accept a note for $80,000 instead of $70,000 and persuading the broker to accept his $6,000 commission over a two-year period, she could not bring herself to offer these terms. When I offered to do it for her, Nancy finally agreed, but she insisted on being out of the room during the negotiation. The seller and broker agreed to the scheme. Nancy has her boutique, but she is still embarrassed that she didn't invest a dime of her own. I don't fault Nancy, because she's the kind of person who feels uncomfortable proposing terms that go contrary to convention.

> **E-Z TIP** If you cannot develop a no-cash-down mentality, rely on a negotiator (a lawyer, accountant, or even an astute friend with a business background) to go to bat for you.

Better yet, if you can develop a no-cash mentality, I guarantee you'll never make another down payment.

The time is always right

You can read this book from cover to cover 48 times and memorize every word, but what good does it do you if you don't put it into practice?

> **note** If you really want your own business, you will face only one real enemy—procrastination.

The procrastinator always has an excuse. How many times have you heard someone say, "The time is just not right." "The economy is bad." "Money is too tight." "All the good deals are already taken." "There's a depression coming." "I want to make sure there won't be a war in Poland." The list is endless. Year in and year out the procrastinator rationalizes while someone else makes the money. Don't be a procrastinator. If you are one of the many who periodically falls victim to basic inertia, this book may be the prod you need to begin acting on your dreams.

Take the all-important first step and set up an action play, a timetable for progress toward your own business. The sooner you start the quicker you will achieve financial independence and security. If I said, "Be at my home within the next hour and I'll show you how you can increase your income by $30,000 annually," how long would it take you to drop this book, get out of your easy chair, and scramble to your car? Not long. Why shouldn't you display the same enthusiasm when I simply say, "I have a business for you that will increase your income by $30,000"?

Every day that passes without action on your part is a day you could have been making more money, expanding your wealth, and challenging yourself with your own business. Nobody's going to knock on your door and say, "I have a great no-cash-down business for you." That's for you to seek, find, negotiate, and win.

Key points to remember

- Don't take the ads and brokers' listings at face value—there are no-cash-down deals everywhere.
- You have to show the seller how to sell on no-cash-down terms.
- Be flexible. Look for deals in every type of business that interests you.
- Pick the business that's right for you. Satisfy yourself.
- Develop the no-cash-down mentality. You can't get a "yes" to a deal if you aren't willing to risk a few "no's," but you must also learn to recognize an impossible situation when you see one.
- Don't procrastinate. Act now. You won't be any wealthier next year by just reading books.

2 Playing the business acquisition game

Chapter 2

Playing the business acquisition game

> **What you'll find in this chapter:**
>
> - Avoid being intimidated by sellers
> - Choose a business that will be profitable
> - Be objective, not emotional
> - What you see is what you pay for
> - Use effective brokers to help

Before you can jump into your first no-cash-down deal, you must know how to play the game of buying a business. Then you can sharpen your approach to concentrate on no-cash-down terms. If buying a business mystifies you now, don't despair; you have plenty of company. Few people buy more than one business in a lifetime. By the same token, few people will sell more than one business in a lifetime. Most business deals involve two rookie players—one wanting to sell and one wanting to buy, while the ever-present coaches—the accountants and lawyers—yell from the sidelines. Perhaps a business broker plays referee keeping the game in motion until he walks away with a hefty commission check.

> *note* You want to match your wits and knowledge with a seller, and chances are he won't know any more about selling than you do about buying.

Who will win? Of course each side declares himself the winner when the papers are signed, but only time can tell who really won or lost. That's when the true scorecard is announced.

When the seller hands you the bill of sale he acknowledges his satisfaction with the deal. If he bargained to sell for $100,000 he can declare himself the winner when the $100,000 is paid off. That is, unless the business increases in value overnight to $200,000. Then he's back in the loser's corner.

But your score depends less on the deal you carve out than on what you do with the business once you own it. Millions of buyers have fumbled on buying the business, but nevertheless won the game by making nothing but money from the day they received the keys. This chapter has one goal—to put you on the winning path without giving up points at the beginning of the game.

You'll meet the players, learn how you can expect them to play the game, and what you must do to come out a winner. But what I have to say is what you the buyer must know. I won't clutter the pages with the complexities of reading financial statements or a synopsis of the Internal Revenue Code. That's for your teammate, the accountant, to worry about. Certainly there is a maze of legal considerations. Why do you think you'll have an attorney coaching you? So I leave the technicalities of the game to your coaches. But you're the businessperson. You will scout out the deals. You will lock horns with the seller. And it's you who will eventually have to decide whether all the plays can end in a deal that can win for you.

You're only as good as your team

Buying a business requires teamwork. Putting together the team that can win the game for you is your first step. Working beside you will be your two coaches—your accountant and attorney. If it's a large enough deal you may even expand your team to include a consultant or other person who knows the ins and outs of the business and can give you some objective business advice.

E-Z TIP: Avoid a common error. Put together your team before you start the game, not when the game is half over.

Too many buyers are afraid to spend a few dollars by hiring the talent they need when it's most important to them—when the deal first comes into sight. Here's why going it alone, for even part of the game, is a serious mistake. Your advisers can help you negotiate and even prepare for the most effective negotiations. Even if you can negotiate well you may overlook many technical issues that have to be resolved, and this means more time and money down the drain. And how do you know when you're giving away valuable points if you don't know what those points are?

Every lawyer experiences it. He receives a call from an anxious client who says, "I just agreed to buy a business and I want you to draw up the papers." The next day the rookie buyer shows up to tell you the details and sure enough it's all botched up. Usually the attorney will find 326 things wrong. Perhaps the deal itself makes sense, but the flaw is on how it was put together. In any event, it's back to the drawing board.

Sometimes a client is like a lamb who has just done battle with a ram—and the lamb thinks he's won! A few days ago one of my clients, Richard P., proved the point once again. He came running into my office with a huge grin. He had agreed to pay $80,000 for a store selling designer jeans. Dick announced that it was a great deal and the best part was that the seller would finance $50,000 for three years at 24 percent interest. Dick would only have to secure the note with a mortgage on his house.

I hated to disillusion Dick, but I personally knew the sellers. They never dreamed of getting more than $50,000 for their run-down business. It was in such trouble that I doubted it would survive more than a few more months. And it never could pay back $50,000 in three years. But there was Richard. He would risk losing his house and his hard-earned cash because he figured he was smart enough to go onto the playing field without his coaches.

You may say, "He didn't sign any papers, so what's the harm?" Plenty. The store could have been a good deal for Richard—if he could have picked it up for $40,000 on very lenient financing terms. And such a deal could easily have been negotiated at the outset. But what can I do now? It's tough to call the seller and say, "I just committed my client to the insane asylum but he will pay $40,000." You never get back points once they're thrown away.

Believe it or not, Richard is a genius compared to some clients. They confuse lawyers with schoolteachers. They don't want advice when it can count. They want a report card.

> HINT
>
> You can't appreciate what good coaches can do for you unless you have them for the entire game.

Here's how this type operates: They'll walk into their attorney's office, throw signed agreements on the desk and ask, "How did I do?" My only hope can then be that the seller will want to tear up the papers just as badly once his lawyer reviews them. If you want to be a do-it-yourselfer, you are about as smart as the patient who performs his own appendectomy and then calls in the surgeon to stitch him up.

Here are some pointers on finding the right advisers and cultivating them so they'll do battle for you:

- Teamwork requires the right chemistry among the players. It's a matter of meshing personalities. Never underestimate its importance. I consistently do my best deals for clients who are on the same wavelength. We can successfully "wheel and deal" because we do work as a team.

- Forget your brother-in-law who just won his law degree from Podunk U. Do you have a lawyer who's competent for the deal you have in mind? All lawyers are competent; we're just competent in different fields. Your brother-in-law may be a great criminal lawyer,

but does he really know a mortgage from a promissory note? Select advisers who have at least a five- to ten-year track record with business deals. Lawyers for commercial banks usually know what they're doing. The Commercial Law League lists attorneys in every state that specialize in this type of work. You can get that list at any law library.

- Don't let size fool you. Your best lawyers and accountants don't always come from the biggest firms. There is no correlation between size and competence. And you may find smaller firms and even sole practitioners giving you better service at more reasonable rates.

- Since timing can be critical in a business deal, make speed a top priority in selecting advisers. Lawyers can be the world's biggest procrastinators. Give them a deal today and they'll have the papers for you in two months. In two months the seller may have found a basketful of reasons why she won't sign. Make certain that your team is ready to move when the starting whistle blows.

- Listen to your advisers, but don't let them grab the ball from you. Your accountant can guide you on the financial and tax matters, and your attorney has only to protect you legally. You make the business decisions.

- Your advisers have to get paid. Don't try to save a few dollars by economizing in this area. Discuss fees before you start, but don't expect a precise fee quote. No lawyer or accountant knows precisely how many hours a deal will require. Still, you can establish hourly rates.

- If money is tight, discuss it candidly. Many attorneys will take a chance on a client and defer billings until the client lands a business and has the money to pay. If he/she thinks you have what it takes to succeed, he/she may gamble with you—and who knows? Perhaps you'll end up as one of his/her richest clients.

With a good team on your side you're less likely to contract killer diseases that can be fatal to your pocketbook.

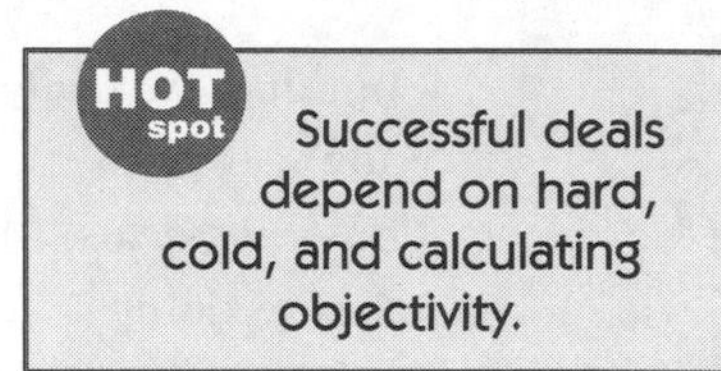

HOT
spot
Successful deals depend on hard, cold, and calculating objectivity.

These diseases run rampant among rookie players. Buyers with strong egos aren't necessarily stupid; they just do stupid things. They let their ego and emotions guide them while their intellect takes a little vacation.

Most first-time buyers are "hot-to-trot." Why shouldn't it be a big fantasy land? They never had to meet a payroll. But raw eagerness can be particularly dangerous with no-cash deals, when you don't have the sobering influence of drawing your savings from the bank. Protect yourself from emotion and ego. Emotion is for lovers. Objectivity is for businesspersons.

Egomania is easy to spot. Those who are afflicted ignore reality and can't be bothered with numbers. Show the problems and pitfalls to the victim and your advice goes in one ear and out the other. Forget the aesthetics, the excitement, and the glamour. You want a business for one reason—to make money for you. Everything else is secondary.

Related to egomania is what I call the *eager beaver syndrome*. The two diseases often strike simultaneously. Those stricken by the eager beaver syndrome not only must have their fantasy business, but they must have it today. Is there a cure? Sure, bankruptcy. But that cure is even more painful than the disease. Bankruptcy, however, does tend to develop an immunity for the next time around.

Diagnose yourself:

- How many businesses did you look at before you fell for the one under consideration?
- What is there about the business that interests you?

- Do the numbers work?
- Have your advisers given the deal the green light?

You get the idea. Sit back and take that long, hard look at the deal. Buy it for all the right reasons, not the wrong ones. With your team in place and your intellect operating at full speed, you're now ready to go out on the playing field and engage in hand-to-hand combat with your opposition—the sellers.

Tackling the sellers as they pull their predictable plays

Sellers come in all shapes and sizes, but they all play the same little games. Why not? They want your money and as much of it as they can finagle out of you. Study this lineup of opposing players to learn their favorite plays.

- The "I don't want to sell" tactic is a common play. It's almost a religious ritual preceding every sale. You spot an interesting business in the paper. You pay the seller a visit. There he is sitting back with his hands behind his head and he says, "I don't really want to sell, but as long as you're here I'll listen to what you have to say."

This play is designed to intimidate you and put you on the defensive. The rich, successful seller sits in his money tree listening to you grovel for his business. No matter how many months he has beat the bushes for a buyer, there he sits trying to get and keep the upper hand.

I first fell victim to the "I don't want to" seller 20 years ago when I was a rookie player. My prey was a large gift shop that I was anxious to buy with two equally "rookie" partners. What a sight. The seller was a real veteran of the playing field and we immediately fell victim to his never-ending protestations about not wanting to sell. His wife was also a "don't want to" type. Between them we were convinced they must have a real money-maker for them to be holding on so tightly. For weeks we chased. We did everything but beg, although from time to time I would hear whimpering from one of my partners. And the ante kept going up and up. Playing "hard to get" paid big dividends for this seller. In retrospect we probably paid 30 percent more for the business than would have been necessary had we been smart enough to see his play.

I learned the hard way—with hard cash. But I never forgot this lesson. Now when I come against this play I know how to handle it—listen and then inform the seller that I wasn't interested in buying, but "if you are willing to sell in a hurry, I might be interested in picking up a few assets."

That usually does the trick and brings them tumbling down from their high perch.

- The "I've lots of interested buyers" play. This type of intimidator playing hard-to-get will get you bidding against yourself every time. of course the other "interested buyers" are wishful thinking on his part, but what you don't know can't hurt him—only you. And he can make it look like the real thing—for instance, arranging a phony telephone call from his secretary, while he engages in a one-sided conversation with yet another anxious buyer.

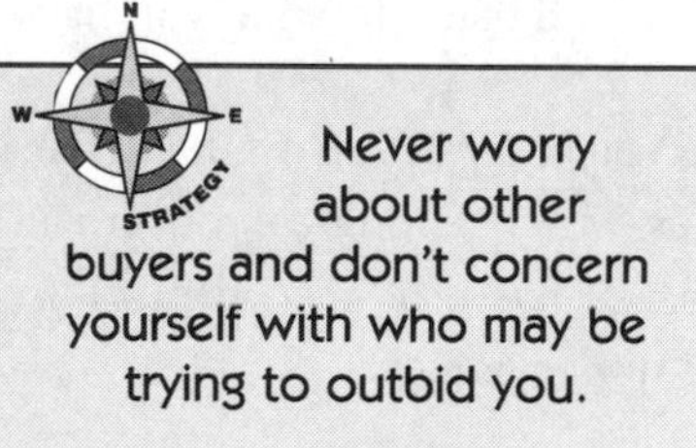

N
W
E
STRATEGY
Never worry about other buyers and don't concern yourself with who may be trying to outbid you.

If you play a few rounds of the game you're bound to meet this type. Let this player know that you can't worry about the other buyers. Besides, two can play the same game. There's more than one business on the block. Play some oneupmanship. Hand him your card and tell him to call you when things quiet down. Expect a call the next morning.

- The "just testing" gambit. Some sellers play "let's pretend." They pretend their business is for sale so they can waste your time and money. They may go down to the wire with you—but never sign.

Why do they do it? There are lots of reasons. Maybe they want constant reassurance that their business is saleable at a given price. Others think they want to sell, but suffer from their own emotional roadblocks when it comes time to pack up and leave it all behind. Others simply enjoy the game itself but never intend to relinquish the ball. Finally, we come to the seller who plays "let's pretend" and puts his business up for sale at an exorbitant price. If he finds a sucker he'll sell, but not for a penny less.

HOT spot The "tester" is a most dangerous player. He can drive you absolutely crazy; and it's almost impossible to spot him until it's too late.

I have found only one method for ferreting out the sellers from the testers. The testers never spend any money as they play their game. The solution: When you suspect you're up against a tester, ask him to have his attorney draw up a contract for you to review. That, of course, means money out of his pocket. This is when the tester knows it's time to call it quits.

Are there other players on the field with still other games? Sure, but with a little experience you'll be able to handle anything they can throw at you. And after all the posturing and positioning is through you'll have an honest-to-goodness seller to play the game with. That's when the game can really get tough because now you're down to basics. And what can be more basic than price?

Pay for the steak—not the sizzle

What's a business worth? Is there a magical figure like five times profit? Twice a company's net worth? How about 60 days' sales? Put away your calculator because that's all baloney. Ask anybody who has knocked around the business world and he'll tell you a fair price is whatever a seller can get you to pay.

How can it be a precise science? Consider the variables: Supply and demand, geography, reasons for buying and selling, available terms, growth potential, profitability, condition and value of assets all have to be factored.

The only logical conclusion you can draw is that a "fair price" is in the eye of only the beholder.

I see it all the time—businesses being sold for a fraction of what I consider a fair price. Others go for what I perceive as exorbitant prices. I handle quite a few pharmacies in my legal practice. In a one-week period two stores were sold. One grossed $450,000 a year with a solid history of profits. It quickly sold for $50,000. Two days later I sold another drugstore with sales of $175,000 whose owner could hardly earn a living. The buyer was happy to pay $80,000. There were no factors that could explain the variance. Time and time again I've seen prices that defied rhyme or reason. From it I've learned to disregard the graphs, charts, formulas, and calculations that the academicians will tell you about in their textbooks, or the uninitiated will espouse.

It all boils down to reality. If you're a seller you know what the business is worth to you, and if you must sell you'll eventually go for the best price you can wangle after you have had the business on the market long enough to determine the best available offer. If you're a buyer you'll have to figure out what the business is worth to you. You'll be guided by two quick calculations:

1) Will the business give you sufficient profits (including salary) to justify the investment?

2) Can the business pay for itself?

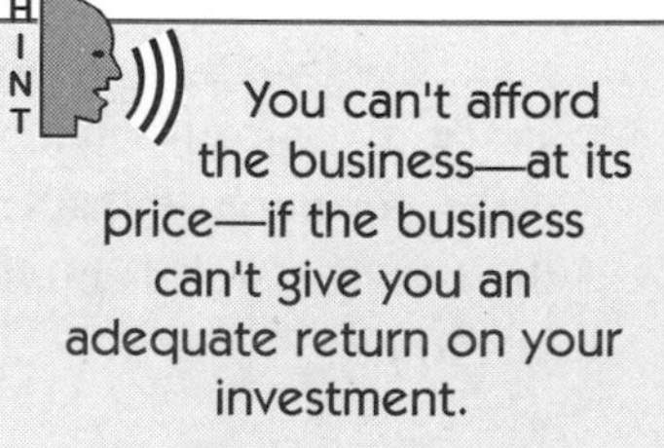

HINT
You can't afford the business—at its price—if the business can't give you an adequate return on your investment.

Take a hard look at the numbers, and be conservative. Even if you're going in with no cash down, you still will have an investment after the business is paid down. And what are your time and energy worth? The business can't afford itself if the profits and cash flow are not sufficient to pay off the loans. If it doesn't have this capability either bring the price down to a level that can be paid from profits or forget it.

Come up with an affirmative answer on both of these questions and the price is mathematically justified. That doesn't mean you should jump for the deal. Now it's time for you to play a few of your own games to get the price down even lower and pick up points before you even start.

Watch out! Sellers will sell you the "sizzle" hoping you'll overlook the fact that the steak is overpriced.

Recently a client, Harvey S., was negotiating to buy an auto parts store grossing $220,000 a year. By our estimation the business couldn't be worth more than $110,000, but the elderly seller wanted $165,000. We pointed out the low volume and anemic profits, but the seller wouldn't budge. He finally came out with the "sizzle." "When Harvey takes over, I know the business will grow. He's young and energetic. I wouldn't be surprised if the store climbs to $500,000 a year in no time at all. Then the store will be worth $165,000 or more." I could muster only one reply—"Mr. Seller, go back to your business. You build it to $500,000 a year and then we'll pay $165,000 for it." You can pay a seller only for what he gives you and nothing more.

> **HOT spot** Never pay a price based on potential. Why should you? It's your brains, your energy, and your ambition that will develop that potential.

Don't forget the lease

Al Lowry, in his excellent book, *How to Become Financially Successful by Owning Your Own Business* (New York: Simon & Schuster, 1981), gives some valuable advice.

He cautions buyers to look at the lease first. I agree. Negotiating a business deal is really the process of negotiating two separate deals. You'll acquire the assets of the business from the seller, but assets may be worthless without a lease, and a lease can involve substantially more profits than the business itself So the price of the business must relate to the value of the lease.

CAUTION
Don't take the lease for granted, particularly in today's crazy real estate market.

Look what happened to the Rodmans. When they first considered buying a large hardware store they asked about the rent. The seller said it amounted to $1,200 a month with two years remaining on the lease. Since that temporarily satisfied the Rodmans, they spent two months negotiating the deal, agreeing to a $250,000 price. Knowing they would need a new lease, they next visited the landlord, who demanded $3,000 a month—$1,800 more than the seller was paying. Over a ten-year period the rent increases alone would tally over $180,000. The deal fell apart. Unfortunately, the Rodmans spent thousands of dollars in professional fees, not to mention the time and frustration. Build your deal like a house—from the foundation up.

Cloak and dagger stories

If you want to see real cloak and dagger stories turn off your TV and skip the movies. They're child's play compared with what you'll experience as you try to put your deal together. Here are several more hurdles you'll have to jump before you get to the goal line.

First we come to secretive sellers. They won't show you the books and financial data until you give a deposit. And how can you give a deposit before you check out the business? A vicious cycle. But there are solutions. Put your cards on the table. Tell the seller about yourself and he'll be more likely to open up to you. Go slowly. Sellers don't want "lookers" tipping off employees and customers that the business is for sale. Let him know you're a "buyer" and

> HINT
> Beware of the hard sell. If the seller is too pushy, step back and take the time you need to evaluate things. You may find the seller has something to be pushy about.

not just another "looker." Respect confidentiality. If the seller thinks you'll blab his numbers all around town he'll stay as closed as a clam. Don't get discouraged if negotiations bog down—it's par for the course. Keep your anxiety level in line. Seldom will a buyer and seller move at the same speed. Some sellers may move and make decisions at a snail's pace. Others will want the deal done "yesterday." Let your lawyer set the pace for you. He/she may have a better idea of what's happening with the other team.

"Red tape" can give you gray hairs, and every deal has it. The typical deal involves more than just you and the seller. For a deal to come together other interests may have to be satisfied—a landlord holds out for a higher rent; the deal can't close without approval from some licensing agency that will take its sweet time; an internal squabble amongst relatives on the seller's side as they fight about who will get what share of the sales price. You name it and it can happen. Tackle the problems as they come up and take them one at a time. Buying a business is a process—not an event. But to get that process going you first have to find the deals.

Look and you will find

Businesses for sale are the easiest things in the world to find. Why shouldn't they be—they're all for sale—at a price. But that gives you a message. No matter how many deals you come across the trick is to hunt for the deals that make sense and will put money in your pocket with no cash down. So you have to develop a screening process that will bring you the deals that are right for you. I have found good no-cash deals from just about every source. There are diamonds in every coal pile. Here are some of the best methods for finding some diamonds without having to dig through mountains of coal.

Turn a broker into a bloodhound

Business brokers typically work for the seller, but there's no law that says they can't work for you. They can be persevering bloodhounds who can save you a lot of legwork as they scout out deals to your specifications. A friend of mine, Hal, really knew how to motivate brokers to bring him the deals.

Hal would select one broker in an area. He wouldn't necessarily select the biggest brokerage firm, as he knew that bigger does not necessarily mean better. But his bloodhound was aggressive and devoted to the task. Hal had a simple approach. He would tell the broker what he was looking for and he always put the cards on the table. It had to be a no-cash-down deal.

Hal would routinely give the broker leads to follow up. That's a switch, of course, as it's ordinarily the other way around. But Hal had a different technique. He knew that with leads in front of him the broker would be set on his path and could follow up. At the end of each week Hal would meet the broker and review the facts of each deal.

Hal told me about one buyout where this routine really clicked. Hal was interested in buying dry cleaning shops. Hal already owned several and figured several strategic acquisitions couldn't hurt. So Hal would scan the newspapers and the trade journals for dry cleaner listings. He would keep his ears open to pick up rumors of people in the business who may have reason to sell. One day Hal heard of a dry cleaner on the east side of town who had just been divorced and was thinking of moving to Florida.

Fed with this information the broker went to work. He would disclose to the seller that he represented a buyer but never revealed Hal as the buyer.

The broker met several times with the seller and obtained information that Hal could never get. The seller confided that he was anxious to sell in a hurry. The broker negotiated that into a lower price. Over dinner the broker convinced the seller that his down payment requirements were out of line. On and on it went. The broker kept working on the seller, and what started out as a $100,000 asking price with a $40,000 down payment was finally sold to Hal for $64,000 with only $10,000 down.

Hal didn't use a broker the way most buyers do. Obtaining leads is the easy part. Hal knew that the broker would be looked upon by the seller as an objective neutral; perhaps even a confidant. When the broker told the seller the price was out of line he listened. Nothing Hal could say would have been as convincing.

You can turn brokers into your bloodhounds. Have them work and negotiate for you—not the seller. If they're on your side they will earn their commissions many times over,

Have the deals come to you first

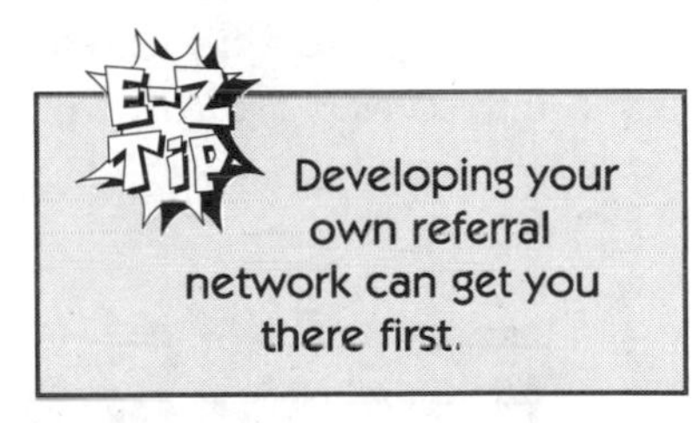

E-Z TIP
Developing your own referral network can get you there first.

Don't look for diamonds after everyone else has sifted through the coal. You have to be first in line to latch onto the worthwhile deals. That's why conventional sources of leads such as newspaper and broker listings usually feature the no-go deals. The very best deals don't have to be advertised. With some word of mouth circulation they're grabbed up before they have to be advertised or listed.

Let's say you want to buy a liquor store. What kind of referral network would you develop? Liquor wholesalers should be your first stop. Tell them what you're interested in and follow up. They know the industry and usually know what stores are up for sale. But the best way of really getting the leads is to stay close to the salespeople who call on the retail

HINT: Cultivate a few key salespeople. With a small incentive they'll keep you well-fed with leads.

accounts. They're in the best position to know the scuttlebutt. Believe me, it works. I do it all the time in the drug field. I can call any one of ten salespeople for drug wholesalers and find out anything I need to know about any drugstore in the state, including what's for sale.

Read the casualty lists

For no-cash-down deals there's nothing like the casualty lists—businesses in trouble or owners having every good reason to want to bail out—on your terms.

There are several ways to find out who's in trouble. Trade publications such as *Bankers and Tradesman*, available in every library, publish names of companies that have been hit with tax liens or creditor attachments.

If you're really ambitious, you can take a trip to the courthouse and check the receivers list. This will disclose companies about to go under as creditors are pressing claims. Your lawyer can show you the ropes and then it's happy hunting.

Have them knocking on your door

What could be better than sitting behind your own desk while an anxious seller tries to sell you her business. You can then reverse all the intimidating games sellers play on you. A simple newspaper ad can bring them knocking.

John K. wouldn't do it any other way. He buys all kinds of run-down businesses, gets them on their feet, and quickly sells out at phenomenal profits. He has but one cardinal rule—he never uses his own cash.

Here's the ad that John uses to bring them in:

I want to buy any type retail business in Boston area.
Immediate cash available. Phone . . .

John has it all "psyched" out. He knows the down and outers will come a-calling. The lure of "cash available" is, of course, a come-on; for once John gets the seller into his office he finds a way to do the deal without cash. You can modify the ad to a specific type of business to narrow the field to your needs.

One $35 ad a week in the Sunday classified section draws 20 to 25 calls. John does a preliminary screening by telephone and usually ends up meeting five to six prospects. John tells me that he only closes about one deal a month because that's all he can handle. But to hear it from John, "There are plenty of good no-cash-down deals that I have to turn away—and to think there are still people out there working for a living who believe it takes money to get into business!"

Key points to remember

- You don't win by buying the business. Victory comes only with making money.
- You may be the businessperson—but you're not the entire team.
- Leave your emotions at home. Buying a business demands clear-headed objectivity.
- Sellers can intimidate you if you don't know the plays.
- There's no such thing as a right price. Ask yourself, "What is the business worth to me?"
- Don't pay for what you will do with the business; pay only for what you're getting.

- Buying a business is a process. Put it together one piece at a time.
- Brokers can be your bloodhounds, but they have to be working for you.
- To do a deal you have to find the deals. And there are plenty out there—if you know how to look.

Who needs cash?

Chapter 3

Who needs cash?

What you'll find in this chapter:

- Understanding creative financing
- Building a financial plan with others' money
- Matching financing to the deal
- Convincing the seller of the deal's advantages
- Being creative in your deals

"Any idiot with money in his pocket can buy a business, but it takes a genius to do it without cash!" That quotation does not appear in any other book because I coined it myself. However I've modified it since I first spouted it 20 years ago because I no longer believe that it takes genius to buy a business with no money down. Experience has taught me otherwise. Ordinary people with no prior business experience have done it. Wage earners who don't know the difference between a profit and loss statement and a balance sheet have done it. Housewives who have never written a check have done it. I've witnessed a group of high school kids do it. As each no-cash-down deal unreeled before my eyes, the more I realized it takes less genius than know-how to succeed.

Robert Allen recently authored the best-selling book about buying real estate without cash called *Nothing Down* (New York: Simon & Schuster, 1980). The author travels around the country giving seminars on "How to Buy Real

Estate With No Money Down." According to Allen, *You can give me $100 for living expenses, put me in any city, and within 72 hours I'll buy several good pieces of real estate with absolutely no-cash-down.*

Although I am not an authority on real estate, I believe every single word of Allen's pitch because the same holds true for starting or buying businesses. In fact, I'll do Allen one better. I'd accept a challenge that you can put me in any city (keep your $100; I'll pay my own living expenses) and in a few days I'll not only own a few good businesses, but I'll have money in my pocket to boot!

Allen wasn't bragging. He knows a smart buyer can forget cash when buying real estate. I am not bragging either; you can buy a business just as easily as I. Once you learn the methods in this book you may even do a better job of it. Want in on a secret? It's a lot easier to get into business without cash than it is to buy real estate. You'll be amazed to see that it is as easy to buy without cash as it is with a pocketful of money to hand a seller. In this chapter I'll teach you the basic formula you need to start on the road to freedom and wealth.

Price is nothing but a word

Lesson 1

An asking price can intimidate the untutored who believe it's well beyond their reach.

If you scan the want ads you'll encounter numerous businesses sporting astronomical price tags of $50,000 to $1 million. You may figure you might as well proceed to the comics, because you couldn't scrape together $40 to take the family out to dinner. Don't be intimidated by numbers on a newspaper page. Price is symbolic. A $100,000 price does not mean that $100,000 must come out of your pocket. As you will see in this chapter, none of it has to come out of your pocket.

In reality, price tags send you an entirely different message. They say "Mr. Buyer, I want to receive the equivalent of $100,000. My business can generate the cash, and your job as the new owner is to see that it does."

Take a sample ad and test it in this light:

Restaurant for sale.
Sales over $500,000. Price $140,000.

How can you get the seller $140,000 from his own business? Let's start with zero (that's where you always begin with no-cash-down deals) and gradually build up to $140,000 using somebody else's money.

How many ways can you stack your financing blocks until they reach $140,000? Too many to count. Perhaps you can do it with one giant block by persuading the seller to lend you the entire $140,000. On the other end of the spectrum, you could borrow $1 from each of 140,000 different people, in which case you accomplish the same goal with lots of small blocks. However, chances are your successful strategy will involve a logical blend of different sized blocks which in the end equal $140,000. Five different buyers competing for this very same restaurant on no-cash terms would construct five different financial pyramids.

Buyer #1

$ 75,000	From a bank loan secured by the business
40,000	Seller financing
10,000	Assumption of sellers' liabilities
15,000	Loans from suppliers
$140,000	Total

Buyer #2

$ 90,000	Seller financing
30,000	Bank financing
20,000	Money invested by partners
$140,000	Total

Buyer #3

$ 60,000	SBA loan
20,000	Seller financing
20,000	Assumption of seller's liabilities
10,000	Loan from business broker
10,000	Loan from supplier
20,000	Borrowed from business cash flow
$140,000	Total

Buyer #4

$100,000	Seller financing
40,000	Investment from partners
$140,000	Total

Buyer #5

$ 60,000	Bank financing on business
30,000	Seller financing
5,000	Loan from business broker
10,000	Sale of certain business assets
10,000	Personal loan
10,000	Borrowed from cash flow of the business
5,000	Supplier financing
10,000	Assumption of seller's liabilities
$140,000	Total

In the following chapters I show you where those building blocks are and how you can use them to put together your deal. But, for the time being, focus on what every smart no-cash buyer knows: The total is only the sum of its parts, and the parts are too numerous to count.

HOT spot Each financing method achieved the purchase price using capital from sources other than the buyer's own checkbook.

Build from the ground up

Lesson 2

Building your no-cash-down financing pyramid requires one careful step at a time. You'll start at the bottom plugging in the largest building blocks first, gradually climbing to the top by adding a small block here and another there. Let's give the concept life in the case of the $140,000 restaurant.

After the usual buyer-seller dickering, my client Barry decided the restaurant was perfect for him and the $140,000 price was fair, so it was time to start building our financial pyramid using everybody else's money.

The seller, an elderly gentleman we'll call Conroy, was a typical seller—reasonable and willing to listen, but also concerned about getting his money. Here's how our negotiating session went, as one-by-one we piled the blocks in place:

I started by asking Conroy what financing was available if we agreed to pay $140,000. Conroy sat back, pondered the question and replied, "I suppose I could finance about half the price." Immediately we had our first $70,000 building block through seller financing. Next we concentrated on the other $70,000. My next question upset Conroy at first. I said we needed to know about the business's existing debts. Conroy answered, "None of your business! It's my responsibility to pay off my creditors from proceeds of the sale." I countered that Barry might assume the debts as part of the purchase price. "Wouldn't you, Mr. Conroy, wind up with the same amount of money?" Conroy had to agree, handing me another building block—existing liabilities totaling $30,000. Deducting it from the seller's price, I immediately locked the "assumed debt" building block in place. Now we had commitments for $100,000—$70,000 through seller financing and $30,000 through assumption of liabilities. But we still had $40,000 to go to reach the top of our no-cash-down pyramid.

I knew a bank wouldn't lend the last $40,000 on the business itself because Barry would already have assets tied up as collateral to secure the seller's $70,000 loan. But what if I could persuade Conroy to subordinate his $70,000 note to a bank loan that would have priority to the collateral? I asked Conroy if he would object to our obtaining a $40,000 bank loan with his $70,000 note in line behind the bank if Barry defaulted. Conroy objected. He wanted to be first in line in the event of default. Though I couldn't disagree with him, it was time for a little give and take. I reminded Conroy that we were willing to pay the $140,000 asking price. "Mr. Conroy, you probably expected us to haggle the price down to $130,000, maybe even $120,000. But we'll pay the full $140,000—if you'll let us secure a $20,000 bank loan, with a first mortgage on the business. If Barry defaults you'll have to pay off the $20,000 to take back the business but in reality that $20,000 merely represents the difference between $140,000 and a reduced price you were willing to accept." Conroy agreed. It would be no trick to get a bank to lend $20,000 with a $140,000 business as solid collateral. Our financial pyramid began to take shape:

$ 20,000	First mortgage to a bank
70,000	Second mortgage to the seller
30,000	Liabilities to be assumed
$120,000	Total

We had negotiated for half an hour and we had $120,000 of the $140,000. We could visualize the top of the pyramid. All we needed was a $20,000 capstone.

But where could we get $20,000? In typical no-cash deals the big dollars that finance 60 to 70 percent of the price will fall into place quickly, but the last few dollars can be the hardest to find. Fortunately there are scores of sources you can tap.

We approached a wholesaler who supplied produce to the restaurant. He willingly lent $5,000 to be paid back over a year's time. Now we had only $15,000 to go. The restaurant had two cigarette machines provided by a vending company from which Conroy earned $8,000 a year in commissions. If the vending company would lend Barry $5,000 we'd give them a one-year concession lease and they could repay themselves from commissions otherwise due Barry. They agreed. The gap was narrowing. We had $130,000 in place.

Barry figured out several ways to raise the final $10,000, but one method was all we needed. He figured the business did $10,000 a week in sales, so he gave Conroy an interesting proposition. "Look Conroy, I'm only $10,000 short. Why don't you take an additional $5,000 out of next week's receipts instead of paying it to creditors for current orders. That will increase my assumed liabilities from $30,000 to $35,000. For the final $5,000 I'll give you my personal check if your attorney will hold the closing papers in escrow until it clears. It'll only take a few days." Barry knew he could "borrow" the $5,000 needed to cover his check from sales generated after he took over.

Within two weeks Barry was his own boss and now reports record sales for his new restaurant. He's able to draw $35,000 a year and still pay the kind folks who provided the building blocks for his no-cash pyramid.

Let's review Barry's pyramid:

$ 20,000	Proceeds from a bank loan
70,000	Financing from the seller
35,000	Seller's liabilities assumed by Barry
5,000	Supplier loan from the produce wholesaler
5,000	Advance commissions from cigarette company
5,000	To come from the business cash flow to cover Barry's check
$140,000	Total

Follow Barry's example. Once you realize that price is nothing but an objective to be reached through individual building blocks, always follow through on that second step—build from the ground floor up.

Ignore down payment demands

Lesson 3

Forget down payments. Pretend the words don't exist, because in reality they have absolutely no meaning when it comes to structuring your 100 percent financial pyramid. Here are two reasons why:

1) A seller will quote a down payment demand based on his perception of what is needed to finance the deal, and based on his further perception of the "building blocks" that will be available to you to finance the rest of the deal.

2) A seller is telling you what he wants to walk away from the closing with, without even worrying about where your building blocks are coming from.

These are the only interpretations you can give the words "down payment."

Now let me show you why these words mean positively nothing. If you accept the first interpretation you immediately see that the seller is dictating what must come out of your pocket to satisfy his idea of what your pyramid will look like.

For example, a seller may put his business on the block for $150,000. He does some quick calculations—putting your building blocks together—and concludes that the buyer can take over an existing bank mortgage for $50,000 and he'll finance another $50,000. That is his idea of the financing. You will need $50,000 of your own (the down payment) to reach the $150,000. To the seller that's simple enough. All the buyer needs is $50,000 and he can take over the business.

But once you know the building blocks that are at your disposal you can build your own financial pyramid. Why go along with his design?

Analyze your position in that example. The seller did give you some valuable building blocks—$100,000 worth to be precise. But you can be the architect for the remaining $50,000. Without even knowing all the methods that the following chapters will give you, some obvious answers can come to mind if you recall what Barry did. Try it out. What building blocks do you see?

Posed with that problem, here's the approach I would take:

- Negotiate the $50,000 bank loan to a higher amount, if possible. That would give me a bigger building block to start with. Chances are that the original loan was higher and has since been reduced to the present $50,000. Why shouldn't the bank consider bringing the loan to its original balance?

- Try to get the seller to increase the seller financing amount from $50,000 to a larger amount; that's a negotiable item. If you can increase it to $60,000, that's an additional $10,000 coming off the down payment.

- Inquire about accounts payable. That's a building block sellers always forget—but can be effectively utilized in at least 80 percent of business takeovers. If the liabilities are $15,000 they would have to be paid by the seller from your $50,000—so why not use it as your building block by assuming it?

- Perhaps you now have $135,000 to $140,000 of the purchase price firmly in place. For the other $15,000 to $20,000 you can use some of the methods Barry employed—or any other method described in this book.

When you're through the deal may look like this:

$ 70,000	Bank loan (increased from $50,000)
60,000	Seller financing (increased from $50,000)
15,000	Takeover of liabilities
5,000	Cash flow from business
$150,000	Total

At this juncture you may say—what if the bank won't increase the loan to $70,000? What if the seller won't finance more than $50,000? What if the seller doesn't have liabilities to assume? Then what happens to that hypothetical pyramid we just built? I have a simple answer: We design another pyramid.

There are thousands of possibilities and combinations available to you. Maybe another bank will lend $70,000 if the existing bank won't. Or perhaps you can't do better than $50,000 in bank loans so you're back where you started. Then it's time to concentrate on the $50,000 down payment component since you can't improve on your existing building blocks of $100,000.

That $50,000 may be whittled away by smaller building blocks. A loan from the business broker. Have the seller create liabilities for you to take over. Exploit some hidden assets. Cultivate some supplier financing. The list is endless.

The fact is that most sellers do not know the most creative ways to finance the business they're selling and they do not strain themselves to find the best ways. For these reasons they should never be counted on to properly engineer your pyramid. Don't forget—it's so much easier for them to say you need $50,000 for a down payment. Now we come to the second subliminal message in down payment demands—the seller wants it as his "walk-away" money. That's another fallacy. In real life what the seller puts in his pocket bears no direct relationship with what comes out of yours. Let's go back to our seller demanding $50,000 on the supposition that if you have it, he will get it.

What if you're that imaginative buyer who finds the $50,000 from all those other sources? The seller gets his $50,000 and he doesn't care where you get it.

That's one common misconception with the term *no-cash-down*. The average person takes it to mean that reciprocally the seller ends up with no money at the time of closing. Nothing could be further from the truth. Of course with many no-cash-down deals a seller will agree to finance 100 percent of the purchase price, so that will be the end result. But it's certainly not a requirement to building your financial pyramid.

Remember Conroy who sold out to Barry? What if Conroy had said, "I need all cash, period!"? That's not unusual. True, Conroy would have deprived Barry of a useful building block, but we would have found others for our no-cash approach.

A bank might have lent $70,000 to $80,000 against the business. We still could have assumed $35,000 in payables. The produce wholesale and cigarette company would still chip in its $10,000, and Conroy would still agree to hold a $5,000 check for a few days. The balance would simply require a little creativity. But as you can see, it will never require your down payment!

You make your own miracles

Lesson 4

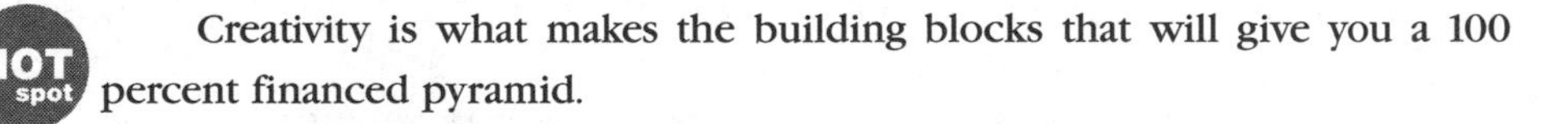

Creativity is what makes the building blocks that will give you a 100 percent financed pyramid.

The human mind is complex and can create amazing ideas if you work it hard enough.

Pose to the average buyer the problem of buying a $240,000 business and you get the stock answers: Borrow from a bank, ask the seller to hold some paper, try the Small Business Administration, or call your mother. But those conventional answers won't help you much if you want the business for no cash down. Sure, it may get you 50 to 80 percent of the purchase price, but what do you do for the other 20 to 50 percent? That's where creativity can work miracles. I showed you how Barry did it. Although his story does not represent the most creative possible solution, nothing more was needed to reach the 100 percent mark. You may need even more imaginative ideas to find the last few dollars to cement in place at the top of your pyramid.

In Chapter 1, I described the no-cash-down mentality. In subsequent chapters I offer more examples of no-cash-down creativity. Some of the cases in this book may appear contrived to make a point, but I assure you that's not the case. The solutions you see are solutions that really worked; and they only scratch the surface of no-cash-down creativity.

Barry and I tried creative brainstorming as we pondered his $240,000 restaurant before the financing fell into place. We knew we could raise $200,000 from the seller, banks, or other obvious sources, but we weren't sure about the other $40,000. So we fantasized as we threw our ideas back and forth. Some were practical, others ludicrous.

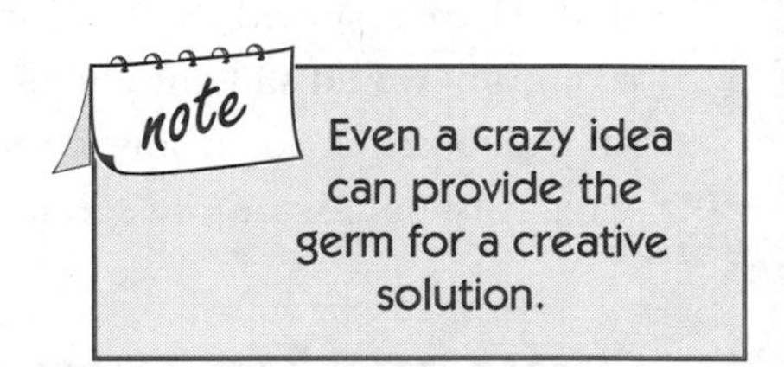

note
Even a crazy idea can provide the germ for a creative solution.

Barry hit me with a barrage of possibilities. "Let's sell stock in the company. No, wait. Let's lease out the basement for a disco and collect the year's rent in advance. Hold it, how about this? We'll ask Conroy to become a silent partner if he knocks $40,000 from the price."

On and on he went, one idea springing from another. Barry was in a frenzy when he blurted his ultimate crazy idea. "Why not sell 'dinner memberships' to everybody in town? For $10 a member they would be entitled to one free dinner for each one purchased." Barry loved his idea. "Imagine, if I sell 4,000 memberships, my customers will buy me my own restaurant!"

Barry will never have trouble closing no-cash-down deals because he has the creativity to find solutions. If one doesn't work, he has two more to back it up.

It can be those last few dollars that stand between you and your business. Every deal offers its own creative solutions if you only use your imagination. You can be on top of your pyramid while others are still contemplating the base.

Lesson 5

This book contains a ton of building blocks for 100 percent financing startups and takeovers. Which blocks you use will depend on the deal: what's most readily available and what gives you the greatest economic benefit. There is no one right way. As you turn to Chapter 5, and learn about the takeover of troubled companies, you will find that your obvious building block will be the assumption of all the bills the company ran up. It wouldn't make sense to consider borrowing $50,000 from a bank to pay off $50,000 to creditors that already represent your built-in financing. In Chapter 6 you'll see how suppliers can help you finance your business. It is possible that you can couple supplier financing with some larger building blocks such as seller or bank financing as discussed in Chapter 10.

> **note** The characteristics of the deal, will give you valuable clues to the building blocks that are most logically available.

Perhaps you'll walk into a business with excess inventory or other assets. By learning the techniques in Chapter 7, you'll be able to grab hold of yet another block that can create your pyramid. If you keep your eyes open, you'll find building blocks everywhere.

HINT

Once you are fully familiar with all the sources of money that can take the place of your own cash, you may find that the available building blocks can actually exceed 100 percent of the purchase price. It may sound farfetched but it's absolutely true. Experience will not only let you design a 100-percent financed pyramid, but in many cases have those building blocks compete against each other for a place in the pyramid.

Building the best pyramid

Lesson 6

Every source of financing has its own characteristics—its own advantages and disadvantages. As you go through this book you'll see the strengths and weaknesses that each building block offers. The best building blocks will:

- Require little or no collateral.
- Carry the lowest interest rates.
- Demand no personal liability.
- Provide the longest payback period.

E-Z TIP: Build your pyramid with the building blocks that will give it the greatest strength.

No one source of financing will display all these characteristics. Bank loans may give you an adequate payback period, but the downside is your personal liability. Taking over the seller's debts ordinarily won't involve your personal liability, but may require a speedy payback. Partnership funds will satisfy all these points but require you to give up profits for your entire business career.

So as you look around for your building blocks, go for the one that meets your requirements. Putting together that perfect pyramid requires financial and legal guidance, so be sure you have your advisers helping you.

Reaching 100-percent financing is only a mathematical exercise, Obtaining it through building blocks that give you a strong pyramid that will survive is the real objective.

Give your pyramid this acid test. Can it pay the obligations? Is the level of personal liability acceptable? Can profits be increased through lower interest rates offered by other building blocks? Don't fall victim to a faulty design!

Does it really work?

Lesson 7

The approach to no-cash-down deals outlined in this chapter does work. Every case you'll read in this book proves it because each is a true story, with only the names changed. There are thousands of others who have landed their own businesses without a dime of their own by following the same no-cash-down formula.

> E-Z TIP
> Most businesses can be purchased or started without cash given the necessary know-how, creativity, and perseverance.

The most important lesson in this chapter is that you have to believe it can work for you. Possibly not in every deal, but in more than enough deals—in any line of business—to get you what you want and sooner than you think. You'll see how others have effectively used all the building blocks that can put you in a business of your own; and they'd all tell you the same thing, "Who needs cash?"

Key points to remember

- Anyone can buy with no cash down once they know how.
- Price is only a word. You can reach it with creative financing.
- Build your financial pyramid one step at a time using everyone else's money.
- No two deals are alike. Match the financing to the deal.
- Design your own pyramid. Sellers aren't thinking in no-cash- down terms, but you must.
- Always start from the ground and work your way to the top.
- You can get the seller his money with no-cash deals.
- Use creativity to find your building blocks.
- The no-cash-down formula does work—if you believe it and use it.

Negotiating to win

Chapter 4

Negotiating to win

What you'll find in this chapter:

- Negotiate from the seller's point of view
- Achieve both buyer's and seller's objectives
- Investigate the background of the deal
- Reduce seller resistance
- Overcome "seller's block"

Wouldn't you love to possess the sophistication of Henry Kissinger, the wit of Will Rogers, the financial genius of J. Paul Getty, and the persuasive power of Dale Carnegie? Even if you did, you wouldn't necessarily negotiate more effectively because you must bring to the bargaining table your unique personality and skills. No matter how many books on the subject you read, negotiation boils down to one objective: Winning what you want from someone while convincing him he's getting what he wants. You can accomplish your objective only through your unique style.

Successfully negotiating a no-cash-down deal is no different. First you must discover what the seller wants, then you must figure out how to satisfy his needs while achieving your goal of not investing your own money. Always assume the seller's point of view. I recall the dramatic tale of a small Manhattan tailor shop. A developer bought the building housing the shop and announced his intention to demolish it and construct a high-rise condominium complex.

This building enjoyed numerous shops as tenants, most with three- to five-year leases yet to expire. The developer offered each tenant $3,000 plus full moving expenses in exchange for the lease cancellation. All but one accepted. The tailor wanted no part of the deal. When the developer raised his offer to $5,000 and one year's rent in any other building, the tailor said, "Not interested!" Despite increasing offers that eventually hit $25,000, the tailor remained adamant, until the exasperated developer said, "What do you want?" The tailor quietly replied, "$500,000." The developer choked. "How dare you demand $500,000 to vacate this crummy little shop? You only pay $175 a month for it. "Easy," countered the tailor. "I hold a lease, so you can't evict me for five years. Unless I move, you can't knock down the building and build your high-rise. I figure it'll cost you at least $1 million in lost income over the next five years. I'm not greedy. I only want half of what I'll save you by giving up the lease." The tailor got his $500,000.

The moral of the story? While the other tenants thought only in selfish terms, our tailor friend focused on the developer's position. What does he want? What's in it for him?

Negotiating no-cash-down deals requires careful preparation until you know the other side's position. You must investigate all the facts necessary to neutralize that position. Then you will discover certain tactics that will strengthen your bargaining position. You may call it a game, but remember the stakes. It's a game that you can't afford to lose if you want to win no-cash-down terms.

Investigate, investigate, investigate

Don't let appearances mislead you. The business that looks too good to be true probably isn't. The seller who gives one reason for selling may really have different reasons. If you research every possible aspect of the seller and the business, you can dramatically lower an asking price or down payment.

Susan learned this lesson the hard way. She wanted to buy a beauty salon. The seller wanted $80,000 with $40,000 down. After limited negotiation and virtually no investigation she purchased the business at almost the asking price. Two months later she received a letter from the landlord's bank, which held the mortgage on the building housing the salon. The letter indicated foreclosure and eviction. Eventually she had to pay triple rent for a new lease. Of course, the seller saw it coming and bailed out, leaving Susan a victim of her own impatience.

CAUTION It happens every day—buyers act in haste and repent at leisure. Many businesses are sold because of hidden problems or a potential disaster lurking around the corner.

The bankruptcy courts bulge with cases involving unwitting buyers who didn't bother to investigate thoroughly. Fraud doesn't just occur in such grandiose schemes as sellers enticing gullible buyers to purchase the Eiffel Tower or the Brooklyn Bridge. Most people fall victim to minor-league trickery. A seller claims $600,000 in sales when it's closer to $300,000; a seller who forecasts a banner year, knowing a major competitor plans to move in next door; a restaurant owner "forgets" to say the health department threatens to shut his doors.

I'd conservatively estimate that fully half of all businesses for sale involve serious problems which sellers cheerfully cover up or laugh off as a minor irritation. You've heard the term *caveat emptor*. It means "let the buyer beware." When it comes to buying a business, "let the buyer beware" rings truer than ever. By the time your dream business turns into a nightmare, the seller is sailing in the Bahamas on a yacht purchased with your hard-earned cash.

There's nothing wrong with taking over a business with some problems, as long as you identify them in advance, know you can solve them, and use them to negotiate the best possible deal. You can turn almost any problem into an opportunity.

I hate to admit it, but I've learned many memorable lessons on the losing end. Several years ago I had a client who owned a coffee shop in a large office building. Despite a successful history, it was about to decline and fail because the landlord decided to convert 60 percent of the building to residential condominiums.

My client offered the business for sale for $60,000, concealing the fact that half his customers would soon vanish. However, every prospective buyer quickly found out about it and said goodbye. Then along comes Rube. That was his real name and I thought it fit perfectly. He acted as if he couldn't count to twelve without removing a shoe. The perfect candidate! I quickly drew up the legal papers and appeared at the closing with a big smile on my face, whispering to my client, "We really have a live one!" After Rube examined the papers, he slowly turned to the seller and said, "I asked you to terminate all your employees." My client said he had. "Did you tell your suppliers the business is changing hands?" Again, a "yes" answer. "I suppose you've completed your arrangements to move to Florida?" "Why, of course," shot back the seller, "I'm scheduled to move in two weeks."

Then Rube dropped his bombshell in my lap. "Counselor, do you see a $60,000 purchase price in the contract? I'm sorry to inconvenience you kind folks, but I can't go through with the deal with what I recently learned about the landlord's plans for this building. And I feel terrible because your client has fired his help, and is all set to skip to Florida. So, to prove I'm a gentleman I'll pay $24,000, or $6,000 more than the auction price the place would command if I didn't buy it. I'll just relocate the equipment to another location." Old Rube turned out to be damned smart because he had investigated and converted a potential headache into the soothing chime of cash registers.

Most sellers will protest they don't really want to forfeit their goldmine, but poor health or a brother in Los Angeles who won the Irish

HOT spot

"Seller pressure" can dictate what kind of deal you structure. How badly does the seller want out? The greater the "seller's pressure," the better the deal.

Sweepstakes or a sick wife makes it time to get out. I accept the seller's story at face value only when he's 85 or older and negotiates with a nurse at his side. Be a detective. A few hours of inquiry can save you thousands of dollars and provide just the ammunition you need for a no-cash-down deal.

The Man from the East

If you're going to romp in the jungle of "Modern American Business," you'll have to resort to just about anything, as long as it's legal, to drive the best deal you can.

To neutralize the hundreds of sellers' tricks, you'll need some tricks of your own.

The "Man from the East" is one of the best. You may recognize it as the "Straw Man," "Front Man," or "Pathfinder," but regardless of the title, each works in the same way to test the water, establishing a threshold from which to negotiate a good deal.

Consider the Man from the East your personal pathfinder. He can offer ridiculous terms and not worry about offending the seller and killing the deal. If he does succeed in getting the seller to concede some major points, he passes this information on to you. When the Man from the East finishes pushing the deal as far as he can, you, as that "new interested buyer," can step right in. The water has been tested with someone else's expendable toe. The following situation demonstrates the value of the Man from the East far better than any textbook definition.

What is the worth of a small lounge grossing $800,000 a year? There's no right answer, because it depends on what a willing buyer will pay. Let's say our seller places a small downtown Boston lounge on the market for an arbitrary price of $300,000, and the Reilly brothers are willing to pay it. However, their willingness doesn't mean they want to spend a lot of their own money. Rather, they may want to play the negotiating game. To set up the sell they recruit three close friends to act as "Men from the East." The first approaches the seller, feigning interest and offering a top price of $140,000. Then the second arrives and offers $160,000, while the third isn't as charitable. He spends three hours explaining why he wouldn't pay a dime over $120,000. All this confuses the shaky seller who contracts a bad case of "owner doubt." Isn't the lounge worth $300,000? Perhaps he overestimated its value. If the best he can get from three prospective buyers is $160,000, maybe he should grab it and run. The stage is set.

The Reilly boys offer $180,000. The seller's ears perk up. He counters with $100,000 with $10,000 down, thinking it a lot better than $160,000. Finally, he agrees to $240,000 with nothing down. Had the Reillys hit the seller before their "Men from the East" softened him up, they wouldn't have succeeded with such an offer because the seller would still have believed his asking price fair. Everything is relative. Compared to prior offers, the Reillys looked good. What did it cost the Reillys to save thousands of dollars? A few hours of their friends' time.

The "Man from the East" can help land no-cash-down deals. He can prod and probe to see just how far a seller will retreat. He can explore every angle. When he's through, you can step in, assuming the role of the new buyer.

HOT spot

Entering negotiations without knowing how far a seller is willing to go creates a disadvantage you cannot afford.

Overcoming "seller's block"

A psychological problem I call *seller's block* prohibits many sellers from understanding no-cash-down deals. Although it is a mental condition, seller's block can present as formidable an obstacle as a 300-pound all-American tackle looming between you and the goal line. You can't go around it, so you must overcome it.

Here's how seller's block works. You're sitting around the negotiating table, slowly but surely chipping away at the financing until you have accounted for 100 percent of the purchase price without a nickel coming from your own pocket. Suddenly the seller freezes. The fact that you're taking over his beloved business with everybody's money but your own dawns on him, and he begins to resist the deal.

Don't be surprised when you encounter seller's block. No matter how logical a deal may be from the seller's perspective, he forgets to think about himself at this point and starts looking at you as if you're another John Dillinger and he's your next heist. He may not admit it, but he believes you're up to no good.

By the time I had completed my third no-cash-down deal, I was fully familiar with seller's block. I had seen it in operation three times, the last of which serves as a classic example.

The seller wanted to dispose of her small tobacco and wholesale business. Grace had had the business on the market for over a year but couldn't find a buyer. At long last John arrived, willing to pay $400,000 for the business. They hassled over terms.

John had it all figured out. The seller had previously agreed to finance $300,000 over seven years with 15 percent interest, leaving only a $100,000 balance. John proposed to assume $40,000 of Grace's business liabilities as part of the price, and the broker agreed to lend $20,000 of his commission. That reduced the key money to $40,000, which John proposed the seller finance with a short-term note, payable in one month from the business's cash flow. Grace had only to wait 30 days for her $40,000 down payment. To protect Grace, John offered to provide her a mortgage on his house, but she resisted. John tried everything to convince her, saying, "Aren't you getting everything you want? I'm paying your price. All I'm asking of you is to wait 30 days for your money. It's fully secured!"

Grace blew up. She stood up, poked her finger in John's face and shouted, "Young man, who do you think you are? If you think you're going to take over my business without investing a cent of your own, you're crazy!" She stormed out. Seller's block prevented her from accepting a perfectly rational deal that satisfied her own objectives. A couple of weeks later I ran into Grace's attorney who confided that while driving Grace home from the meeting she insisted that, "only a fool would sell to a buyer with no money of his own to invest." After all, when she bought the business ten years earlier, she had needed a $40,000 down payment.

I reminded Grace's lawyer that John was investing $40,000 represented by a bona-fide mortgage on his house, which has plenty of equity. If Grace didn't need the $40,000 immediately, what did she have to lose? After a few moments he said, "She has nothing to lose. With her it's the principle of the thing." That's what I wanted to hear.

I said, "Would your client lend my client $40,000, secured by his house, if he hands her $40,000 at the closing?" He called Grace, discussed it with her for 20 minutes, and called to say we had a deal. The subsequent exchange of $40,000 checks represented one of the most ridiculous deals I've ever seen. Both Grace and John ended up with what they would have had under John's proposal, but they added an unnecessary step to overcome seller's block.

Seller's block can be as simple as a man's being ashamed to admit to his wife or friends that he gave up his business to someone who didn't invest a dime. Some sellers think about the hard-earned cash they originally invested in their business, resenting the fact that you are smarter. Whatever the case, you must recognize seller's block when it arises. Try to find out exactly what's bothering him and stress that he's getting everything he wants from the deal. Don't let him think you're outsmarting him. You simply know an imaginative way to skin the proverbial cat. Be patient.

HOT spot A well-structured and logical no-cash deal can eventually erode seller's block.

Here are a few simple arguments that you can raise when you encounter seller's block.

- Ask the seller what he wanted from the deal. Isn't he getting it? Turn the deal into the basic fact that the seller is obtaining just what he wanted. Why should it matter to him whether the money is coming from you?

- If the seller is financing the deal, show him how he's protected. Remind him of his security and what his options are if you default. Once he's convinced he has little risk, resistance drops.

- Show him that you are investing. It may not be your own money on the line, but what about your personal guarantees and what you stand to lose on default? This demonstrates a financial commitment on your part that nullifies any thoughts that you're trying to steal his business or get something for nothing.

- Finally, show the seller your plans for the business. Let him know what time and effort you will spend to build and improve it. Once convinced that you mean business, he'll be in a better frame of mind to give you his. Once your position is effectively set forth you'll no longer look like Dillinger. Instead the seller will see you for what you are—a sincere buyer who is smart enough to satisfy his needs without spending a dime of his own.

Sell yourself

E-Z TIP

The successful businessman, like the successful salesman, sells more than the deal; he sells himself.

Why do some salesmen consistently outsell others? How do some businessmen pull off deals others can't? Your business terms and all the necessary numbers may make sense, but if the seller has trouble

> **HOT spot** Remember, sellers are people with the same likes, dislikes, prejudices, and concerns as everyone else.

relating to you personally, your job will be twice as hard. You must handle people properly to build the confidence and trust vital to most business deals. The chemistry of people can make or break a deal. You must learn to adapt your unique personality to the sellers. Some sellers will become lifelong friends, while others will never give you the time of day.

Regardless of the seller's temperament, you can learn to appear more credible, reducing his resistance. Use common sense and cater to the psyche of the seller.

Harvey can show you how not to win friends. He thought he was a skillful negotiator, but it turned out he didn't know the first thing about handling people.

Harvey wanted to buy an average gas station for sale by a nice enough guy for whom it represented years of hard work. Harvey knew he could make the station profitable, but he didn't have a down payment. Harvey had seen the gas station but had never met the seller, because all negotiations were completed between the lawyers by telephone. The night of the closing all the legal papers were in order and needed only the buyer's signature. What could be easier? In walked Harvey. The seller and his wife greeted him with cordialities but Harvey had decided to impress everyone with his brilliance. He turned to the seller and said, "The first thing I'm going to do is paint that dump of yours. How did you survive without opening on Sundays?" On and on he went, trying to prove what a great station owner he would be by knocking the seller. After listening to Harvey's insulting comments, the seller got up and walked out, leaving Harvey to his old job sorting mail at the post office. The world is full of Harveys. They never learn diplomacy. Those who understand human nature don't take lessons from a book. Those who don't cannot learn it from all the books in the world.

Contrast Harvey's approach with Mark's. Mark understands people. He never discusses the numbers relevant to a deal until he has formed a friendly relationship with the seller. Once the bond of confidence and trust exists, everything else falls into place. Mark owned a Cape Cod restaurant. Although he was new to the business, he had already enjoyed modest success and the business had tremendous potential. Before long he discovered a larger restaurant for sale for which the seller wanted $200,000 with $60,000 down.

Mark met the seller at the seller's restaurant, engaging him in constructive dialogue concerning their mutual business interests. They compared menus, costs, customers, and suppliers. Mark even gave him the recipe for his own restaurant's best-selling chocolate dessert. At Mark's invitation the seller went to see Mark's operation the following week. They never discussed a business deal. Instead, Mark asked the seller's advice on classic restaurant problems and flattered the man by allowing him to demonstrate his broad knowledge. After a couple of months they became fast friends. When Mark finally presented his no-cash-down deal, the seller instantly agreed to let Mark take over his restaurant with 100 percent financing. Mark's story proves an important point. When two people agree in principle, they can work out even the most unusual terms.

Business deals are like romances—the best ones have as a foundation the "courting" period. It's people getting to know each other, and building a friendship, or at the very least a like, trust, and understanding of each other. In this book I refer to the negotiating table. That's only a figure of speech, for that big table in a lawyer's or accountant's stuffy office is absolutely the worst place to negotiate. The smart buyers avoid the austere environment, and instead try to build the deal slowly and gradually in an atmosphere more conducive to negotiation. That's why the IRS allows tax deductions for business entertainment. They know that more deals—and the best deals—are signed in fancy restaurants than in business offices.

So sell yourself! Once the seller sees you as more than just another buyer, that down payment can become the most insignificant part of the deal.

Know the bargaining basics

Every deal has variables. To control one you sometimes have to abandon another. That's what makes the negotiating game so fascinating. Like tennis, thc winner simply scores more points than his opponent.

To readers of this book the most vital variable is the down payment, so no cash down must be the one point you never sacrifice. Give up anything else, but never budge on this one. Consider the vast numbers of variables open for negotiation in the typical business deal. The following chccklist can guide you at a negotiation session:

- price business assets to be sold
- duration of financing
- interest on notes
- security for notes
- personal guarantees on notes
- seller's agreements not to compete
- assumed liabilities
- brokerage commissions
- closing dates
- lease (if seller is landlord)

Since this list just scratches the surface, rely on your attorney, who will have most of the other important questions at his fingertips. A seller may demand a down payment but he will probably be willing to concede it for other variables of equal or greater value to him.

Let's take a test run. A seller offers his business for $200,000 with $40,000 down. How much will you have to give away to get it for nothing down? Start with price. You offer $178,000 with $20,000 down (don't worry about the $20,000, you're not signing papers yet). He counters with $190,000 with $30,,000 down. Progress! You switch to financing terms. He'll accept payments over seven years at 16 percent. You chip away. You'll agree if he drops the down payment to $20,000 and increases the note to $170,000. He agrees. But you're not through. You say you won't provide a personal guarantee on the note. He'll have to accept your corporation's note so you incur no personal liability in the event of default. He balks. You mull it over, saying you'll provide your personal guarantee if he accepts $10,000 down and drops the interest to 14 percent. He goes along with the $10,000 but holds out for 16 percent. You concede. Finally, you tell him he has to agree not to compete with you within ten miles for ten years. You're adamant. He says that's too restrictive, so you reply, "Okay, make it five miles instead of ten, but only if we shave $5,000 off the price and down payment. I'll pay the remaining $5,000 for the down payment within 80 days after closing."

That's how a typical negotiation proceeds. It may extend over weeks, or even months, or it may consist of a few telephone calls or letters. Regardless of the situation, the essentials remain the same.

- Slowly but deliberately concede minor points in return for the down payment until it disappears.
- Never forfeit a point without winning a concession of equal or greater value to you.
- Never commit to any point until all the points are settled.
- Issue outrageous demands you're prepared to concede. If you must give away anything, always sacrifice what's meaningless to you.

Seasoned negotiators are a joy to behold. They throw appropriate glances at the right time, pause for the ultimate dramatic effect, and light the pipe or cigarette at the perfect moment. Their voices rise and fall with persuasive inflection, all the while bartering away meaningless points for crucial ones.

Not everyone can play the negotiation game effectively, but other methods can work for almost anyone wanting to achieve the no-cash-down objective.

Give the seller more than he wants

Put yourself in the seller's shoes. Pretend that you want to sell your business for $200,000 with a $80,000 down payment. Assume you don't need cash from the sale and will accept an offer of $180,000 with $60,000 down. You'll carry a note for $120,000, but you will refuse to lower the price below $180,000.

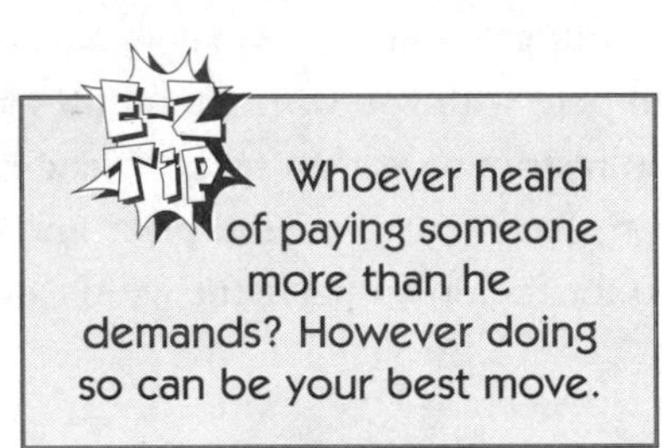

E-Z
TIP
Whoever heard of paying someone more than he demands? However doing so can be your best move.

How would you react if a convincing buyer simply put it on the line and offered you $200,000 with nothing down? You would essentially "lend" the buyer the $60,000 at a fair interest rate. When all is said and done, you will receive $20,000 more for your business plus interest on the $60,000 loan. Not a bad return!

Now, look at the deal from the buyer's point of view. Sure, you're paying $20,000 more than if you had the $60,000 down payment. But consider how insignificant $20,000 can be in light of the long-term positive cash flow of your business. If the business is worth 180,000, it is worth $200,000. But $20,000 can induce the seller to strike a no-cash-down deal.

About 10 percent of all no-cash-down deals implement the premium price approach. A recent example involved a small chain of dry cleaning stores for which George asked $500,000 with $250,000 down. For five months my client Ed negotiated with the seller. Finally, George agreed to a $450,000 price with $200,000 down. Ed never confessed that he didn't have the down payment. As long as George believed Ed enjoyed strong financial backing, he would continue to negotiate, but slick negotiations, like good comedy, require artful timing.

One day George and Ed were playing golf to celebrate their "deal in principle." At the eighth tee, Ed turned to George and said, "George, do you plan to invest the $200,000 down payment I'm going to give you?" George replied, "Who knows? I suppose I'll stick it in a money market account or bank certificates paying 16 percent interest." Ed timed it perfectly. Casually he asked George if he'd consider investing the $200,000 in a solid and secure business deal at 16 percent over seven years. In addition the borrower would pay a $30,000 finder's fee. Of course George was interested, for it would pay off better than conventional investments. The rhetorical nature of the question gave Ed an out if the seller wasn't interested. But Ed moved in for the kill. "George, I'm that borrower. For me to buy your business I'd have to borrow the down payment on those same terms from a relative. I'd rather give you the benefit of the deal." Then he delivered the clincher, "What could be safer than lending against your own business?"

Soon Ed took over the six-store chain with annual sales of $2,400,000 and profits of $200,000, or $1,400,000 over seven years. For such income Ed paid a $4,000 a year premium for seven years. Wouldn't you pay a few extra dollars to own a business that will plop 50 times as many dollars into your own pocket?

The "walk away" and other tricks you won't learn in school

Most people trust what they hear. If somebody tells you she's going to buy your business and will hand you her $20,000 check at the closing next Wednesday afternoon, you'll probably believe her. I don't suggest you shouldn't, unless you're dealing with the champion of all negotiating scoundrels, the "walk away artist."

> **note**
> The walk away artist doesn't do anything that can land her in jail, but she does know how to land herself in a business of her own without investing a cent.

She works like this: She negotiates the lowest possible down payment, then encourages the seller to make irreversible plans in anticipation of the sale. As in the example earlier in this chapter of Rube, who understood seller psychology, the walk away artist sets up the seller so it's difficult, if not impossible, for him to back out. Administering the *coup de grace*, she threatens to walk away, disclosing at the closing that she has a last-minute problem. Her uncle from Peoria was going to loan her the down payment, but he died suddenly. Full of regret, the buyer offers a short-term note; otherwise, she'll have to walk away from the deal. What can the seller do? Not only is he all psyched up about selling—he made plans dependent on the sale going through. His wife can't wait for their long-overdue vacation; his employees threw a farewell party the night before, and he's incurred $4,000 in legal expenses to bring the deal this far.

My favorite walk away artist landed three no-cash deals using that technique.

In one case he purchased an appliance store, making his agreement conditional upon negotiating an acceptable lease. He even promised a $40,000 down payment. To the seller everything looked great until the day of the closing, when the walk away artist complained, "The landlord saddled the lease with a horrendous cost-of-living index escalator. I don't see how I can go through with the deal and still hand you $40,000 down. I hate to do this, but the only way I can cement the deal in light of that lousy lease is if you add $40,000 to your note." Of course he snagged another unwary seller. Despite variations of the theme, the tune is always the same:

- Make the agreement conditional upon some external factor—a lease, other financing, or your accountant's approval of the books. This gives you the legal right to terminate the agreement and walk away from the deal if you cannot satisfy the condition.

- Don't tell the seller about your terrible "problem" in advance.
- At the closing present the problem, then negotiate it away in return for the down payment.

Devious? You bet! But I'd rather call it effective negotiating.

The sabotage trick

Back to the jungle! With the sabotage trick you show up at the closing with panic all over your face. You've just heard that a competitor is coming to town, or the major tenant in the block is going down the tube. You're shaky about the future of the business based on these new facts. With your escape clauses you can walk away and you don't see any choice but to do just that. Now watch the seller come around. He's now doing the selling. Your fears—imagined as they are—will require quite a bit of pampering to get you to sign. And what would better persuade you to slowly give in than a condition that the seller slightly structure the deal to finance the down payment? A client, Pat, recently used the "sabotage" trick to its optimum advantage. She was negotiating for a one-half interest in a well-established real estate firm for a price of $250,000 and $60,000 down. She thought the price was high, but the seller wouldn't budge. So it was time to depress values, and what better way is there to lower the value than to show a new real estate office opening up across the street.

Pat got her friend to rent a vacant store across the street on a monthly rental of $350. Then Pat signed the $250,000 agreement full of escape clauses. The day of the closing her friend with strategic timing put up a big sign "Coming—Acme Realty—10 Full Time Brokers and the Lowest Commissions in Town." Pat showed up at the closing hysterical. The seller had deceived her! He knew all the time that Acme was opening up across the street and never told her. The seller was becoming equally hysterical. On one hand he had a buyer who was not only ready to walk away, but she was also accusing him of fraud. On the other hand he believed he really did have an honest-to-goodness first-rate competitor about to open. After all, he knew nothing about Acme until the sign went up two hours before the closing.

After three hours of crying, threatening, and all-around hysteria, the seller, realizing his plight, agreed to sell for $200,000 with nothing down. Pat's argument was that she now needed the $50,000 to throw into advertising to outdo that Acme crowd. It worked! At the end of the month, Pat's friend took down the Acme sign and the store is still vacant. For $350 in rent and $100 to paint the sign, Pat saved $50,000 and it all came off the down payment.

More pressure tactics that can work for you

Motivating a seller requires both the carrot and the stick. As with donkeys, sometimes the stick can be the more potent force. Think of all the pressure tactics that can and have worked in persuading a seller to sell out—on your terms. Here are some highlights of more dirty tricks that have done the job:

- A buyer who would hire away the key right-hand man of a sickly owner of a restaurant.
- A competitor who literally stole a business by having a common supplier commence legal action to collect $60,000 on a long overdue bill from a target business. The seller couldn't pay up so he had to do a quick sale.
- A competitor who undercut prices and grabbed up three key accounts from the seller's business. Faced with going under, the seller was relieved to salvage something on no-cash-down terms.

HOT spot Remember, if you want to get into business, you have to show the seller why it's in his best interests to sell out. Sometimes you have to help his self-interests along.

- The buyer who threatens to go into direct competition unless the seller sells on more favorable terms. You get the idea. I don't recommend strong-arm tactics, for they can come back to haunt you, but I won't moralize, I'll leave that to you.

Foolproof ways to cement the deal

note

There's a critical time gap between the day you shake hands on a no-cash-down deal and the day you actually get the keys. Remember Murphy's Law. If something can go wrong, it will (and at the worst possible moment).

Until you cement your deal you run numerous risks of the seller finding a buyer who will offer a better deal to his brother-in-law convincing him to hold out for stronger terms.

Every deal is subject to sabotage, and the most common deal- killers are lawyers. Unimaginative lawyers speak a strange vocabulary limited to "can't," "won't, "shouldn't," and "don't." "I went over the deal with my lawyer and he says don't do it, so I guess I'll have to call it off." I can count on the fingers of one hand the times a seller's attorney proposed a better way to accomplish everyone's objective. That means too much work. They'd rather say "don't" and let the seller go back to work, biting his nails waiting for the mythical "better deal" to fly in the window. Still, deal-killing lawyers are legitimate players in the game. Learn what to expect from them, because you can neutralize them with your own sharp lawyer.

The "invisible" players who aren't even in the game will give you gray hairs. Every seller seems to have an uncle in New York City who knows everything there is to know about business.

E-Z TIP

Don't let the seller off the hook. When he agrees to your deal, legally cement it.

Before you even start negotiating a deal have your lawyer incorporate you. Since you'll need to do this when you go into business, have it ready to use for wheeling and dealing. With your corporation in place, you can immediately put your deal in writing. Real estate brokers call it a "binder"; it does just that, legally binds both parties to the terms. Be careful. A simple business binder requires both technical skills and consummate psychology. Leave the drafting to your lawyer. Brokers have a bad habit of acting like lawyers and may offer to do it, but politely decline. They're not trained to draft agreements, and, more important, they aren't working for you.

The simpler the binder agreement the better, because "legalese" sends sellers to their own "deal-killing" lawyers. Rely on your attorney, but keep him in the background. Your corporation will sign as the buyer, giving you a distinct legal advantage. If the seller defaults, he is liable to you for breach of contract. If you default or walk away from the deal, your corporation is liable. What can the seller collect from a corporation that exists only on a piece of paper?

The binder gives you some chips with which to play the game. All the verbal agreements in the world aren't worth a crow's feather. Until you get it in writing, you don't have a deal.

A final word on negotiating to win

There's no "right way" to negotiate. What works on one seller may fail with another.

That's what makes it fun. It all boils down to knowing people—knowing how to satisfy their objectives while you satisfy your own. Unlike tennis, every good negotiation produces two winners—you and the seller.

Key points to remember

- Every negotiation starts and ends with achieving the objectives of both buyer and seller.
- Put yourself in the seller's shoes. Negotiate from his point of view.
- Investigate the deal. Never accept a deal at face value. Detective work can save you thousands—and add to your negotiating ammunition.
- Values are relative. Use the "Men from the East" to reduce seller resistance to your terms.
- Destroy seller's block with common-sense arguments.
- Sell the seller on yourself! Trust and confidence enhance your no-cash-down proposition.

5

How to turn a seller's nightmare into your personal fortune

Chapter 5

How to turn a seller's nightmare into your personal fortune

What you'll find in this chapter:

- Understand the key to a healthy business
- Learn how to create a winner from a loser
- Watch for troubled companies
- Reduce debt for instant equity
- Don't be intimidated into settling for less

Nothing can make money for you like a bankrupt business. Sound farfetched? Believe me, it's not. Particularly if you have what it takes to turn it into your very own perpetual money machine. And here's the best part—there are thousands of troubled businesses that you can grab without investing a dime. Someone else's problems can work for you. I don't care what size or type of business you want; it can be in Boston or Los Angeles. The techniques for buying it—and making money with it—always follow the same principles.

Look around. There are plenty of examples:

- A grocery superette now doing $600,000 a year, taken over for its liabilities only. It provides its new owner with $60,000 a year income—with no-cash-down.

- A nursing home bought right out of the bankruptcy court earns its owners $120,000—again with no-cash-down.

- A glass installation company picked up by an imaginative buyer from a foreclosing bank now produces $100,000 a year—with no-cash-down.

HOT spot Companies in trouble can present fabulous opportunities for no-cash takeovers.

Some of the very best deals involve companies just one short step from the auctioneer's hammer—imaginatively exploited, they have created more than one millionaire.

There's no such thing as a bad business

Father Flanagan of Boys Town was fond of saying, "There's no such thing as a bad boy." The same applies to businesses. Every business, like every boy, has redeemable virtues. It may be that the business as it is is a loser, but the company's insolvency may be due to nothing more than its losing money year after year That may well be an indictment of its management rather than of the business itself. In reality a bad business is a victim of incompetent management unable to utilize assets, capture customers, expand markets, or control costs. In other words, the present management may not be effectively making the thousands of decisions necessary to make that business a winner.

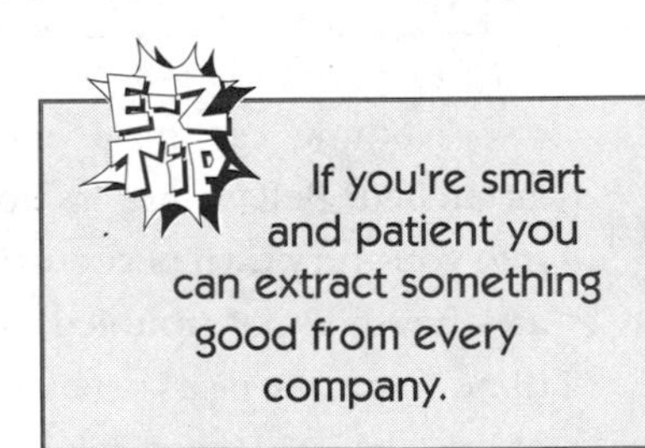

E-Z TIP
If you're smart and patient you can extract something good from every company.

In my legal practice I handle quite a few business bankruptcies. Almost all of these bankrupt businesses could have become profitable operations in the right hands, though some major surgery may have been required. The right management team can do wonders with even the most insolvent and desperate companies. I could write five books on this subject and still not cover all the business failures that were nothing more than management failures.

Last week our firm liquidated a printing plant. Why did it fail? The problem involved three partners who wasted all their time fighting with each other. That same equipment in the hands of an aggressive printer would have the company making plenty of money overnight.

Two weeks earlier we auctioned off a supermarket. It sported a great location, but its owner was too busy being a playboy to tend to business, spending only 20 hours a week on the job. A strong, no-nonsense businessman could easily have increased the gross profits from $2 million a year to $6 million.

Another story involves a men's clothing store. It was owned by a hard-working and knowledgeable haberdasher, but he made one mistake which did him in. The location was in the town's worst location. This same physical plant relocated to a high-traffic mall could have flourished.

The list goes on and on. Some managers don't deserve the title. Management may fall apart due to illness, marital problems, or any one of the other human weaknesses and frailties. Management is people. Businesses fail because the people who run them fail. The toothpaste on a druggist's shelf doesn't fail. The Campbell's soup on the grocer's shelf certainly didn't fail, nor did the haberdasher's neckties. These are the tangible assets of the business. They only do for a business what good management makes them do.

That's how you should think about a troubled company. In your mind separate its problems from its assets. What could you do with it? What changes could you effect in the company to rescue it? How could these very same assets in your hands be transformed into a moneymaker for you?

Now I'm going to reveal a painful but essential truth. If you cannot effectively diagnose and turn around a company in your area of expertise you probably shouldn't be in that business. The management skills necessary to make an insolvent company solvent are the very same skills required to keep a business solvent. The only difference is that with an unprofitable company your management will change its direction.

Management skill must come from you; nobody is going to tell you how to do it. You're on your own. Forget about your accountant and your lawyer. The accountant may give you some basic financial navigation and keep a log of the voyage in the form of financial statements. But he/she can't sail your ship for you. Your lawyer might be able to get you the business, organize it, negotiate the lease, and get rid of creditors. After that he or she is off to the next case. Employees? There may be a few good ones in the pack, but they'll expect you to call the shots. If they can run the business better than you they will soon have their own businesses to run. So where do you turn? At best, management books and courses can only give you broad concepts. As a full professor of management I can assure you that 99 percent of all business texts are written by Ph.Ds who have never stepped outside the warm cocoon of academia. They have never met a payroll. As theoreticians they may be fine, but they won't or can't tell you how many shrimp should go into a shrimp cocktail or whether antifreeze will move at $5.75 a gallon. It all comes back to you. Remove bad management and plug in the good. Given that metamorphosis, any business can become a good business.

Do you remember in the first chapter when I said, "Know thyself"? I encouraged you to ask yourself hard questions about the kind of business you are best suited for. Now, before we move on to the nitty-gritty of taking over problem businesses, I pose one more question: Can you provide management that can make your business fly? The answer is a key to knowing thyself.

The current mania for how-to-do-it business and real estate books creates the impression that any idiot can buy an apartment house (or business), and will tomorrow be enshrined in the millionaire's Hall of Fame! Though I'm all in favor of liberal optimism and motivating those who have what it takes to become successful or more successful, I long ago abandoned looking up the chimney for Santa Claus or under my pillow for the tooth fairy's quarter.

CAUTION Take all those evangelical books and success stories with a big grain of salt. Know your limitations. Move on a sure footing. Have realistic confidence in yourself, emphasizing realistic.

There are some would-be entrepreneurs I'd never encourage. For example, a former student of mine who is now a pharmacist keeps badgering me to find him a drugstore. Despite the fact that I have found plenty of good deals, I never tell him about them because I'm convinced he'll never make it in any business. Academically bright, in the real world he's helpless as a baby. He has not been able to hold a steady job for more than three months, and he spends most of his time blaming everyone but himself. Perhaps I'm wrong to discourage him, but I think it's as wrong to encourage those who cannot make it as it is to not encourage those who can.

HOT spot Regardless of what you've heard about problem businesses, if you have what it takes to start your own dream business, you have what it takes to turn a troubled business into a winner.

Spotting the problem business

Every business has problems; it comes with the territory. In this chapter we'll look at businesses that are more than just a little sickly, businesses that are in fact terminally ill and teetering on the brink of bankruptcy.

On Sunday mornings while semiconsciously dining on my usual toast and eggs, I scan the auction pages of *The Boston Globe*. Where the casual reader sees restaurants, motels, stores, and manufacturing plants scheduled for auction, I see more than that—a lot more. Each of those businesses represents a failed dream and a discouraged owner who must start from scratch. Each spells lost savings and personal disaster. I visualize the many thousands of dollars owed to creditors. A dismal vision indeed. Only the obituaries rival the auction pages for misery. Unfortunately, however, although people cannot come back to life, businesses can and often do. And they often do it without one cent of cash invested.

Since the auction pages are a final farewell, they don't give us the necessary time to move in and structure a no-cash-down takeover deal, so we want to spot the problem business at an earlier stage. There are basically three ways to discover a company in trouble:

1) visible signals

2) financial statements

3) external information

Visible signals can first tip off problems in a company, particularly in the retail segment. I can stroll down Main Street in any town and with fair accuracy predict who's in trouble, and by how much.

The first item I examine is inventory. When I see low inventory levels it means one of two things: Either the owner is operating hand to mouth and without adequate credit to stock the store, or he is so conservative in merchandising that sales and hence profits are bound to suffer. Distinguishing between these possibilities can be easy. A merchant who goes from a $100,000 inventory level to $50,000 is draining off inventory to cover cash flow or operating losses. Sometimes the dummied inventory signal flashes. You've seen it—the twelve across but one deep assortment of soup, one gondola devoted to $25 worth of Kleenex. It reminds me of the bald man who tries to cover up his hair loss by a strategic arrangement of his remaining hair. The rest of the physical plant can confirm the story. There may be non-working light fixtures, peeling paint, unkempt premises, or defunct equipment. All represent visible signals of trouble.

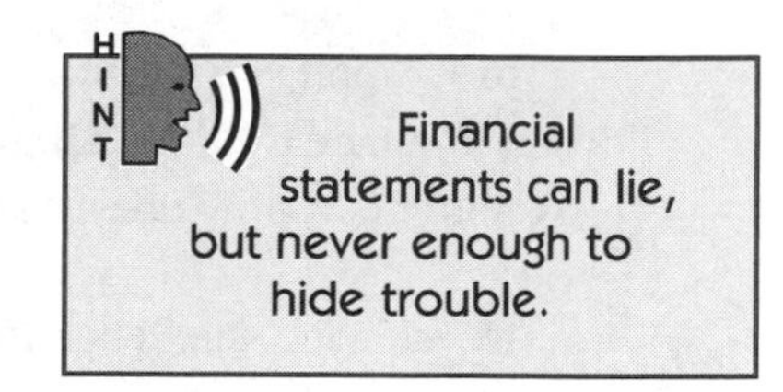

HINT
Financial statements can lie, but never enough to hide trouble.

If you lack such expertise, you need to study an accounting text to learn to read financial statements. Keep your accountant at your side while you look at the balance sheet. How much debt is owed? How old are payables? Can the business make all its note payments? To what extent are creditors closing in? Next examine the profit and loss statement. How much did the company lose, and for how long? How much is the owner taking out of the business according to the books?

What do you think he's taking out off the books? In ten minutes you should learn two important things:

1) just how much trouble the business is in, and consequently, how desperate the seller is likely to be

2) how to structure the takeover

That brings us to the third clue, external information. It takes a good detective to bird dog a potential deal.

Perhaps you can elicit some stories from one of the business suppliers. You might interview the company's landlady to see if she is owed back rent. Sometimes the firm's employees are the best source of such information. Has anyone's payroll check ever bounced? No one can hide problem businesses. They're as subtle as crackers in bed.

What—me in trouble?

They always say it. Then they gulp hard and argue vehemently that they've got the best thing going since the hula hoop. Finally they assure you the only reason they would think of selling is the wife who must relocate to Yuma, Wyoming to cure her impetigo. Sometimes the sellers even believe their own words.

In Chapter 3 we discussed the fragile seller's psyche. Sellers are human beings and hate to admit failure. Why should they? To do so would bruise their egos, and it certainly doesn't strengthen their bargaining position.

Never back the seller into a corner to force him to break down and confess that he's on a first-name basis with the process server. Instead, figure out what it will take to make the seller give you the keys to the store. You must develop insight into human nature. If you keep lifting his head higher and higher, increasing his self-esteem with well-timed flattery, you'll have him eating out of your hand. Downplay the money angle. Don't forget his position. He probably has already seen a dozen potential buyers who tried to knock his business, demoralize him, and knuckle the business away from him. I have one client who has taken over seven businesses for no cash down in ten months. They were all in trouble. He used the following approach. First, he told the seller, "I've fully analyzed your company. Since I'll have to put a lot of money into it to develop its full potential, I can offer you very little for it. However, you are its most important asset. I'm only interested in it if you stay on. I can provide the money the business needs but your continued involvement is essential for this business to succeed."

Imagine sellers waiting for my client to tell them they are behind the eight ball and should thank heaven for anything short of bankruptcy, when all of a sudden they hear praise for their management genius. It's easy after that.

Of course, some sellers say, "I'm glad you want me to stay on, but I'm committed to another job after two weeks." With that, my client replies with relief: "Too bad! I really want you, but perhaps you can teach me some of what you know in two weeks."

So much for the psychology to use on the seller of the problem business. Later we'll discuss how you can put money into their pockets if they insist, but first let's discuss how you can capitalize on the seller's mistakes to finance your takeover.

Getting liabilities to work for you

If a company has $100,000 in assets but also has corresponding liabilities, what should you pay the seller? The answer is obvious—nothing. You can give her $1 for her interest in the company and assume all the assets and liabilities. Now you own the business with nothing invested. That's why troubled companies offer such interesting takeover targets like built-in financing.

Let's explore liability takeovers. First, you find that perfect boutique, then you analyze it from every direction until you're convinced you can make it successful. It's in obvious trouble. The seller says she's asking $150,000, but the books show it owes trade creditors $120,000. At best the seller can only clear $30,000 at the asking price. Once the seller admits this you have locked in $120,000 worth of financing. Later chapters in this book will show you how to get any other necessary monies without dipping into your own cash.

Look at Harry's story. He wanted to own his own business after having worked for a large commercial bakery for years. Finally he discovered a bakery that was in trouble. After a little homework he found that it had liabilities of $80,000. With that information he started negotiating. The seller wanted $100,000. Since Harry valued the business at $60,000, he asked, "How do you arrive at a price of $100,000?" The seller exclaimed, "I have bills of $80,000 and want $20,000 for myself." The seller was unrealistic. If his bills were $180,000, would he ask $200,000?

Harry nursed the deal along. Finally, after months of negotiation, the outstanding bills mounted to $96,000, which was far in excess of the value of the business, but was to Harry only a temporary statistic. The seller, finding himself deeper in the hole, agreed to sell for the debts and a job for himself.

The formula for liability takeovers is simple:

- Calculate outstanding debts. This may involve notes, taxes, accounts payable, or expenses payable. The character of the debts is not as important as the total. The total indicates what the seller would have to pay off if he found an all-cash buyer.

- Accept the debt as part of the purchase price. The deal may require little or no other down payment. Your lawyer can handle the legal complexities, which can pose serious problems.

If the seller is incorporated the problem is minimal. All the seller has to do is transfer his shares of stock in the corporation to you. If his business is a sole proprietorship, he must actually sell the assets. In that case, he must notify creditors of his intentions unless the buyer agrees to assume the debt. A creditor who holds a security interest or mortgage against the assets must grant his permission before a transfer can take place. Bankruptcy is complicated, so leave the details to your attorney.

Some sellers are reluctant to transfer liabilities because they are personally accountable for them. If you fail to pay them, creditors can go after the seller. For example, a seller may have guaranteed a bank note for $100,000 which you assume. If the company subsequently fails, yielding the bank only $20,000, the seller would be liable to the bank for the $80,000 balance. The seller may sue you, but that doesn't relieve him of the responsibility.

Personal liability factors, if they exist, pose a stumbling block to liability takeovers. You can handle that problem in one of two ways: 1. Convince the seller that if he doesn't sell, the business will not make it and he will face a residual liability. With you at the helm, however, he has a much better chance of paying off the debt. It's all a matter of alternatives. 2. Consider personally guaranteeing to pay off the debt yourself, giving the seller legal contractual recourse against you if you don't pay it. Limit your guarantees to an amount consistent with the value of the deal. If you believe the business can have a value of only $30,000 to you, then the guarantee should be limited to $30,000 or less.

Again, let your counsel handle these problems.

Putting cash in the seller's pockets

No matter how bleak his financial picture a seller hates to walk away from a deal without something. If he does not care about being off the hook on personal liabilities, or doesn't worry about saving face in the community by saying, "I sold the business," rather than, "I filed for bankruptcy yesterday," you may have to enrich the seller. Usually it won't take much and you can establish an easy payment schedule. The trick is to give him something more than he would get by putting the company into bankruptcy. After all, why should he otherwise go through the hassle of selling when he could turn the business over to his creditors to liquidate?

> **note** There are stubborn sellers. No matter how great their debts, they won't part with the keys without cash in their pockets. For them, no amount of flattery will replace cash.

Here's how to convince any seller that a sale is better than bankruptcy:

- Offer the seller employment. Many sellers will gladly turn over a business if they have a job lined up. A steady paycheck from you, free from the headaches of running the business, may be just what he wants. Knowing where his next paycheck is coming from can be quite an inducement. A word of caution—don't sign long-term contracts. If he's a good worker he won't need a contract. If he's not don't burden yourself with an unproductive employee. You'll have your hands full straightening out the business as it is.

- Offer a small percentage of future profits. If he's convinced you'll save the company, he'll envision a bigger payoff later. A few years ago I noticed an ad in the *Wall Street Journal* that caught my eye:

Wanted: Insolvent Companies. We will pay cash to the sellers.

Intrigued, I wondered who in their right mind would give a seller anything in exchange for taking over debts in excess of assets? I called and made an appointment for my next trip to New York.

When I arrived I was ushered into an enormous office decorated in Early American Rich. Immediately the "big man" and his cadre of lieutenants surrounded me at an oak conference table. Fortunately I had a client with a troubled toy distributorship who faced almost certain bankruptcy. A likely candidate, I thought. I pulled out my client's financial statement showing assets of $1,000,000 and liabilities of $1,600,000.

After my presentation they asked a few superficial questions, then retired to deliberate. When they returned to the smoke-filled room, they offered to take over the company as is. The seller would simply transfer his shares and receive a contract entitling him to 20 percent of the profits for the next three years.

I raised all the usual objections. After all, profits are no more tangible than the smoke in the room. But they had a better argument. What did my client have now? A failing company heading for bankruptcy. The possibility of something was better than certainty of nothing.

We didn't go along with the deal because I had other plans for my client's business, but that's not the point. Other sellers in similar circumstances did. These buyers acquired 15 companies with combined volumes of $44 million a year without one cent invested, and they have a net worth to go along with it. Watch the *Wall Street Journal*. They're still advertising—and anxious to take over troubled businesses that can make them plenty of cash. Here's how they do it:

Instant equity—yours for the asking

If you find a business with $200,000 in assets and $300,000 in liabilities, you may say, "Who needs it? The debt exceeds its value." Although you are right mathematically, go one step further to see the magic of instant equity at work.

> **note** Thousands of people have made fortunes taking over problem companies, which provide not only no-cash-down financing opportunities, but also instant equity.

What if you could reduce the liabilities to $60,000? Your equity would be $140,000. If you could take over that same business for nothing, and reduce the debt from $300,000 to $60,000, you'd enjoy instant equity of $140,000. (The $200,000 assets minus the $60,000 liabilities.) You could sell the business for $200,000, pay off the $60,000, and pocket $140,000. Maybe you would prefer to borrow $120,000 against the business. After paying creditors their $60,000 you would have $60,000 for yourself and still own the business with a $80,000 equity. On the other hand, you may want to build the business so it can give you a fat paycheck. Either way, you win.

> **HOT spot** Businessmen make phenomenal fortunes taking over sick companies, reducing debt, then cashing in their equity through a quick sale.

Suppose your objectives are different. You're reading this book because you want a business of your own for the long haul. The mechanics are the same. You take over the company and clean up the debt, generating instant equity along with a healthy solvent business. By then you can concentrate on making a profit.

Don't forget profit. Don't become involved in any business unless you know you can make it a money machine. Making the business solvent is the only prerequisite for the fiscal health required for long-term profitability.

Unless you want to be a wheeler-dealer, trading in instant equities won't give you what you want, if what you want is a profitable business of your own.

Three quick ways to a solvent business

Does it all sound too simple to you? How hard is it to reduce liabilities? How do you do it?

note

It isn't as difficult as you may think. Every day, in every city, hundreds of companies strike deals with creditors who are willing to walk away with as little as two cents on the dollar. Understand their alternatives and the concept is easy to understand. Creditors will accept any amount beyond what they would receive if the business were liquidated. It doesn't matter what you owe them. For example, you might owe a creditor $10,000 or $50,000, but what's relevant is what he would pocket if the business were auctioned off. Offer him just a bit more. If he accepts, the rest of his debt is discharged. Watch how this worked for Donald K.

A good-sized hardware store was for sale in a Boston suburb. Since Donald had worked for a competitor in the next town, he wasn't surprised when he heard this store was for sale. For several months the owner had been ill, and the business was going downhill. The financial statements showed liabilities of $400,000 and assets worth $140,000. Although the company's debts tripled the amount of assets, that didn't discourage Donald. He knew he could make the business successful. Several weeks later he paid the seller absolutely nothing for it, then he went to work on the creditors who were bombarding the business with lawsuits demanding payment.

Donald's lawyer called in a well-regarded auctioneer who handled many liquidations for the bankruptcy court, instructing him to appraise the assets and determine what they would bring if the store were auctioned. The answer was $40,000. That's right—$140,000 in hardware inventory, fixtures, and equipment would net only $40,000 under the hammer.

Armed with that information, Donald convened a creditors' meeting and presented the financial facts of life. The business owed creditors $400,000. If the business underwent bankruptcy and liquidation the creditors would split only $40,000, giving each less than a dime on the dollar after court costs and auction expenses. Donald offered them 20 cents on the dollar, payable over two years, or twice as much as they could otherwise hope to get. Oh sure, the creditors grumbled and mumbled. They always do. Nobody wants to forfeit 80 percent of what is rightfully theirs. But what choice did they have? Logic prevailed and $400,000 in debt shrank to $80,000. Donald had instant equity of $60,000 and easily paid the creditors their $80,000 out of future profits.

Is Donald's story unusual? No. Here are a few highlights from some instant equity deals I have witnessed recently:

- A gift shop with a $50,000 inventory. A debt of $60,000 was slashed to $15,000, producing $35,000 instant equity.

- A garment manufacturer with inventory and material worth $800,000 and equipment worth another $200,000. A debt of over $4 million was dropped to $300,000. The new owners picked up a $700,000 instant equity.

- A shoe store with inventory of $100,000 and debts of $90,000 generated an instant equity of $70,000 after creditors agreed to cancel $60,000 in claims.

One of my favorites involved a pet shop featuring puppies for sale. They had $300,000 in liabilities. How much can you auction a cocker spaniel for? Creditors didn't want to chance it, so they walked away for $6,000.

Lawyers commonly use three methods to reduce debt:

1) Composition agreements offer a quick and informal out-of-court settlement. The insolvent company convenes its creditors, reviews the fiscal alternatives, and negotiates a compromise which is usually a

percentage on the dollar payable from profits over time. Most creditors must agree to it before it's binding.

2) Invoking Chapter 11 of the Bankruptcy Code is a more common method to rehabilitate an ailing company. Under its protection a company is fully shielded from creditor action. The debtor buys time to negotiate a plan of arrangement, which is nothing more than a composition agreement under the auspices of the bankruptcy court. If a majority of creditors accept the plan, it binds all creditors. Chapter 11 grows more common all the time. It worked for the giant Penn Central Railroad, and it can work just as well for a small luncheonette.

3) The Dump Buy-Back. I didn't invent the idea, but I will take credit for the term. Suppose you tell the creditors you'll give them 10 percent but they won't listen to reason. They want it all, or at least more than you want to pay them. You let the company be auctioned, borrow enough from the bank to win the assets at auction, and pick it up for a small fraction of its real worth. The creditors disappear and you own a business of your own. Whatever your approach, hire an experienced bankruptcy lawyer. He'll guide this phase of the deal. Leave the creditors to him. Your job is to make the business profitable.

Remember the story about the toy dealer who had assets of $1,000,000 and liabilities of $1,600,000? The New York buyers knew what they were doing. If the deal went through, they would have put the company right into Chapter 11. They figured they could reduce the debt from $1,600,000 to $400,000, producing instant equity of $600,000. With their management team operating, the company made the projected $160,000 a year profits. Not a bad return on a no-cash investment with no risk. Do you believe me now? A seller's nightmare can be your dream come true.

At my no-cash-down seminars the question invariably pops up, "If it's so damn easy and profitable—why doesn't the seller do it for himself?" That's a legitimate question. Sixty percent of all troubled businesses do not sell out. Their owners stay with it and fight to save it, struggling to reduce debt and effect a turnaround just like a new owner. Many of the other 40 percent grow tired and mentally beaten, while still others realize they haven't got what it takes to make the business profitable. Believe it or not, many businesspeople throw in the sponge because nobody, not even their lawyers, showed them ways to save the business.

Forget the 60 percent who won't turn their problems over to you. There are still plenty waiting out there.

Unquestionably the best time to take over a troubled business is when it's still in the seller's hands. The sooner you can get it the better, because terminal cases are harder to handle. Perhaps you didn't realize that flower shop around the corner was in trouble until you heard they filed bankruptcy. If you had only known! Your green thumb could have done wonders with it.

Contrary to popular belief it's never too late. Some great no-cash-down deals have been plucked right out of the bankruptcy court. When I say *bankruptcy court*, I mean any form of liquidation under insolvency, a receiver appointed by the local court, or an assignee under an assignment for creditors. The IRS may have seized it for nonpayment of taxes. A bank may be foreclosing. It doesn't matter. Everyone's objective is the same: Sell assets to pay creditors. Regardless of who's involved, offer them more than the assets would bring at auction because you want them to finance you. If creditors have a choice of receiving $40,000 now or $40,000 over three years, they'll always go for the immediate money. So offer $50,000 over two years at 18 percent interest. They'll start listening. If the offer is attractive enough, they'll finance you.

Even bankruptcy courts anxious to close out cases will entertain time-payment offers that benefit creditors.

> **HOT spot** There is no 11th commandment that says, "Creditors shall auction thy goods." Offer a better deal and everyone can come out ahead.

Our firm recently faced liquidating a stereo shop to satisfy creditors. Our auctioneer expected it to bring about $80,000. Suddenly a buyer offered $100,000, payable over three years with 22 percent interest, all adequately secured. It made sense. We agreed, and the buyer expanded into video cassettes. Business is booming! His former creditors are selling to him on C.O.D. terms and making a profit. If we had auctioned, they'd have enjoyed one less customer.

Refinance and put money in your own pocket

Once you have generated instant equity by eliminating debt, consider refinancing. You may have cash on hand to develop the business or expand into other businesses, but refinancing provides the advantage that such proceeds are not taxable.

One of Boston's largest food wholesalers built its business this way. They searched for small wholesale food distributors in trouble. They'd assemble a no-cash-down takeover, followed by a quick composition agreement or Chapter 11 to minimize the debt. Then they'd refinance with a bank that would lend them 70 percent of the asset value. Last year they completed an impressive acquisition—a company selling exotic foods such as venison and bear meat to gourmet restaurants. They sold over $3 million a year. Its major assets were refrigeration and processing equipment. To replace the equipment would cost over $400,000, but the auctioneer said he'd be lucky to get $80,000. Inventory was negligible since porpoise livers have a very short shelf life. Liabilities amounted to over $750,000. The owner was happy to sell because the buyer offered him a carefree position in another division of the buyer's company. Creditors wound up with $70,000. Borrowing $300,000 against the assets, the buyers paid the creditors and kept $210,000 for themselves. Was it a good deal? You bet. The major asset wasn't the equipment but the customer accounts, which never had a value at auction. Today the gourmet distributor does $5 million with $500,000 profits. The successful buyers are negotiating to take over a fish processor doing $8 million a year and will be delighted to employ their $210,000 obtained on refinancing to swing the deal.

Why debt-ridden companies can be your best bet

Problem companies possess distinct advantages over other forms of no-cash takeovers. An army of angry creditors can induce the seller to hand you the keys, and you can benefit from instant equity. The best part, however, is the negligible risk factor when taking over a debt-ridden company.

If you buy a business for $100,000 with nothing down by following the methods explained in this book, you'll probably be personally liable for the $100,000, because sellers will demand your personal guarantee. If the business makes it you have no problems. But what if it doesn't? How much must you personally fork over if the business doesn't prosper?

When you assume liabilities you can avoid personal exposure. You're taking over the business subject to its debts. That doesn't mean you personally agree to pay them. If the business fails you can walk away. No down payment, nothing to lose: a winning combination!

Key points to remember

- A business never fails. Only management fails. Good management can turn around even the worst situation.
- Make sure you have what it takes to turn a loser into a winner.
- Be on the lookout for companies in trouble; they're easy to find if you know how to spot them.
- Flatter the troubled seller. Help him save face while you save money.
- Let the debt be 100 percent or more of the asking price.
- When you reduce the debt you have instant equity, even if it's only on paper.
- Don't let creditors intimidate you. They'll take a fraction on the dollar.
- Refinance your instant equity for easy money in your pocket.
- Put yourself in a no-risk position—what can you lose?

6

Creative supplier financing: Yours for the asking

Chapter 6

Creative supplier financing: Yours for the asking

What you'll find in this chapter:

- Negotiate for supplier help with financing
- Show the supplier how his help benefits him
- Create a fair deal for all
- Avoid getting "locked in"
- Shop among suppliers for the best financing

Your business should be that proverbial money tree. Not only will it put money into your pocket year after year, it will also put money into the pockets of your suppliers. Those kind folks will benefit immensely from selling you merchandise inventory for that money-making business of yours. In fact, no matter how much money the business can earn for you, it may earn even more for your suppliers.

This brings us to a simple proposition. If your suppliers stand to profit from doing business with you, why not call upon them to advance some money that can put you into that business? You have plenty of persuasive arguments. If suppliers see the profit potential your business represents they'll quickly advance some cash to help with the down payment.

Imagine yourself negotiating for a $1 million-a-year market. The seller wants $100,000, but will finance 70 percent of the price, leaving you to find the down payment of $30,000. With a little research you discover that the supermarket buys about 60 percent of its merchandise from one grocery wholesaler. Assuming the supermarket has a gross profit on sales of 25 percent, total annual purchases will be about $750,000. This translates into the grocery wholesaler selling you 60 percent of that $750,000 in purchases—$450,000 in merchandise—year after year.

Stick a price tag on that $450,000. What is it worth to the supplier? A little more research uncovers that grocery wholesalers take a 10 percent gross profit. With these numbers in mind you have a bargaining chip.

Why not walk into the supplier and lay the chip on the table? You want him/her to lend you the $30,000 in return for your continuing business with the company. It not only gets the $30,000 back, but the company will also win $45,000 in profits each year that you're in business. That comes out to a 150 percent annual return on the loan—a whopping return for even the most greedy among us.

Supplier financing is high on my list. In fact, I've yet to see it fail. My first experience with supplier financing was many years ago when Bill F., one of my more entrepreneurial clients, called to say he had found "his perfect second liquor store." Bill already owned one thriving liquor store, but since he had bought it only two years earlier, it was heavily mortgaged. He couldn't squeeze a dime out of it to help finance the purchase of his second store. Bill told me the seller of the second store wanted $400,000, all cash. Bill had already lined up a bank to lend him $240,000 and the business broker agreed to finance his commission of $40,000. Additionally, the seller would let Bill assume about $40,000 in outstanding liabilities. The problem was the $80,000 down.

> **HOT spot** Properly engineered, supplier financing can work in any business that deals in products, particularly one that relies on a primary supplier.

Bill wanted me to come along on a visit to his major liquor wholesaler in case some legal questions arose. Bill glowed with confidence as we walked through the door of the liquor wholesaler to meet the president of the company. After the usual pleasantries, Bill immediately dropped his air of confidence and adopted a look of despair. It was a good act. Turning to the wholesaler he said, "I've got a problem and want to go over it with you. As you know, I'm buying about $1,200,000 a year from you. I came across a second store I want to buy, but the current owner buys all its merchandise from your competitor, Company X. He spends about $1,000,000 a year on merchandise.

"Well, when Company X heard I was interested in buying the store they were afraid they'd lose the account to you. So they made an interesting proposition. They would lend me $100,000 to finance the purchase of the second store if I continued to buy from them, and they would give me an additional 2 percent discount if I gave them the business from both stores." While the liquor wholesaler mopped his brow and looked for the nearest window to jump out of, Bill continued the scenario, "I couldn't understand their giving me an interest-free loan of $100,000 and additional profit of $44,000 a year (2 percent of combined purchases of $2,200,000) until they explained that a high-volume customer like me would be more than worth it to them." With that, Bill went into his finale, "I knew I had to come to you with it, because all things being equal, I owe you the opportunity to match their deal, since I want to continue to do business with you if at all possible." With that, Bill looked despairingly at the floor, pretending to be the victim rather than the victimizer.

After a few minutes of grunting, groaning, and halfhearted attempts extolling the virtues of his company over Company X, the president asked us to wait a few minutes while he conferred with his managers. Upon his return he announced that he would lend Bill the same $60,000 interest-free loan, grant the same two percent extra discount, and would do even better. He would increase Bill's existing credit line and send in his merchandising team to upgrade the stores' displays. Bill looked up and blurted, "That's great. I couldn't sleep all night thinking I might lose one of my best friends as my supplier. But, just one more thing—Company X was also going to give me a dealer's bonus of a free trip to San Francisco for the liquor dealers' convention.

I assume that will be your policy too?" Even that didn't break the camel's back, for the president said, "Sure." We exited amidst another flurry of pleasantries.

Walking to the parking lot I asked Bill why he didn't tell me about Company X's offer. He laughed and said, "There was no such offer. I never even spoke with Company X. My friend the president would never know that, since he is a bitter competitor of Company X. They don't compare notes. Besides, I bet I could have gotten that deal from Company X. Even if my friend had turned me down on the $100,000, I knew he would have to come up with something, and I could have saved face by simply accepting his lesser offer out of the longstanding friendship and loyalty." Then he delivered the clincher. "You know I only needed $60,000 to close the deal, but I figured why not go for $60,000? If I got it I'd have another $20,000 working capital. In any event, it was a point from which he could always work me down."

Bill played the game perfectly, using a blend of psychology, logic, and business reality (I won't moralize over his little white lie). Bill had his supplier in a bind. The supplier knew that Bill's account was worth the interest on the $100,000 loan and that the extra 2 percent discount was a small giveaway for the additional volume represented by the two stores. The outcome was inevitable. Soon Bill owned his second store without plunking down a dime of his own. In his pocket was $20,000 to boot!

Suppliers may be the most logical source of your down payment, considering the benefits they can derive. This is not a new concept. Whole industries have been built with suppliers financing businesses which will increase the retail volume of the supplier's products.

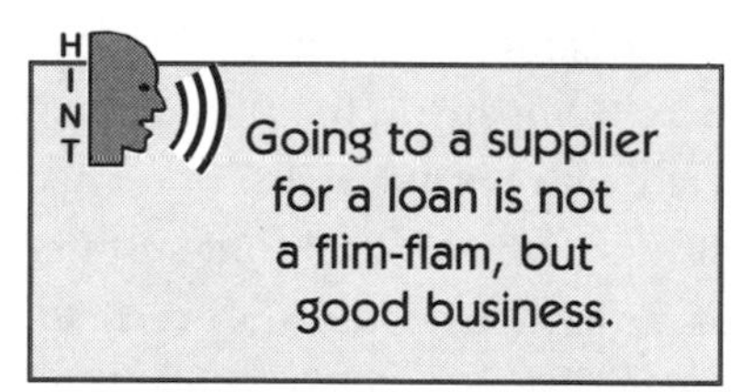

HINT
Going to a supplier for a loan is not a flim-flam, but good business.

Supermarket chains now set up convenience store franchises with practically 100 percent financing. It's not altruism. The supermarket chain serves as a supplier and makes its profit as a wholesaler. Do you want a car dealership, boat dealership, or even a sewing machine dealership? Perhaps

100-percent financing is available to you. The suppliers face little risk. If you fail, they reclaim their goods. But if you succeed, they have a flourishing money tree as you push their products and keep their factories humming. Although franchiser financing can be an attractive way to get started, this chapter will focus on dealing with suppliers who are not in the franchising business, because other types of suppliers can, and usually do, offer more attractive alternatives.

How to structure the supplier loan

Everybody in a deal must perceive a sufficient benefit. Otherwise it just won't happen.

I recommend this approach since it has proven successful time and again:

- Define your primary supplier. Most businesses purchase a substantial percentage of their inventory from one category of supplier, the rest from a scattered number of secondary sources. You want to tap the primary supplier since your account means a lot to him. It's worth much less to secondary suppliers.

- Calculate the approximate amount of annual business he will get from you.

- Determine his percentage gross profit on all sales to you. Don't concern yourself with his expenses or net profit since his expenses are basically fixed; he will usually value your business in terms of gross profit. If you have any experience in a business you will know what the operating profit margins are at various levels of distribution. If not, you can find the answer easily enough by asking those who are experienced or by scanning the trade journals or

E-Z TIP: Everything in business (and life) operates on the "value for value" system.

reference guides that publish comparative financial statements for specific industries.

- Multiply the percentage profit by the annual volume. This will show the supplier's annual profit from your account. We call this number your *supplier profit*. For example, if a supplier of paint stands to sell you $300,000 in paint products in one year and his gross profit is 20 percent, he has a supplier profit of $60,000.

- Once you have calculated your supplier profit, start the negotiating process.

- Induce your supplier to lend you money in return for the supplier profit. How much money can you justifiably request? A good figure to shoot for is at least six months' supplier profit, and that's conservative. I have seen suppliers commonly lend amounts equal to one year's profit, and in some cases as much as two years' profit.

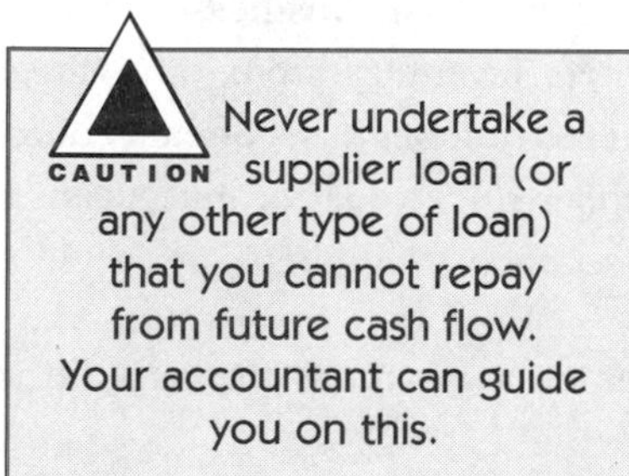

CAUTION
Never undertake a supplier loan (or any other type of loan) that you cannot repay from future cash flow. Your accountant can guide you on this.

Consider the other terms of the supplier loan. For example, what's the payback period? Your supplier will want repayment as quickly as possible, while you want extended payments. How about security? Like any other lender, your supplier will be concerned about the safety of his loan. Be prepared to offer a mortgage on business assets, and, if necessary, a personal guarantee. Your attorney should negotiate these items.

Your buying commitment is essential. Your supplier isn't lending money because he loves you. He's doing it because he wants your business and its resultant profits. He will expect a buying commitment wherein you guarantee to buy a certain quantity of merchandise for a specific period of time. If you fail to satisfy the buying commitment, he has the right to demand immediate payment on the unpaid balance. This is a key point. Play it straight. Don't take his money then try to switch suppliers. Not only will it stimulate quick legal action but could blackball you within the industry.

After all is said and done, how good a deal you get depends on many variables, some of which you cannot control. The competitiveness of the industry is one major factor. Competitiveness is determined not only by the nature of the industry but by geographic considerations. For example, look at the wholesale drug business in the Boston area. No fewer than nine full-line drug wholesalers literally slit each other's throats for the rapidly dwindling number of drugstore accounts. Discounts, bonuses, giveaways, credit terms, and other creative forms of buyer inducements run wild. I could probably get a supplier loan on unprecedented terms from any of these suppliers. On the other hand, take me to Wyoming and there may be just one wholesaler, Without question I would have to approach him with hat in hand just for a cup of coffee. Later in this chapter I'll show you how you can get suppliers to bid for your action, provided enough suppliers exist for an "auction" game.

Your success with supplier financing also depends on your *clout*. By "clout" I mean your value as an account. A large-volume account obviously justifies a bigger loan than a small-volume account that represents only marginal profits to the supplier. What can you do to enhance your clout? If you plan to expand, tell your supplier. Let him/her visualize how he/she will benefit from your burgeoning business by helping you grow. If you're in a position to feature lines that are particularly profitable to the company, sell the supplier on it. For example, tobacco jobbers earn the highest profits on sundry merchandise such as household items, film, and school supplies. Liquor wholesalers generate the greatest profits on private label or house brand liquors and wines. Don't "cherry pick" only the lean items. Remember, your supplier will think selfishly. For you to tap the supplier "money market" you must satisfy its financial needs.

> E-Z TIP
>
> Show the supplier what your account can be worth to him/her. How much money a supplier will lend is proportional to how much profit he/she thinks your account will generate.

There's one final ingredient—you. Suppliers are no different from other prospective lenders. After all is said and done, the nod of the head will only come if people have confidence and trust in you. Tell them about your prior experiences, your plans for the business, and anything else that can convince the supplier that you have the know-how and desire to make the business go.

One of the best ways to instill confidence in a supplier is to offer the endorsement of one of his more valuable customers. If you're friendly with one of his better customers, have him arrange the meeting. You'll know people in the industry and chances are they're not competitors. Better still, bring him along to the meeting. This offers two advantages. The introduction serves as an endorsement, and the supplier may treat you more favorably to maintain the good will of your mutual friend. Essentially you're "borrowing" some of your friend's clout.

> **HOT spot** If expansion is in your plans it can provide you with a dynamic sales tool.

Suppliers enjoy solid and long-lasting business relationships with their customers. They also want to know about your potential growth. A year ago Bill had one liquor store. Today he has two. Perhaps five years from now Bill will have five stores. Today's chains and conglomerates are yesterday's mom and pop operations. As you grow so do his sales and profits.

Watch out for the "lock-in"

Borrowing from suppliers presents some dangers. You want a "value-for-value" deal, but that excludes paying an outrageous price for the loan—the major factor to watch out for in dealing with supplier loans.

Some years ago I heard a pitiful story at a management seminar for nursing home operators. As businessmen generally do, they were comparing notes in a session on food costs. One participant volunteered that he received an 8 percent rebate from his food supplier. Another countered that his supplier gave him 10 percent. Around the table it went until it became obvious that food suppliers customarily grant 8 to 11 percent discounts. Finally, they got to Mildred, an owner of one of the larger local nursing homes. Mildred sat back, looked around, and confessed she had been in business for two years and never received any discount from food suppliers and was shocked to learn that such discounts existed within the industry. Her anger accelerated when she heard two other participants claim discounts from her supplier. Under questioning, Mildred admitted that her food supplier had loaned her $20,000 towards the down payment on her nursing home. When she confronted her supplier the next week, he reminded her of this as a defense for her "missing" discounts. She bought it, figuring, "You can't expect any food man to lend me $20,000 and give me his best price on top of that!"

Mildred was the victim of what I call supplier "lock-in." She felt so obligated to her supplier for the $20,000 loan that she allowed herself to throw away many thousands of dollars in earned discounts. What did the supplier loan cost Mildred? To start with, she paid the money back in one year with interest at the prevailing lending rate, at that time 10 percent. Over two years of doing business with this supplier she purchased $600,000 in food, forfeiting $60,000 in discounts at 10 percent, and she stood to lose $30,000 in lost discounts per year. Mildred unwittingly paid over 300 percent interest for her loan.

It's worth repeating: Suppliers are not and should not be an altruistic lot. But steer clear of any supplier loan that carries a price tag of lost discounts or a waiver of any other customary trade term or concession. Losing these erodes your profits and makes the true cost of the loan outrageous. Make this clear when negotiating the loan. Offer your steady business (and its resultant supplier profits) in return for the loan. If you have to pay it back with a fair interest rate, fine. To become a supplier's indentured servant is the last thing you need. Incidentally, Mildred's story had a happy ending. Her attorney notified the wholesaler that, whereas Mildred did not agree to the waiver of discounts her competitors were receiving, his actions constituted price discrimination violating the Robinson-Patman anti-trust laws. Mildred would be entitled to damages equal to three times her lost discounts, or $180,000. Within ten days, Mildred had a settlement check for $90,000. She then switched to another supplier who gladly granted her a 12 percent discount. Greed always has its price.

Have them bidding for the action

Comparative shopping is nothing new. You shop several car dealers before you buy a new auto. You may even comparison shop for your weekly groceries to make sure you're getting the best deal. If such acquisitions warrant comparative shopping, a deal that may involve a million dollars in a business career deserves the same consideration, but considerably more care, cunning, and effort. You want the very best deal you can get from a supplier, both in terms of the loan and subsequent trade concessions. Let me guide you through the bidding morass by telling you about the no-cash-down techniques of a friend's client, Mr. E., who put himself into the movie theatre business with no guidance and lots of imagination.

> **E-Z Tip**
> Learn to play one supplier against the other and have them bidding for the action.

A theatre was available with full financing, except for the $40,000 down payment. Mr. E. convinced the seller to have the theatre sell gift certificates for future admissions at a 25 percent discount with the proceeds going to the seller, though Mr. E. would redeem and honor them after the closing. The promotion generated $24,000. But what about the other $16,000?

Whom should we turn to?

Movie theatres have only two primary suppliers—film distributors and candy jobbers. Since film distributors have a strict cash and carry policy and a generosity akin to Attila the Hun, Mr. E. opted to tackle the candy jobbers. A quick trip on the adding machine disclosed annual wholesale candy purchases of $200,000. Since candy jobbers make a gross profit of about 16 percent, the successful bidder for Mr. E.'s candy business could earn a supplier profit of $32,000 annually. With this ammunition, all Mr. E. needed were the targets.

In the telephone directory Mr. E. found fewer than 15 candy suppliers for theatre sales. With his numbers in mind he approached all 15 candidates, insisting on the best trade prices, on top of a substantial loan. As expected, the bids ranged from "Sorry, not interested" to $30,000 interest-free and not due for repayment until Mr. E. stopped doing business with that supplier. It was a great deal for both parties. Mr. E. got his loan with enough leftover cash to renovate the theatre, and the supplier got a lifetime customer.

The best bid requires a little haggling. Prepare to go back and forth, playing one supplier bid against the other until you hear the best deal. Adopt the attitude that you're doing the supplier a favor—your business. A small repayable loan is a small price for him to pay. Remember—you will hand him a lot more money over the years than he will hand you.

Use the "captive supplier" theory

Some businessmen are blessed. They give a supplier so much business that the supplier would go broke if the account were switched, setting up the possibility for highly advantageous supplier loans for expansion.

I know a printing company that expanded from a small print shop doing $300,000 a year to a mini-conglomerate engaged in all types of printing services with a volume well in excess of $6 million. The owner accomplished all this through effective supplier financing. Here's how it worked.

My printer friend initially gave a local print shop about $120,000 a year in subcontract work. This $120,000 represented most of his business, without which he would die.

When the printer saw an opportunity to buy a graphic design shop for $20,000 down, he tapped the logical source for the money, the subcontractor who could not say "no" and take a chance on losing his account.

Don't fail because you forgot to ask. Suppliers seldom offer to loan a down payment on a business, but they do have the money. It can be yours, and it represents one of the most logical sources for your no-cash-down deal, but you must ask!

Key points to remember

- Consider supplier financing for the down payment.
- Sell the supplier in terms of "supplier profit," and what your account can mean to him,
- Negotiate a supplier loan that represents a fair deal for both sides.
- Avoid supplier "lock-in." Pay back the loan but don't give away your profits.
- Shop around and have suppliers bidding for the action.
- Use leverage with a supplier dependent upon your continued business.
- Look for opportunities where potential suppliers will set you up in your own business.

A little cash flow

Chapter 7

A little cash flow

What you'll find in this chapter:

- Use cash flow to cover the down payment
- Use a short-term note for the down payment
- Calculate potential cash flow accurately
- Increase sales to stimulate cash flow
- Encourage the seller to accept a down payment from the business

Let's talk about what you're most interested in—money, money, money. Before you start making it, you may have to find just enough of it to get into your own business.

Now here's an interesting statistic that will show you just where that money can come from. The average business rings up in its cash registers in two or three weeks an amount sufficient to cover an average down payment. Think of it. Imaginatively handled, the money the business accumulates in only a matter of days can be yours to satisfy the seller's down payment demands. There's no rule stating you can't "borrow" some of those dollars piling up in the register. In this chapter you'll find out how you can turn those dollars into your own down payment.

How to use cash flow for a down payment

This approach requires two steps. Although there are variations, the basic gambit is always the same:

1) Determine the cash flow potential of the business (the difference between cash receipts and what must be paid out).

2) Structure the deal so the seller gets his down payment out of cash flow.

Follow the case of Sandra P. She wanted to own a large restaurant with an annual volume of $700,000, for which the seller wanted $200,000 with $80,000 down. The seller would liberally finance the balance for ten years at 10 percent interest. The only problem Sandra encountered was the $80,000 down payment, so she decided to chip away at it. The broker agreed to finance $10,000 of his $20,000 commission. That left $70,000 to worry about, $20,000 of which two friends agreed to lend her, bringing her down payment to $50,000.

Sandra's accountant prepared a cash flow statement for the first month. It projected cash sales of $70,000. Actual disbursements for that month would be $2,000 for rent and $14,000 for salaries. Therefore the business would generate a $54,000 surplus cash flow in less than a month. Sandra didn't intend to pay any suppliers for the first month since she was starting clean without bills and figured they would extend her one month's credit. That was all she needed.

Step one of the cash-flow approach completed, Sandra knew she could draw the $50,000 down payment from the business within the first month. Step two was the bigger problem: How could she persuade the seller to wait 30 days for the $50,000? This seller expected it at the closing in the form of a certified check. Sandra found a way out of her problem. She promised to pay the seller $12,500 a week for the first month, allowing him to hold his bill of sale and the closing documents in escrow until he got his $25,000. If Sandra missed a payment by a day the seller could immediately step in and take over.

How could the seller lose? What did he risk? After those questions wore down his resistance, Sandra hit him with the clincher, telling him she wanted him to work for her in the restaurant for the next month at top salary. Not only could he acquaint Sandra with the business, but he could also monitor the operation to make certain everything went according to plan. Sandra honored her word and today grosses $1,200,000 a year and nets over $140,000 with her restaurant.

To prepare a cash flow projection, recruit a good accountant who can give you the magic numbers quickly. It's not hard. First, calculate the projected income for several weeks. Be conservative. If you overestimate your income, your financial commitments to the seller will be in jeopardy. Include all sources of income.

Next, determine the amount of money you absolutely have to pay out in that same time period. Be pessimistic so you build in a comfortable margin of error. Your big question is how little can you pay suppliers—and how long can you stall? That depends on many factors: the credit rating of the business, industry custom, and your ability to persuade creditors to give you sufficient credit before you start paying your bills.

> *note* Ongoing operating expenses such as rent, payroll, and utilities must be paid when due.

Subtract your anticipated expenditures from your income to find the surplus cash you should have on hand at any given time for your down payment. I recommend you project your cash flow on a weekly basis.

Sometimes you only have to calculate cash flow for a weekend. I learned that lesson from Jane R., who negotiated the takeover of a cheese shop. After considerable negotiation, Jane worked the seller down from an initial $60,000 down payment demand to $10,000. The formal closing of the sale was set for

1 P.M. Wednesday. My client called me the preceding Monday to insist I delay the closing until Friday at 3:00. Though it wasn't a convenient time for me or the seller's attorney, we assented. Friday came. By 3:30 we were in the midst of completing the documents when Jane suddenly excused herself and ran to make phone calls from the next office. After waiting 20 minutes for her return, I went to retrieve her. She pulled me aside and said, "Stall the closing until 5:00. Don't ask why—just do it." Bewildered, I revisited the conference room and desperately manufactured half a dozen legal obstacles that needed resolution. Everyone at the seller's end of the table grew edgy and impatient. At 5:00 my client dashed in, completed the paperwork, and handed the seller a personal check for $10,000. The deal closed amidst farewells and best wishes for the upcoming three-day weekend. I turned to my client and asked, "What the hell was that all about?" With a smile she said, "My $10,000 check had no funds behind it. But I'll cover it bright and early Monday morning with the weekend receipts from the business. If we had closed the deal before 5:00, the seller could have called my bank to see if the check was good—goodbye deal!"

I don't necessarily recommend that technique, although it did work for Jane and probably for many others. Picture all the businesses that generate such a tremendous cash flow that two or three days' sales could cover a conventional down payment. Fantasize over the hundreds of supermarkets, discount stores, and other rich cash-flow ventures you could take over, if they'd hold your personal check for a few days.

Sometimes sellers grow impatient to get their hands on the down payment you intend to generate from cash flow. As in most activities involving people, timing can mean everything. The seller may be willing to wait a few weeks for his money, but the business may not generate sufficient cash flow quickly enough to satisfy him. When you meet an inflexible seller flip to the other side of the coin: increasing cash flow.

Plug yourself into this situation: You find a men's clothing store for which the seller agrees to accept a $40,000 down payment in two monthly installments of $20,000 each. He won't budge. Based on projected income, the business can only generate $20,000 in surplus cash flow over the two-month period. Since expenses are fixed, increasing income may be the only answer. What would you do? If you answered, "Run a sale. Increase the next two months' receipts by at least $20,000," give yourself a masters degree in maximizing the income stream. When you successfully pull it off you will have earned your Ph.D.

A little promotion can double or possibly even triple a business' income during a sale. This may be just the answer, particularly if the business has excess inventory. More about this in the next chapter. I watched one company expand into a formidable chain by using just that method. Zeroing in on prospective takeovers with heavy inventory, it negotiated the smallest possible down payment spread over three months. Then it called in its own promotional staff to run wild sales campaigns. Stores formerly doing $40,000 a week suddenly shot to $100,000 to $120,000. When inventories decrease to an acceptable level, the sale stops. However, proceeds easily satisfy the down payment.

> HINT
>
> The approach of income-maximizing does more than get your down payment in short order. It notifies your customers that new management means more than "business as usual."

Use the escrow method to gain control

Let's return to the conference table for a moment. After hours of strenuous negotiations the seller shows no sign of backing down. He's adamant, "$30,000 down or no deal!" He rejects all your ideas about paying from cash flow over the next two months. He wants your check at the closing.

It's time for counter-strategies. Another victim of seller's block, he has no intention of handing you the keys until he sees your money. Confronted with this impasse, try "the escrow method." Before I explain how it works, a word of caution: The escrow method requires consummate legal skill. Confide in your attorney so he/she can properly word the agreements.

To implement the escrow method, insist that your down payment not be deposited in an escrow account until certain post-closing conditions are satisfied. If and when all conditions are satisfied, the deposit will go straight to the seller. Here's the trick: An escrow check is only held, not cashed, during the escrow period. That buys you time to accumulate cash flow from the business to cover the check.

A local car wash recently changed hands through the escrow method. The buyer promised a down payment of $40,000. His attorney argued that the deal should be conditional upon the buyer's obtaining a transfer of the car wash franchise, which would take two months. Naturally, the buyer's attorney didn't want to hand the seller $40,000 he might have to fight to get back if the franchise transfer failed. Therefore, he provided in the agreement that "the buyer's down payment check of $40,000 shall be held intact by buyer's attorney pending transfer of the franchise, and in the event the franchise transfer is not approved, the escrow check shall be returned to buyer upon rescission of the sale by buyer."

Notice the key words: the payment check "shall be held intact." The check "shall be returned to buyer." This insures that the check will not be deposited into an escrow account, where it would be cashed and bounce, of which fact the escrow agent would notify the seller. Under this wording, the escrow agent merely holds the check without knowing that there are not sufficient funds to honor it.

Such legal subtleties make it vital for an attorney to guide you every step of the way. You can easily justify the escrow method—you may need permits for the business; perhaps the seller must repair some equipment; contingent claims may arise against the business. An astute seller may go along with some escrow arrangement, but he may demand a certified check, or that the money go into an interest-bearing account to produce interest pending its release.

Avoid this. It is less a matter of right or wrong than of matching wits with the seller. The trophy goes to the smartest player.

A similar method can also work for you. It involves handing the seller a series of postdated checks for the down payment. Legally this doesn't give the seller much more protection than a short-term note calling for periodic payments, but it creates an important psychological advantage. Though many people are skeptical of a promissory note, they respect your personal check, assuming it will clear. They don't have to worry about your mailing it on the due date, for they already have it in hand.

This provides a good backup strategy if the escrow method fails.

Some pointers on cash flow manipulation

Everybody juggles cash flow. We delay paying some bills so we have enough to buy groceries. It's the great American game. It's also a game you'll have to play with your new acquisition if you want to quickly raise a lot of money for your down payment. Study these pointers for manipulating cash flow to accomplish that objective.

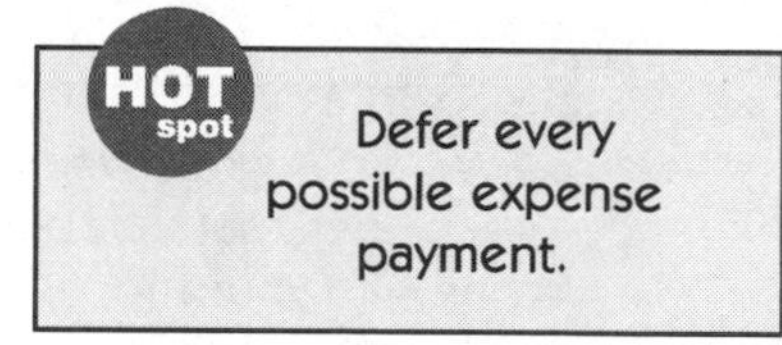

- Your cash flow projections may include a weekly payroll. Consider the resultant increases in short-term cash flow if you can persuade some high-priced employees to defer salaries for a few weeks. It's especially possible at the executive level. This short story proves it. An elderly couple wanted to sell their employment agency for $30,000. They would accept a long-term note for the balance if they received a $15,000 down payment. Buyer B. knew that three high-priced employees each earned $500 per week. B. convinced the seller to drop the down payment to $20,000 and increase the note to $40,000. Next, B. approached the employees, asking them to defer their salaries for one month provided he returned that back pay over the next year with interest and a handsome year-end performance bonus. He was in luck. The employees agreed. With that information, the buyer went back to the seller and said, "I'll give you a check at the closing for $8,000 and four postdated checks for $3,000 each, due one week apart." It was a deal. By deferring their salaries these employees actually helped their new boss buy the business. Incidentally, the $8,000 towards the down payment didn't come out of the buyer's pocket either, because he lined up a client who agreed to advance the agency an annual $8,000 retainer.

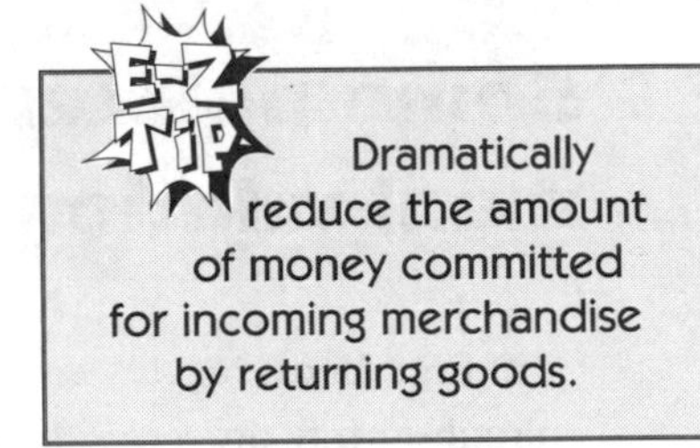

E-Z TIP
Dramatically reduce the amount of money committed for incoming merchandise by returning goods.

- Every business with inventory is saddled with dead or excess stock it can return to suppliers for credit. Accumulate any merchandise that should be returned for credit and use the credit to offset the payments for future shipments. Any business that can defer payments to merchandise suppliers can stimulate a sizeable cash flow into the seller's pocket.

HINT

Aggressively negotiate credit terms with your suppliers.

- Every credit dollar is another dollar you can give the seller toward the down payment. The credit game is not for the timid player. Some of the biggest and most prestigious companies in the country have mastered the techniques of optimizing cash flow by holding creditors at bay. Even the federal government gets cash today in exchange for a debt to be repaid in the future. Look at our social security system. Have you ever fended off a bill collector by saying, "Your check is in the mail." Show me any business that buys $50,000 worth of goods a month, regardless of its credit rating, and I'll show you how an experienced and forceful buyer can haggle at least one month's credit. That $50,000 can cement your no-cash-down deal. In the previous chapter we discussed how to wring cash from your supplier. In this chapter you're pursuing credit. There's no monetary difference between the two; the only difference is when your supplier gives you that money.

How cash flow can solidify any deal

Many sellers will say "I want my cash up front." They don't want to hear about short-term notes, escrow of deposits, or any other technique that allows you to plunder cash flow for the down payment. Against such a recalcitrant seller, use what I call *advance cash flow*. In this instance it's the seller who does the plundering before he turns the business over to you. This does have advantages. The seller has cash at the closing and doesn't have to worry about your scraping up the money. Also, if the seller enjoys a better credit rating than you, he may be able to pull off the necessary trade credit more easily. A record store in downtown Boston which changed ownership a year ago serves as a perfect example.

DEFINITION

> *note*
>
> Ten percent of all no-cash-down deals use the advance cash flow system.

The seller wanted $75,000 for the business with the buyer assuming an existing $85,000 bank loan. The seller would accept a $20,000 note and the buyer would make a $20,000 down payment. Though the seller claimed substantial buyer interest, apparently none could handle the $20,000 down.

The successful buyer didn't need cash because he employed advance cash flow. He said, "You want to walk away with $20,000 cash and a $20,000 note in your pocket. Fine. Within the next month the business will generate a surplus net cash flow of $20,000. If you don't pay your suppliers during that month, your trade debt will total $20,000. You take the cash, and I'll assume the $20,000 in trade payables as part of the purchase price." A month later the seller pocketed his money and the buyer owned his own business with no money down.

This underscores an important point. A seller doesn't care where his money comes from. You can borrow it from a bank, your Aunt Matilda, or creditors.

Who was cheated on that record shop deal? Nobody. The creditors will get their money, even if it takes a little longer. The seller received exactly what he demanded. But the big winner was the no-cash-down buyer.

Journey back to the statistic at the beginning of this chapter—the typical business generates enough cash in the two or three weeks before or after the sale to equal the down payment. Your down payment can be as close as the cash register.

Key points to remember

- Use cash flow. The average business generates enough cash flow in a two-or three-week period to cover a down payment.
- Offer the seller a short-term note instead of a down payment, then pay it from the cash flow of the business.
- Calculate the cash-flow potential carefully. Your deal depends on it.
- Increase cash flow by increasing sales. It can shorten the period the seller must wait for his money—and reduce seller resistance.
- Cover "escrow paper" from cash flow.
- Defer payments, and put the money in the seller's pocket.
- Let the seller take his down payment from the business. It's better than taking it from you!

8

Use hidden assets to get the keys

Chapter 8

Use hidden assets to get the keys

What you'll find in this chapter:

- Utilize every asset that has cash potential
- Turn excess inventory into cash
- Search for disposable capital assets
- Profit from your location
- Arrange customer financing

Your down payment may be staring you right in the face. You may have some trouble spotting it, for it doesn't look like money. But it can be just as good as money if you have the imagination and know-how to make it work for you. In this chapter I show you how you can transform "hidden assets" into immediate cash to finance your down payment. Every business has them; the trick is to be able to spot those assets with a cash conversion potential and turn them into immediate money for your down payment.

> **E-Z TIP**
> Sellers usually don't need instant cash, but you do. And that is precisely why you should always consider the hidden assets of any business deal as a way of raising the down payment.

You may see possibilities never considered by the seller. After all, sellers can be short-sighted. They have been so close to their businesses for so long that they may not realize the potential gold mine locked up in their hidden assets. They can sit on their assets.

Perhaps "hidden" is a misnomer. The asset may be in plain view. Perhaps it's excess inventory, which is visible enough. Possibly it's a large machine collecting dust in the far corner of the building—that too is hard to miss. When I use the word "hidden" I give it a different meaning. I define a ***hidden asset*** as any asset, tangible or intangible, that can be immediately exploited into a cash generator. The ability to convert hidden assets into a down payment has always fascinated me, especially the fact that the list of assets with a "cash conversion" potential never stops expanding. Just when you think all the possibilities have been exhausted, another imaginative buyer finds yet another.

Although the list is endless, the objective is always the same: turn assets into immediate cash for your down payment.

A checklist that can make you money

Here are just a few assets that sharp buyers look for. Use it as a convenient checklist the next time you scout a business:

- excess inventory that can be sold off
- disposable fixtures & equipment
- concession space possibilities
- customer lists
- trademarks & patent rights
- distributor territories
- advertising & display space available to rent

- real estate & leases that can be sold or assigned
- parking areas to sublet
- subsidiary spinoffs
- prepaid subscriptions or enrollments and other customer financing
- excess motor vehicles
- credit rating to borrow or raise cash
- supplier credits due

Consult this list as you engineer your takeover. Let's review it item by item so you can see just how these assets can give you the down payment.

Watch for excess inventory

E-Z TIP
Look for excess inventory first. It's the most common hidden asset you can tap for a down payment.

Observe how Barry T. turned excess inventory into a $40,000 down payment for a gift shop with a volume of $600,000 a year. The seller demanded a total price of $200,000 based on a $140,000 inventory. The seller would finance $160,000 with a $40,000 down payment. Barry knew that the inventory could be reduced to $100,000 without hurting sales, so he proposed a simple but effective proposition to the seller, asking him to run a sale to reduce the inventory by $40,000. The $4.0,000 cash generated by the sale would go to the seller in lieu of the down payment, and the price was reduced accordingly. With this gambit the buyer walked in without investing a dime.

"Inventory work-down" represents the most common method of exploiting this hidden asset. However, simultaneous sell-off can be an equally effective technique. With it you locate a buyer in a comparable business who promises to buy excess inventory from you at the time of sale. All you have to do is swap checks. Unfortunately, with the sell-off method you often must sell below your wholesale cost. With inventory work-down you can obtain a better price despite a discount.

One of the best no-cash-down deals I have seen involved a furniture store with stock jam-packed from the basement to the roof. The seller posted a $1 million price based on an estimated $800,000 inventory. He wanted $150,000 down and the balance over five years. Along came two promotional-minded young men without a dime in their pockets but a plan that could satisfy everybody's objectives. They informed the seller that they'd give him not $150,000 down but $250,000 down if the seller would accept a deal in which the amount would be paid in five monthly installments of $50,000 each following the closing. To protect the seller, all sales receipts would be deposited in an escrow account requiring the seller's signature for withdrawal.

After the seller consented, the buyers ran a spectacular inventory clearance sale. Within the next five months the new partners sold off over $350,000 in excess inventory, paid the seller his $250,000, and had $100,000 for expenses and working capital.

The steps for converting inventory into a down payment are always the same.

- Determine the amount in excess inventory.
- You or the seller work off the excess inventory in place of a down payment, with proceeds going to the seller, or
- You line up a buyer to take over excess inventory at the time of closing.

Whenever you consider excess inventory as a way to your down payment, you have some interesting statistics on your side. A study conducted by faculty members at Northeastern University discloses that 45 percent of all retail stores studied have an inventory at least 20 percent in excess of that needed to maintain sales. Wholesale and distributor firms averaged just slightly lower. Think of it. Almost one out of every two businesses you'll look at have your down payment sitting on the shelf.

Make capital assets work for you

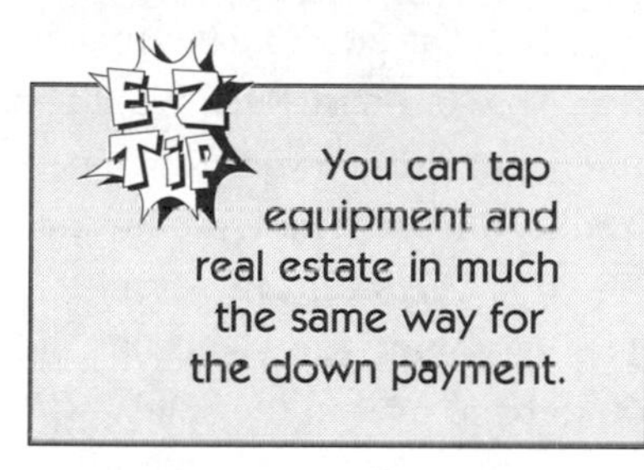

E-Z TIP
You can tap equipment and real estate in much the same way for the down payment.

The "sale-leaseback" is one of the most common techniques. I know a landscaping company that recently sold for $100,000. Its assets consisted of three trucks, assorted gardening equipment with an approximate value of $50,000, and the good will of 100 accounts generating a seasonal volume of $250,000. The seller wanted $150,000 for the business with $50,000 down. At the time of closing the buyer sold the trucks to a physician friend in a high tax bracket for $50,000.

The physician leased the trucks back to the buyer for a monthly rental of $1,000. The $50,000 down payment and a $100,000 note for the balance went to the seller. Since the seller gave up some loan security by agreeing to the truck sale (the trucks would have been additional collateral for the note), the buyer gave the seller a second mortgage on his home instead. Everyone won. The seller had his $50,000 down payment and a fully secured note for the balance. The physician had a tax break from the depreciation on the trucks, and the buyer had his landscaping company with no cash down.

note

The sale-leaseback is common with all types of equipment and real estate, but it works especially well with computers, high technology items, material-handling equipment, and motor vehicles. Time sharing on essential high-cost equipment which you do not use daily presents another way to raise a down payment. Whether it be a computer or a printing press that sits idle 50 percent of the time, why not rent it when it's not working for you? If you have a $50,000 piece of equipment with a capacity to handle three times the work you require from it, you may be able to charge others as much as $25,000 to $30,000 a year in rental fees.

Time-sharing can get you up-front money for your down payment if you know how to get your time-sharing customers to prepay the rental fee. Here's how it works: Assume that the business has a piece of equipment that can be time-shared with another company. It is agreed that the annual rental or time-sharing cost would be $24,000 for the year. Now ordinarily that would be paid at the rate of $2,000 a month. That routine won't finance your down payment, although it is a smart move to increase profits once you have the business. But what if you say to the customer, "Pay the first year's rent in advance and I'll discount the rent by 20 percent." The customer saves $4,800 and you immediately have your hands on $19,200 to hand over to the seller.

More than one enterprising fellow financed the total purchase price of a business through imaginative exploitation of intangible assets.

Here's a classic story that shows the potential cash-generating powers of those intangible assets:

Ralph's story goes back to 1975, when he came upon a company that manufactured artificial brick used for interior walls and household decoration. The business produced over $3 million a year in sales. It distributed its product through lumber yards and major hardware chains. Since the buyer could assume existing bank loans for $400,900, all he needed was $150,000 down payment on the purchase price of $550,000.

The $150,000 down payment was a big stumbling block for Ralph, who didn't have enough money to buy a new car, but that didn't discourage him. He discovered instant cash in hidden intangible assets—cash that closed the deal. Here's how he did it:

First, Ralph learned that the company held international patent rights to the artificial brick-making process. He lined up a Japanese company to license the patent rights for Japan for an advance payment of $100,000 and 5 percent of all Japanese sales.

Next he turned the mailing lists into cash. Over the prior five years, the company had accumulated more than 600,000 names of customers inquiring about the bricks. Who could benefit from these lists? Ralph reasoned that they could be valuable to companies selling related items to homeowners and handymen. He duplicated 50 lists and sold each for $3,000 plus duplication costs, netting $150,000.

When he learned that no product of similar quality existed in Canada at a competitive price, Ralph negotiated for a Canadian distributor to initially pay $75,000 for Canadian distribution rights. Flushed with victory over the Canadian deal, he focused attention on Mexico, where he attracted a similar agreement with a Mexican concern for $50,000 up front. Now Ralph had $375,000—more than enough for the $150,000 down payment.

But there's more. The brick company also held exclusive rights to distribute a special cement filler within the United States. After Ralph analyzed shipping costs to markets west of the Mississippi, he proved that they incurred a loss to the company. Undaunted, he found a West Coast company that was anxious to penetrate this market and was willing to pay $150,000 and a percentage of sales for sub-distribution rights.

Ralph had converted intangible assets into $525,000, but that's still not the end of the story. Ralph imagined all the do-it-yourselfers who might want to learn how to install artificial brick in their own homes to avoid expensive labor costs. So he announced seminars at local high schools. More than 3,000 homeowners flocked to the courses for the small admission price of $10 each. This $30,000, minus modest expenses, gave Ralph $550,000, the full purchase price of his new business. And he didn't give anything away. In fact, each transaction not only put money in his pocket, it improved the sales or profitability of the company

Certainly, Ralph worked like a madman, and he had loads of imagination. Luckily, the seller gave him the leeway to negotiate the deals before the closing.

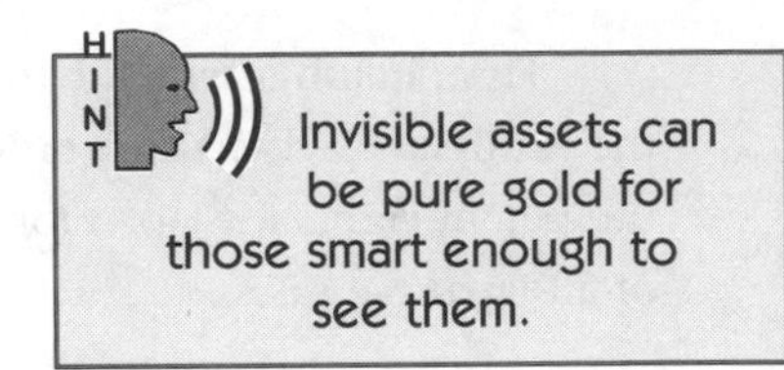

HINT
Invisible assets can be pure gold for those smart enough to see them.

Today the young brick manufacturer grosses $9 million a year with profits of $1 million.

A good lease can be a bankable item

Look carefully at your target business. What is its major asset? It's not the thousands of dollars in merchandise, nor those modern and glistening fixtures, but location. Without location, business assets might as well be sold off for a dime on the dollar. The right location can turn any business into a thriving moneymaker. A lease gives you the location, and believe it or not, can raise the down payment for your business.

The Long sisters developed a successful approach while negotiating to add to their seven-store chain a large suburban supermarket located in a small town. Actually, the store was not a typical supermarket but a modern "general store," selling everything from jogging shoes to antifreeze. It listed for $250,000 with $50,000 down. Either the seller or a local bank would finance the $200,000 balance. Although the Long sisters had made a fortune and could easily produce the down payment, they wanted to continue the no-cash-down style that got them into business in the first place.

The supermarket location provided the key. After visiting several local banks, they persuaded one to rent space within the supermarket for a bank concession at $10,000 a year for six years. The Longs would drop the rent to $50,000 if the bank paid in advance. With the advance rent in hand, the Longs acquired their eighth supermarket without spending a cent of their own. Over the years the bank concession increased traffic in the store, thus enhancing profits. It's an easy concept. Sublease part of your rented space, collecting the rent in advance (at a discount if necessary) and apply it towards a down payment. It can help all kinds of businesses. I've seen a pharmacy near a major hospital rent a concession to a florist, a discount store lease space to a luncheonette concession, and a luggage shop rent space to a travel agency. Only your imagination limits the list.

Sometimes outside space can yield even better opportunities. I once watched Paul T. use an outdoor billboard to pay the down payment on a car dealership for sale for $300,000 with $100,000 down. Paul searched fruitlessly for the cash. Day in and day out he beat the bushes, but he couldn't find anyone to invest, lend, or advance the down payment. Gazing out the window of the dealership he looked up to see thousands of cars speeding by on the elevated expressway. A thought struck him. Who would pay for a billboard on the roof of the dealership? The advertiser would enjoy 100 percent visibility from the entire highway. Without revealing his intentions to the seller, the buyer negotiated from him a lease for the rights to the roof and air space above. The seller agreed to accept delayed payment of three months for the lease. Paul turned around and negotiated a five-year lease with a major billboard company for a total advance payment of $100,000. Paul has his dealership. He was smart, but I had to laugh when a year later the billboard company erected an ad for a competing car agency.

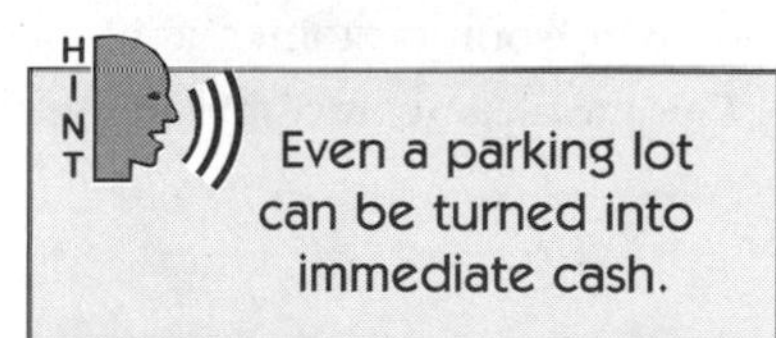

HINT
Even a parking lot can be turned into immediate cash.

I have a client who figuratively turned a parking lot into a thriving restaurant with a volume of $500,000. His story started when he came across a restaurant for sale for $150,000 with $30,000 down. The restaurant was right on one of the busiest beaches of Cape Cod. Our client lined up a married couple interested in leasing the parking lot from 9 A.M. to 5 P.M. each day during the summer months. At 5 P.M. the space reverted to my client, who opened for business at that time. The couple agreed to lease the space on that basis for $15,000 for the season. With the lease in hand, our client assigned it to a bank who loaned him $15,000. The additional $15,000 came from other no-cash-down sources.

More hidden assets to look for

Let's take a typical business with a normal amount of receivables due. The seller wants $100,000 for the business, $50,000 for inventory, $10,000 for fixtures, $10,000 for receivables, and $30,000 for good will. The seller demands a $20,000 down payment. How can the receivables replace half of the down payment?

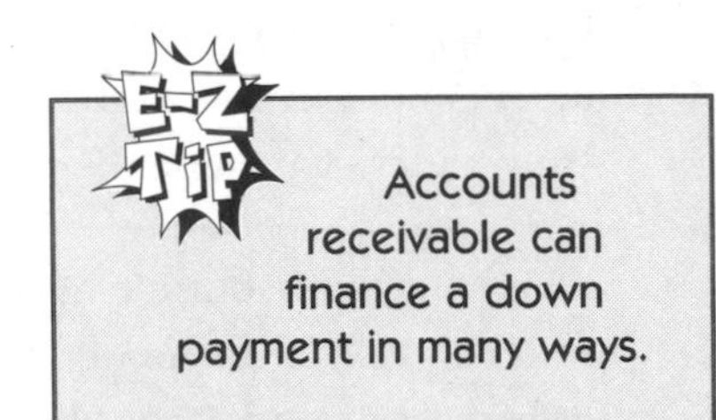

E-Z
TIP
Accounts receivable can finance a down payment in many ways.

Give the seller the accounts receivable and shave $10,000 off the price and down payment. The receivables will turn into cash for the seller within 30 to 60 days, and you will not have to worry about collecting them yourself.

Or you can "factor" the accounts receivable. Through factoring you assign the receivables to a bank or other lender who will offer 80 to 100 percent of their face value depending on how the company sells them. If it sells them on a Urecourse" basis, it guarantees their collectability, while on a "nonrecourse" basis the bank takes all the risk. In the latter case the receivables would still generate $8,000 to $10,000 cash for the seller.

You can also manipulate receivables by offering discounts for immediate payment. Locate a large receivable and offer your customer a 10 percent discount if he pays by the closing date. This cash can contribute to the down payment.

Don't overlook motor vehicles

Another hidden asset to investigate is motor vehicles. Does the company own cars or trucks? Are there any loans against them? If they're paid off you have an easy job. Determine how much you can borrow against them, obtain a loan commitment, and use the proceeds toward your down payment.

The vehicle-financing technique helped my client take over a laundry company. The seller asked $70,000 for the company with $30,000 down. The buyer borrowed against four delivery trucks to implement his no-cash-down deal.

If motor vehicles comprise a substantial part of your business assets, you may have just the flexibility you need. Do a quick analysis. Does the company really need all the trucks it owns? (40 percent of all companies analyzed in the Northeastern University study showed them operating with excess vehicles.) Can you refinance the vehicles? Most businesses do not pledge vehicles as collateral for general business loans and therefore even if the business has a mortgage against its assets it probably will not include the vehicles. If you encounter this situation you can borrow up to the limit on the vehicles.

Vehicles are also a prime candidate for sale-leaseback arrangements. Look for a buyer in a high tax bracket and sell him the trucks for immediate cash, then rent the trucks from him.

Keep these possibilities in mind:

- sell excess vehicles
- refinance the vehicles
- do a sale-leaseback

No matter how you do it, it will bring you immediate money. Are you considering buying or opening a business that serves a particular market segment? Does it offer a product or service that's noncompetitive or unique? If you answer yes to either of these questions, you may take advantage of customer financing.

A few years ago I witnessed a classic example of customer financing. Throughout the country existed drug cooperatives which bought promotional merchandise and coordinated the promotional programs for participating drugstores. Although the stores were individually owned, each advertised under the group name and logo.

It made sense. Collectively the stores could command better prices for merchandise and the concentrated large advertising effort beat all the uncoordinated little ads. An idea whose time had come—30 such co-ops soon prospered.

Then someone got the idea for a "super co-op," a sort of co-op of co-ops, that would buy for all members. After all, if a local co-op representing 100 stores worked better than any one member store, it only stood to reason that the super co-op representing several co-ops could do even better.

The super co-op founders obtained capital by charging each participating co-op a $20,000 entry fee and a percentage of purchases thereafter. Finding money for this business was no problem. The customers gladly paid.

You can apply the concept to less grandiose schemes. I can show you a canteen service entirely financed by customers along its route. This particular service was the only one serving a large industrial park built in a desolate area far outside the city. Since the average American worker cannot survive the day without a coffee break, a young promoter had decided to corner the market but knew it would cost $15,000 for equipment and supplies. He convinced each industrial plant in the park to give him an outright $500 grant and a no interest loan, proportionate to their number of employees. The companies benefited from happy employees and the young promoter had his no-cash-down business.

Some years ago I served as legal counsel for a 350-member pharmacists' association. Everyone in the group complained about extensive internal pilferage, which they combated with independent security services. I proposed setting up our own members-only security operation which would offer better service at lower cost. The idea caught hold. We formed a pharmacy security service, charging each participating member $200 each to produce

$25,000. Everyone benefited and we were off and running without a dime of our own invested.

note

There are hundreds of examples of how customers, representing the major hidden asset of a business, helped finance a startup or acquisition. Here are a few more examples that can illuminate the path:

- Advance orders on a stock market newsletter allowed its publisher to obtain all the funds needed to get started and print and mail the first three issues.
- A flea market promoter rented stalls with advance rents, and with it had enough cash to lease a drive-in movie for weekend promotions of his flea market. He clears $40,000 each summer and started with no-cash-down.
- A company with a new veterinary formula for curing a certain disease commonly found in livestock was capitalized by advance orders from thousands of ranchers. Having customers front-load your startup costs has great potential. Take a lesson from American Express. They have millions of card holders—and each pays a hefty membership fee to join. Multiply that fee by the millions of card holders and you get an idea what advance payments from customers can do for the cash flow—and startup costs of a company. And it can do the same for you. Just ask yourself that one question: What would customers pay you in advance?

Know how to use assets for a down payment

So far in this chapter we have been talking about converting assets into cash for your down payment. But how can you control an asset you do not yet own, and turn it into cash at the precise moment of closing?

The mechanics depend largely on the nature of the transaction and the extent to which you can legally commit to the transaction. I usually advise letting the seller in on your plans. Be open and above-board because you may require the owner's assistance. Your discussions with others about the disposition of assets you haven't yet purchased can get back to the seller, who may resent your wheeling and dealing with his/her property. However, if the plan involves exploitation of intangible assets, such as licensing agreements, trademarks, and marketing rights, you're better off not being too open with the seller.

HINT

Those with the imagination to see hidden assets will find no shortage of no-cash-down deals because they'll see money where others see nothing at all.

I hate to see an entrepreneur all set to take over a company, only to prematurely disclose the entire business plan to the seller. A sharp seller might call off the deal and run with your ideas. Remember Ralph? Do you think the owner of the brick plant would have sold if he had had a road map to $500,000 without selling his company? Let your attorney know what you plan to do with hidden assets. He/she will negotiate the loan terms and other financing according to your needs.

Key points to remember

- Use the checklist on page 144 in any business situation. Don't overlook any asset with a cash potential.
- Turn excess inventory into cash for your down payment.
- Look for disposable capital assets.
- Trademarks, licensing rights, and exclusive products can give you cash.
- Analyze your location—who will pay you for a piece of it?
- If your business offers a benefit to a particular customer group, rely on customer financing.
- Cautiously coordinate your plans with the seller.
- Keep your eyes open. Learn to spot and use hidden assets to get you into your no-cash-down business.

9

More no-cash-down techniques that can work for you

Chapter 9

More no-cash-down techniques that can work for you

What you'll find in this chapter:

- Use the brokers' commission
- Increase borrowing power with multiple loans
- Try gradual ownership
- Consider leasing a business
- Control the lease

At a recent no-money-down seminar someone asked, "Exactly how many ways are there to put together a no-money-down deal?" I thought for a minute and replied, "How many stars are in the sky?" You can combine just the more obvious methods in limitless combinations. The possibilities are astronomical, and we have only begun to explore the universe of no-cash-down techniques. I don't think I'll ever tire of seeing new combinations. Just when I think I've seen them all, along comes another deal involving yet another method. Sometimes the new method works uniquely well for a certain type of business. Other times it's only a brilliant stroke of imagination.

Let's examine some lesser-known but highly effective methods that can give you the keys to your own business with no cash down.

How to turn a broker's commission into a down payment

The typical business seller usually expects less than 30 percent of the sales price as a down payment. But bear in mind that's only an expectation. If you study completed deals, you'll find the average down payment to be less than 20 percent. That's the result of negotiation. The buyer gets the other 80 percent from a bank, seller financing, or both. Your job is to reduce the first 20 percent to zero. The source of that 20 percent may be sitting right there at the negotiating table with you. Look around. You see the seller to your left, but overlook him for a minute. Next to him sits his lawyer. Don't look for his help. But turn to your right. The person with the big smile on his/her face is the business broker, who wants to put together a deal as badly as you do, so he/she can walk away with a 10 percent commission check in his/her pocket. Think about that for a moment. If you want a $100,000 business for which the seller demands $20,000 down, the seller will have to fork over to the broker $10,000, or 50 percent of the down payment.

Don't be afraid to ask the broker to finance half of your down payment with her commission, thereby cutting your cash obligation in half. The seller will still get his $10,000.

Why should the broker lend you her commission? If she doesn't, the deal could collapse, leaving her with nothing to show for her work. Most brokers would rather take their commission over a period of time than lose it altogether.

I've seen broker financing close hundreds of deals, but, as with everything else, timing and approach are crucial. Broker financing will not work if the broker thinks you can raise the down payment from other sources. The broker will insist he/she's not in the finance business. But once you convince the broker there is no other way the deal can go through, he/she will probably agree.

Play fair with the broker. He/she must make a living too. Agree to pay him/her off within a reasonably short time with fair interest on the money. Secure the "loan" with whatever collateral the business can provide. Since brokers handle two-thirds of all businesses sold, opportunities for broker financing abound.

You can use this concept even without a broker if you play "let's pretend" with the seller.

My client, Sam, has plenty of money but fancies himself a top-notch negotiator. In fact, he's one of the best I've ever watched. Look at what he did: Sam had previously taken over two restaurants, in each instance obtaining broker financing after persuading the broker that there was no other way. Now watch the third deal, a $200,000 restaurant he discovered himself. Since he could not turn to the broker for any of the necessary $20,000 down payment, Sam could tap only the seller, an equally sharp and crusty wheeler-dealer. After three hours of intense discussion, Sam had reduced the price to $175,000 with $20,000 down. Then Sam played "let's pretend." Turning to the seller he said, "If a broker were involved in this deal you would have to pay a $17,500 commission. Of my $20,000 down payment you'd get only $2,500. Let's pretend a broker is involved. Reduce the price by $17,500 and the down payment to $2,500 and I'll sign the papers this afternoon."

"Are you nuts?" blurted the seller, "I agreed to $175,000 with $20,000 down because no broker is involved."

Sam sat back and smiled. "True, but a sharp seller like you would have squeezed the broker to lower his commission. Even so you would have agreed to sell for a price that would have netted you, after commission, something less than $175,000 and $20,000 down. who knows what you would end up with after a three-way negotiation. Why don't we compromise? Make it $170,000 with $10,000 down." When the seller finally caved in Sam had his third restaurant. Sam didn't pay the $10,000 either. He persuaded the cigarette vending machine company who maintained a high-volume machine at the restaurant to advance the cash.

Sam's strategy was simple. He reduced the price and down payment by showing the seller how much less he may have settled for had a broker been involved. Why shouldn't the buyer share the benefit of not using a broker?

HOT spot Don't forget that a broker can be your partner in the down payment.

The "multiple-loan" game

Everyone has some borrowing power, but the "multiple-loan" game can legally and easily increase your borrowing power five to ten times. Let's play a multiple-loan game.

Suppose you find a business you want, but after lengthy negotiations exploring all sources of financing, you still need $20,000. Though you have limited personal assets which restrict your borrowing power, you are confident you can obtain a $4,000 bank loan. If one bank will lend you $4,000 on the strength of your signature, five banks will lend you a total of $20,000.

However, there's a trick to it. If you already had a loan, you would have to disclose that liability to subsequent banks, who would say you had exhausted your borrowing power. If you apply to five banks simultaneously, you can truthfully state on each loan application that you have no outstanding loan. Thus you can effectively quintuple your borrowing power.

A word of caution. Always review loan applications with your lawyer. Answer all questions honestly, for illegal false statements can get you into big trouble. However, until banks redesign their applications to include the question "Loans applied for?" you can turn a shoestring into a shoe store.

The gradual takeover

A key employee can take over his employer's business with no cash down if he implements the gradual takeover.

This approach works beautifully on a seller approaching retirement age who wants to gradually relinquish ownership and responsibility.

Ben C. used this technique to buy a prosperous furniture store. He had begun working for the owner ten years earlier as a stock clerk and had advanced over the years to sales manager. When the owner turned 62, he decided to cut down his working hours so he could enjoy more leisure time. He wanted $400,000 for the business, but he was not desperate for a down payment because he did not need immediate funds.

Ben proposed the gradual takeover. He offered to buy 5 percent of the shares of stock each year over ten years. Ben would be able to pay the $20,000 partially out of his own rightful earnings, and the balance from his share of accrued earnings. At the end of ten years, Ben promised to pay the owner the $200,000 balance, giving Ben 100 percent control of the company. Since the furniture store enjoyed twice the assets necessary to collateralize a $200,000 loan, Ben's 50 percent equity of ten years would be sufficient to get the needed money. The deal satisfied both men because:

- The owner retained control of the business for the first ten years. When he reached 72 he could retire and collect Social Security.

- The owner would receive $20,000 a year toward the purchase price, while still drawing a salary and other owner benefits.

- The business was pre-sold. The owner needn't worry about finding a buyer when he wants to retire.

- During the first ten years, the seller could confidently relinquish management involvement because Ben's own financial success rested on skillful management of the store
- Ben would wind up with his own business with no down payment.

E-Z TIP: Few successful business owners want to go directly from full-time work to full-time leisure. Most prefer the gradual wind-down which our Social Security system virtually compels.

If you're an employee who wants to own the business yourself keep these benefits in mind. Every year thousands of businesses go up for sale for retirement reasons.

Ben could have proposed an immediate sale on the same terms, but offered to employ the owner for the next ten years. The owner may have accepted it; many do. However, many others prefer control of their business during the wind-down period, even though they know their business will be in good hands during the gradual takeover.

Life insurance can pay for your business

note

Few people realize that life insurance finances almost as many business acquisitions as bank loans do. I'm not talking about cashing in your policy or knocking on Prudential's door. I am talking about a little-known but highly advantageous technique called "partnership buy-out insurance."

This is how it works. Jill and Joan own a business with a net worth of $100,000. Jill takes out a life insurance policy on her life for $50,000 and names Joan as beneficiary. The women agree that upon Jill's death, Joan will purchase her partner's interest and pay Jill's estate the $50,000 she gets from the insurance. Joan will make the same arrangement with Jill. They can pay the premiums out of the business, producing a nice tax write-off expense.

This approach works equally well between employee and employer. Harry P. purchased a prosperous auto body shop from Angelo S., who was getting along in years and wanted $150,000 for his shop. Harry had worked for him for seven years, and the two men had developed a strong friendship. Angelo agreed to sell to his friend if the sale occurred upon Angelo's death. Then he bought a $150,000 life insurance policy, naming Harry beneficiary. Since Harry would benefit from the policy, he agreed to pay the premiums. Three years later Angelo died. When Harry received the $150,000 insurance proceeds he paid the money to Angelo's estate in return for ownership of the business.

Angelo's heirs didn't have to worry about selling his business because they immediately received $150,000 for it, and Harry got the shop for three years' worth of insurance premiums.

The life insurance gambit requires two essential elements:

1) a seller willing to hold ownership until his death

2) a seller of advanced age. Does the macabre thought of a young employee waiting for an elderly seller to kick the bucket bother you? It shouldn't. We all have numbered days. One leading business journal estimates that 60 percent of all partnerships utilize partnership buy-out insurance. Use some creativity to turn that into an employee buy-out policy.

Perhaps you can combine the gradual buy-out with a life insurance plan. For example, Ben could have negotiated a life insurance plan to finance his immediate acquisition of the furniture store upon the seller's death. If you are an employee with a strong desire to take over your boss's business, contact a life insurance specialist, who may be able to put together a no-cash-down deal the seller can't refuse.

Lease a business—a new take-over trend

Before we go further, I should outline the types of businesses that lend themselves to leasing or purchasing on lease terms. Broadly speaking, they are service businesses whose assets include fixtures and equipment—such as gas stations, printing plants, car washes, auto parts stores, laundries, and vending machine routes. These businesses can be easily leased because by doing so the seller doesn't have to worry about turning inventory over to you. Whether you turn the company into a smashing success or not, the owner has the security of knowing it won't depreciate in value. Notice, too, that these businesses do not rely heavily on good will for success. You cannot lease good will.

E-Z TIP: Ownership isn't everything. You can reap the same benefits from leasing a business as you can from buying it; plus you may receive an added advantage: Leasing can eliminate your down payment problem. People lease cars, apartments, and equipment, why not a business?

note: Why lease a business you'll have to return when the lease expires when you could own it outright? The point is, you can do both.

A properly structured lease can insure that you will eventually own a leased business. Jack M. will show you how it's done. Jack wanted to buy a small vending business consisting of six computer games located at various locations. The seller wanted $30,000 with $15,000 down with the seller financing $10,000 at 15 percent for three years. As it happened, the seller had a $15,000 loan against the machines and would use the down payment to pay it off.

Jack did not have $15,000, so he offered to assume the seller's $15,000 loan. Although that seemed to make sense, the seller rejected the idea because he had personally guaranteed the note and wouldn't be released from liability if Jack defaulted. Thereupon Jack approached the lending bank and asked them to rewrite the note in Jack's name. Since Jack's credit was poor, the bank refused.

The deal was on the verge of collapsing when Jack hit upon an alternative: leasing with an option to buy. Jack proposed to lease the machines for three years in such a way that the rent would equal the monthly payments due the bank plus the $10,000 the seller needed. At any time during the three-year period Jack could exercise an option to purchase the machines for the balance of the note due the bank plus the balance of the seller's $10,000. Mathematically it added up the same way as it would have under the original terms, but Jack's plan allowed the seller to retain title to the equipment until Jack had either fully paid for it or exercised the purchase option. If Jack missed a payment, the seller could cancel the lease immediately. His risk was minimal.

Jack eventually bought the computer games and went on to expand to 15 machines that gross $250,000 a year. Without the lease-option alternative, he would still be a salaried employee. Does leasing seem to be an indirect way to pick up a business? It may, but in some situations it's the only alternative. If equipment is heavily mortgaged, a seller cannot sell it without the consent of the mortgage holder, but he can lease it. If the buyer can't pay off or assume the mortgage, he has no choice but to lease.

Sometimes it doesn't even make sense to try to buy. I recall a recent situation involving two clients who wanted to buy a trailer park.

A young couple, Charlie and Sara, had looked at several before they found the ideal one for them. Located in a small town outside Nashua, New Hampshire, this particular park was for sale for $600,000, and included ten house trailers that could be rented out and eight acres of land that could accommodate 60 others. The seller wanted $600,000 cash at the closing. When we first started to negotiate, I was not optimistic that we could swing a no-cash-down deal. But we took that all-important first step—we investigated. We discovered that the seller owed a $480,000 mortgage on the trailer park to a local bank. The note had 20 years left, at an attractive interest rate of 9 percent. At this time, one could not get a new loan for less than 18 percent.

Turning to the mortgage payback tables, I found that the total payback on a $480,000 note for 20 years at 18 percent was $400,000 more in interest payments than it was at 9 percent. Since refinancing would cost the buyer $400,000, only the bank would benefit from the deal. That was all the ammunition I needed. I turned to the seller and said, "We'll pay you $640,000 for your park. That's $40,000 more than you're asking." Charlie and Sara looked perplexed until I unveiled my proposition. My clients would lease the trailer park and all its assets for 20 years for $640,000 total rent and would have the option to acquire the trailer park outright at any time during the 20 years by paying off the balance of the $640,000 lease. Charlie and Sara would pay 15 percent interest on the $80,000 difference between the sales price and the $480,000 mortgage. The seller would use the rent payments to continue to pay down the mortgage, pocketing the difference in lieu of a down payment. The seller understood the advantages. If she had sold the park for $600,000 she would have cleared only $120,000 after paying $480,000 to the bank. I gave her a $40,000 plus interest "bonus" to finance the $160,000 at 15 percent for 20 years. Had she gotten cash she would have paid a capital gains tax at the time of the sale, further reducing her "walk away money." The lease arrangement postponed her paying the IRS until the time of sale.

But Charlie and Sara were the big winners. They'll save $400,000 in finance charges over the 20 years. Unless interest rates drop to 9 percent, they won't exercise their option to buy until the note is almost paid, then they'll simply pay off the small balance and pick up the deed.

Control the lease and control the deal

That's another way leases can work for you. Using this approach you can pick up a business for a fraction of its value on fully financed terms.

One example is worth a thousand words:

A large luncheonette in Hartford, Connecticut was recently on the market for $350,000. Paul W. negotiated for several months but couldn't get the seller to budge. In the course of the conversations, Paul found out that only several months were left on the luncheonette's lease. If he agreed to pay $350,000, he would still have to negotiate a brand-new lease with the landlord, so he reversed strategies. Paul told the landlord he would like to sign a lease to take effect when the present lease expired. As an inducement, Paul agreed to erect a new storefront and redecorate and upgrade the premises.

Without telling the seller his strategy, Paul got the new lease. Then he sat down with the seller, pointing out that he now held the lease, so the seller couldn't promise any other buyer an ongoing business. Paul presented the seller three options:

1) auction the equipment for $40,000

2) relocate at a new location at considerable expense

3) sell to Paul for $60,000 with no cash down

The seller ranted and raved, but logic prevailed over his emotions, and he sold on Paul's terms.

You may think such a conniving buyer and naive seller are rare, but Paul's is not a unique story. When many businesses are sold, 60 percent or more of the purchase price is for good will rather than for tangible assets. But good will is nothing more than location, and location is nothing but control of the lease.

Was Paul ethical? Before you pass judgment, stroll down any main street or check out the new tenants in any shopping center. Large corporate chains scout top locations for expiring leases. Well before they expire, the corporation moves in and signs up a new lease, turning to the distressed tenant to pick up his assets at slightly better than auction prices. It's just another part of the rough and tumble world of business.

The successful "lease stealer" follows this procedure:

- He finds a business he would like to own, in a key location.
- He checks out the lease by directly contacting the landlord or examining public records on recorded leases.
- He negotiates a new lease with the landlord to take effect when the present lease expires.
- Lease in hand, he negotiates to buy the assets from the soon-to-be-dispossessed tenant, giving him slightly more than auction prices in return for full financing.

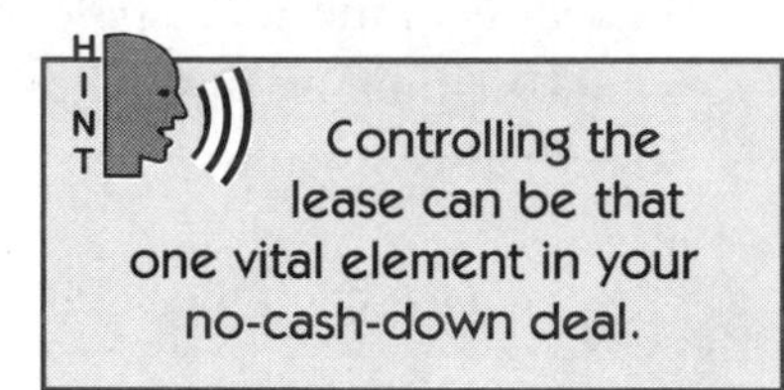

HINT
Controlling the lease can be that one vital element in your no-cash-down deal.

- If the seller won't finance, the buyer obtains 100 percent financing from a bank, considering the low price he will pay for the assets.

Deposits can be dynamite

There are countless deals where customers could and would put up an advance deposit for something you will sell them—when you have it to sell! The trick, of course, is to get your hands on their deposits so you'll have the cash to buy whatever it is you agreed to sell. Does that sound confusing?

I'm now working on an exciting deal for a client. His idea is to buy a 40-room motel in New Hampshire and turn the rooms into time-sharing, or as they are sometimes called, interval, ownerships. You know the arrangement—buyers own and have the exclusive rights to use a unit for a designated time period during the year The motel is for sale for $450,000 and the seller wants all cash. We can get a first mortgage for $300,000 and a high-interest secured second mortgage for $75,000. The broker will lend us back another $25,000 to bring our total financing to $400,000. But we were still $50,000 short of our needed $450,000,

We had plenty of motivation to find that last building block of $50,000, for the deal promises plenty of profits. We estimate that the 40 units can be sold by the week and for 30 weeks of the year. The numbers looked staggering. Each one-week period would sell for $3,000, giving us 40 units x 30 weeks x $3,000 sales price per week. A total sales price of $3,600,000. Against that we have the price of the motel, $450,000, plus renovation and selling expenses of another $250,000. So we have a potential profit of close to $3 million. And all that was standing between us and a fortune is $50,000.

Here's how we solved the problem. We tied up the property for 90 days with a small deposit. Then we began to sell time-sharing units. We told the buyers the full story and asked for a $500 deposit to be placed in escrow with a bank until we had enough deposits to buy the motel. If we didn't obtain the necessary funds, their deposits would be returned with interest. We had no trouble finding 600 buyers—each putting up a $500 deposit. With $300,000 in hand we had ample funds to buy the motel, with the additional money coming from a bank mortgage.

It won't take us long to pay off the mortgage and start pocketing some of the $3 million in profits as the units continue to sell.

HOT spot If your deal is one involving a quick resale, you can look to advance deposits to finance you.

Do you think money grows on trees?

I do. I have one acquaintance that put together the weirdest amalgamation of no-cash-down techniques to end up with ownership of a franchised donut shop grossing $480,000 a year. Here's how he did it:

Last winter a six-acre piece of land located on a major highway came up for sale. Henry spotted it and knew it would be the perfect location for a donut shop. The only problem was that the price was $160,000 and since it was raw land, financing for 100 percent would be impossible to find. Henry gave the seller $1,000 to hold the land for 60 days. Next he found a firewood company to buy all the timber on the land for $20,000, to be removed once Henry took title. Next Henry found a buyer who would pay $80,000 for two acres of the land, leaving Henry with the other four acres. Henry wasn't through. The donut franchiser agreed to buy his four acres for $120,000 and lease it back to him, complete with a turnkey donut shop to be constructed by the franchiser, for an annual rent of $12,000. So Henry had commitments for $220,000 on land that would cost him only $160,000. Henry knew how to wheel and deal with property he didn't even own. With $220,000 in hand he had no trouble paying the $160,000 and pocketing $60,000 as profit. And he was in business with his own franchised donut shop besides. Where others saw trees, Henry saw money. Sometimes money does grow on trees!

HINT

Those who really want to get into business never let the lack of money stand in their way. They have what it takes to grab the initiative and instead find the ways to make it happen.

All the Henrys in this book share a common trait. They don't sit back and wait for somebody to come by and drop a bundle of cash in their laps. That's for dreamers. And as any one of them would say—there's a way into every deal—and every deal has its way.

Key points to remember

- Brokers end up with a big slice of every down payment. Why not ask them to lend you some of it?
- You can increase your borrowing power by playing the multiple-loan game.
- Talk to your boss about selling. He may just be willing to give you gradual ownership.
- If you can't buy, consider leasing. It works for many businesses.
- Lock up the lease—it's better than a down payment.
- Prepaid deposits can give you all you need to buy—and then sell.
- There's a way for every deal—and every deal has its way.

10

Going where the money is

Chapter 10

Going where the money is

What you'll find in this chapter:

- Seller financing is your first choice
- Match your deal with the right bank
- Manipulate the numbers
- Pyramid your borrowing power
- Borrow the right way

Willie Sutton, the famous bank robber, when asked why he robbed banks, replied, "Because that's where the money is." In this chapter you'll see how you can get money from banks and all those other lenders who have plenty of cash kicking around—without a gun.

No cash down may take the place of a down payment, but you still have to find the money to finance most, if not all, of the purchase price. Perhaps you have figured out how to cover the down payment of $30,000 on a $100,000 deal, but where will that other $70,000 come from? Conversely, the $70,000 in financing may be in place; but now you have to scrounge around to find some or all of the $30,000 down payment. In either case you can find lenders who will lend you as much as you need and on whatever terms you need—if you understand loanmanship.

Loanmanship—like robbery—does require its recipient to know where to look. Who has the money? On what terms will they give it up? And what's the one best source for your deal? Those are the basics. To really excel literally having money thrust upon you takes only a few additional tricks. let's start with the basics.

Why seller financing beats the banks

Seller financing will offer you numerous advantages over every other source. You should never even consider any other source of funds until the seller gives you his final "no." The reasons for this advice are compelling:

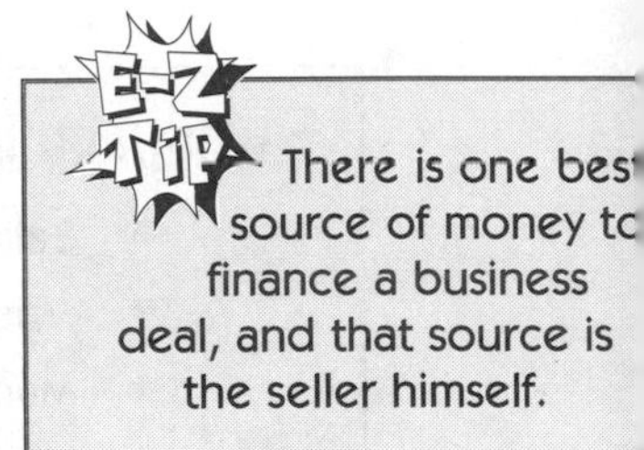
E-Z TIP
There is one bes
source of money tc
finance a business
deal, and that source is
the seller himself.

- "Sellers are not interest-hungry." As I write this book the pri lending rate charged by commercial banks to their best customers soared to over 20 percent. As a small businessperson you won't qua for the prime rate, but will pay anywhere from three to five perc above prime. Go to the SBA and you will pay still an additional one-l to one percent interest. Even friends and relatives will want to hit up for 18 to 20 percent. Why not? They can make that letting th money sit in money market accounts with complete liquidity safety. How can you in good conscience ask them to lend it to you lose money in the process?

But sellers are another breed. They want to sell a business. They're lending you the money to make money from interest. To them its only a in which the deal can come together. And here's a surprising fact—sellers finance you at rates that can cut your interest payments in half. That can m substantial savings to you! I have handled hundreds of deals where most of financing came from sellers agreeing to hold a note for the purchase pr Based on my experience, seller-financed deals outnumber bank-funded d by three to one. With sellers you can bargain for interest rates as low as 10 percent. The typical interest rate paid to sellers on 50 of my latest deals was just under 12 percent. Compare that to the rates charged by your friendly banker!

Why will sellers accept 12 percent? Why not? It's comparable to what their money would earn at the bank. Further, you always have that persuasive argument that if they charged a higher interest they would be making a profit on the loan. They should be more than satisfied with just selling the business. Do a few percentage points on interest seem insignificant? Let's put it in dollar terms. Borrow $100,000 from a bank for five years at 24 percent. You'll pay the bank over $60,000 in interest charges. The same loan from the seller at 12 percent will cost you about $30,000. That's a $30,000 interest differential. What could that $30,000 in savings do for your business? Maybe you'd prefer to think about it in personal terms. Well, it can put you in a top-of-the-line Mercedes. You get the idea.

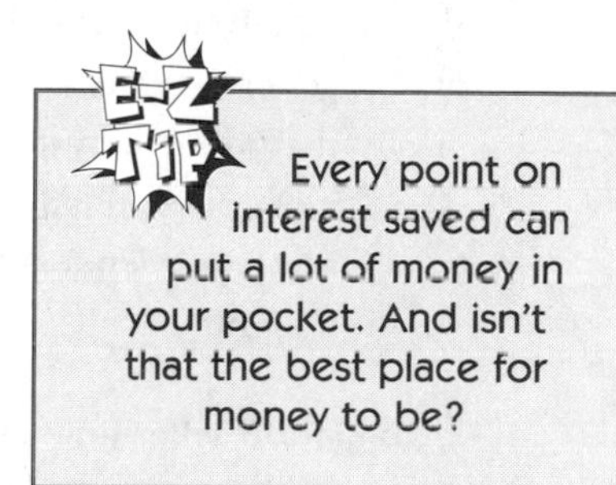

E-Z TIP
Every point on interest saved can put a lot of money in your pocket. And isn't that the best place for money to be?

- Sellers will wait longer for their money. Time is your best friend. The longer the payback period, the smaller the payments. This can mean the difference between success and failure—or perhaps between growth and standing still. Banks are conservative; they may grant loans for up to five years, but seldom longer. Forget friends and relatives—they may say yes to a short-term loan, but check their reaction when you tell them you need it for ten years. So sellers win again. If the deal involves any serious money, the sellers are prepared to wait from five to ten years. On the average, seller notes are written for seven years.

Sellers know the payback capabilities of the business. Besides, we're back to that one all-important consideration—they want to sell the business.

How would you like to buy a business and pay it off over 20 years? I seen it done more than once. Sellers look at it as an annuity. Those ti payments can really make life easy.

> **HOT spot** For no-cash-down deals you'll need every dollar you can find—as long as it's coming from someone other than you.

- Sellers can finance a larger part of the price. A bank might go 50 to 60 percent of the purchase price; the SBA usually stops at 50 percent. And how much can friends and relatives really afford to cough up? But sellers can be generous. Their money is already tied up in the business. Furth they don't have to be as cautious. They know what the business worth. If you fail they can step back in and take it over. Since ba and other lenders can only liquidate, a seller can afford to be m lenient.

Long-term seller financing of 70 to 80 percent of the total purchase pr is the norm, and 100 percent is not uncommon if the deal has the ri ingredients. Later in this chapter I show you how to put those ingredie together.

- Everybody wants collateral. But sellers will accept less th everybody else. Banks and the SBA are hungry for collateral. The gobble up everything you own, including your home, sto savings, and even your pet German shepherd. If you have it the want it. I've seen banks tie up $500,000 in solid collateral fc $100,000 loan. Why shouldn't they play it safe? They're not business to lose money.

Sellers don't have the nerve to demand the same collateral. They want a mortgage on the business you're buying from them and you can exp to personally guarantee the note. Anything beyond that is unreasonable sellers know it. And if you should find a seller who feels insecure holding own business as collateral, you have one hard-hitting argument—"Mr. Seller, if the business isn't adequate collateral for your $80,000 loan, it's not worth the $100,000 I'm paying for it." The logic is overwhelming.

- Here's the best part of seller financing. Sellers can be such kind, forgiving, and understanding folks, especially when business is off and you're forced to miss a payment or two. Now what do you think happens when you skip a few payments with a bank? The loan officer catches hell from the branch manager. The manager in turn has to come up with some answers about your "problem loan" for the president. And the buck doesn't stop there. The president has some explaining to do to the board of directors and a host of regulatory agencies. They can be a humorless, ruthless, and picky bunch. So they foreclose, wipe you out, and make you another statistic. But now their life is easier.

> **note** Consider, now that the business has been sold, do you really think the seller wants it back?

But a seller has only to answer to himself. You are more than a number to him. For starters, you probably have built a personal relationship with him. Perhaps he's even working for you. Besides, why should he foreclose? He knows the business and the meaning of cash-flow troubles. He was probably in the same boat himself from time to time.

With just a little prodding

Here's a typical scenario. You find a business for sale for $100,000. The usual haggling goes on, and finally you propose $90,000, but the seller has to finance $70,000 of the price for seven years at 10 percent. The seller will have no part of it. He wants cash—all cash.

Such a noble idea. Selling a business for all cash can be more than that. It can be wishful thinking. Your job is to convince him that it's the latter rather than the former. No, you're not going to let him off the hook on financing you. No, you're not going to go running to all those greedy banks that will lend you the money—on such disadvantageous terms. At least not yet. Not until you have tried every trick to convince him why he should finance the deal. You know why it's in your best interests.

Here are a few strategies that can turn the most adamant "no" into a "yes."

- Try the bluff. A certain amount of bluffing is intrinsic to every deal. It's all a matter of who capitulates first. The seller will stick with his "no financing" posture as long as he thinks you'll go running off to somebody else to get him the money. That's where the bluff comes in. Let him know that bank financing is out. Either he finances for you or no deal. Faced with that alternative most sellers will come around to your terms.

- Always ask why. You won't always get the truth but you'll have an answer, and that's a start. Do they need the money for other purposes? If that's the situation find out how much they need. Few sellers have to totally "cash out." Perhaps they need some funds—but not all. Now you're closer, particularly if the difference can be made up elsewhere.

- Is the seller's concern the safety or security for the financing? If so you have an easier problem. Elaborate on the security you will offer for the loan. Convince him his downside risk is negligible. Your counsel can set up the loan package in a way that can sell even the most skeptical of sellers.

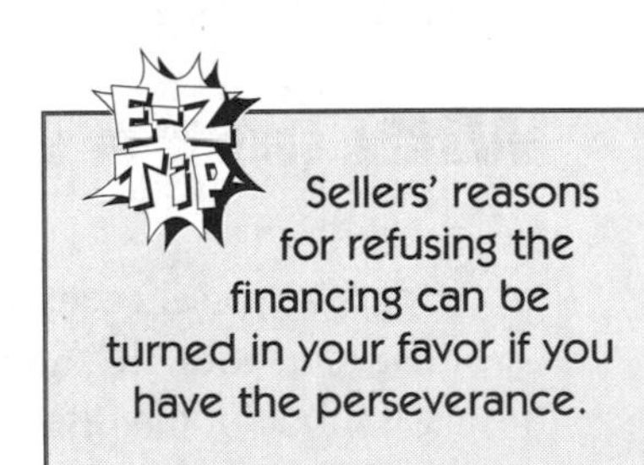

Sellers' reasons for refusing the financing can be turned in your favor if you have the perseverance.

Four points to remember about banks

Even though you can find them on just about any street corner, banks still remain the most misunderstood and intimidating of businesses.

Why all the mystery? It's a rare person who hasn't dealt with a bank. You have a checking account, and chances are you have a savings account or two. Fact is you may be one of the bank's favorite people and not even realize it. Consider that they pay you 7 percent for the use of your money, and turn around and lend it to someone else for 24 percent. How did you think they paid for all those fancy buildings?

But then again maybe you were on the other side of the fence. A loan for a new car? A 20-year mortgage on your home? Sure, you borrowed money before. It wasn't hard. Walk in, fill out an application, wait a few days for a quick credit check and there's your check waiting for you. A business loan, however, is a brand-new ball game. And a lot more is required than knowing how to complete an application.

HOT spot: Forget what you know or think you know about banks.

If you're the average hat-in-hand borrower who continues to be intimidated by all those tall marble columns, you probably are operating on the myths that have given banks the upper hand for years. So let's explode a few myths about banks.

1) Banks are not in the business of lending money. Money's only their inventory. But they are in the business of making money. Profitable loans are what they're after.

2) There's no such thing as a standard loan policy. Banks can and will undertake all kinds of loans, depending on your persuasiveness.

3) You face stiff competition for the bank's dollars. Conversely, how many dollars a bank has to lend depends on supply. But even in the best of times the competition can be keen. For you to win you have to use persuasion on the basis of profits and security.

4) Banks need you as much as you need them—if you have a deal that makes sense. As with any business deal attitude is essential. Remember, at 24 percent interest you're not asking for a favor. The bank will make plenty of money on you, so make yourself right at home.

Open the right doors

Knowing where to shop for your money can be half the battle.

No two banks are alike and neither are any two bankers. You have to find not only which bank is best for you, but also how to spot and cultivate the banker who has both the authority and willingness to write out the check. Let's start with selecting the right bank.

> CAUTION
> Walking into the wrong bank for your business loan makes about as much sense as walking into an Italian restaurant for a chicken salad sandwich.

Banks, like all other businesses nowadays, have their very own specialties. Here's how the field can be narrowed to put you on the right track.

Business loans are the game of commercial banks, while home mortgages and consumer loans are the domain of savings banks, cooperatives, and credit unions.

If you're in the market for a loan under $100,000, concentrate on small banks. Matching size is important. If you walk into a large metropolitan bank you'd be a small fish in a big pond. How important can you be to the big banks when their clientele wheel and deal in $10 million transactions?

Stay close to home. Banks may have legal restrictions or internal policies against lending to businesses beyond a geographic area, usually defined on a county basis.

Banks even offer ethnic differences. Boston, for example, sports two banks chartered primarily to make loans to blacks and Hispanics, while another bank is controlled by those of Chinese origin. Interview a Jewish businessman and chances are he obtained his financing from any one of three banks controlled by Jewish folks. Every ethnic group seems to have its banking affiliations.

Like public restrooms, we have even advanced to "his" and "hers" banking. Several years ago several women got together and chartered a bank exclusively for the purpose of lending to female entrepreneurs, and they're doing a landslide business.

The most important ingredient in the bank selection process is personality. That's right. Banks are more than brick and stone. They're operated by people, and people have likes and dislikes, prejudices and preferences.

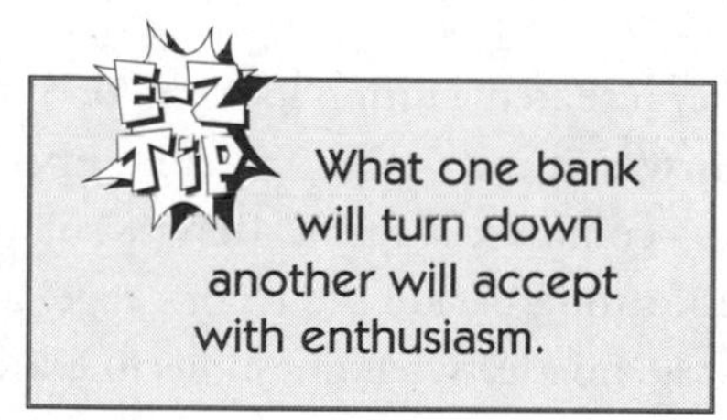

E-Z TIP
What one bank will turn down another will accept with enthusiasm.

All things otherwise equal, the one best place to shop is the bank that is currently used by the business. The seller probably has a working relationship with it and he can arrange an introduction. The bank is familiar with the business and its financial history, and this can get your negotiations off to a flying start.

Spot the capitalist in the crowd

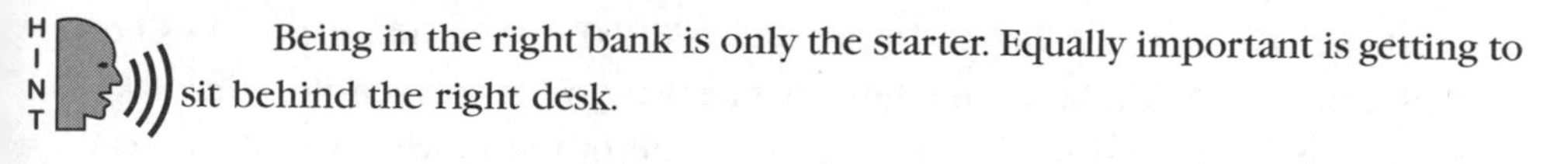

Being in the right bank is only the starter. Equally important is getting to sit behind the right desk.

It's amazing. People will walk into a supermarket, assemble their weekly goodies, and with their shopping cart full, analyze the situation to see which check-out line will get them out the fastest. We've all done it. However, these same people will walk into a bank for a $50,000 business loan and never give a thought about approaching the right banker amidst that sea of mahogany desks.

Choose the wrong desk and you can forget that bank. If a junior loan officer recommends "loan denied," you can bet a higher-up will support her to the hilt. And you can't very well switch loan officers. That is why it's so important to place yourself behind the right desk.

Based on my experiences there is only one "right" desk in the entire bank, and that's the president's. You may have to be a little pushy to get there, but it's well worth it. Going straight to the top has its advantages. You avoid all the $15,000-a-year junior loan officers with limited experience and even less authority. It's all part of the process of not being intimidated. And why shouldn't you be entitled to meet the president on a deal that will give the bank $50,000 in interest payments?

I learned this lesson years ago. I represented a group looking for $50,000 to start a local business. Our first stop was at the desk of a young man with the title "assistant to the vice president—commercial loans." He was so low on the totem pole that he had a steel desk sitting beside the teller's cage. It was clear that he was in over his head and had no idea what questions to ask. After four weeks he still couldn't give us an answer on the loan. So we went right to the top man, and it worked. After one hour of chatting comfortably in the president's office we had our $50,000. We never again settled for less than the president, or at the very least a vice president that had both experience and authority.

Yes, dealing with the pinstripes can be frustrating. I have one client who should have known better. He needed $78,000 to buy into a new business venture. To look at him you'd think that he was poverty personified. He walked into the bank and was ushered over to one of the newer loan officers. My client's loan application was presented complete with scrambled eggs and coffee stains (he made it out while eating breakfast). That was enough to discourage this pinstriper. He turned down the request and completely ignored the $3 million net worth of my client. One quick trip to the president's office did the trick. It may sound ridiculous but that's just what happened.

HOT spot There's nothing like being on a first-name basis with an honest-to-goodness bank president. Why not? You'll see him or her many times during your career.

How to get a bank to say "yes"

Now the fun begins. Imagine yourself sitting across the big mahogany desk saying to the bank president you only need $1200,000 to buy Joe's Diner. You ramble on about what a great deal it is and how much money you're going to make, when he politely shows you the door—without the cash. Where did you go wrong? The answer is simple. You acted like an amateur, and banks don't lend money to amateurs. If you had had the $3 million net worth of my client they may have overlooked your inadequacies as they focused on your assets. But not if you're the buyer going in on nothing more than a wing and a prayer. That means knowing what the bank will look for before it says "yes"—I call them the three Cs.

note You have to think like a pro, act like a pro, and sell like a pro.

1) CHARACTER: Do you have a history of good credit, or are you a deadbeat?

2) CASH FLOW: Does the business offer sufficient cash flow and profit after expenses to pay back the loan? Your best intentions mean little if the numbers don't work.

3) COLLATERAL: What does the bank risk? If your loan defaults, will the bank have sufficient collateral to recover the balance owed? Professionals know a bank will assess the loan application on these three points alone, so they cover them immediately in a clear, logical, and businesslike proposal. Follow this checklist:

➢ Credit and Personal History (Character):

- ❑ Name and address
- ❑ Family status
- ❑ Employment history
- ❑ Experiences in related business
- ❑ Education
- ❑ Personal assets
- ❑ Personal liabilities
- ❑ Military status
- ❑ Bank references
- ❑ Credit references

➢ Financial Information on the Business (Cash flow):

- ❑ Brief description of business
- ❑ Brief history of business
- ❑ Tax returns for two years

- ❑ Projected cash-flow statement for loan period
- ❑ Summary of proposed business changes
- ❑ Lease or proposed lease terms

➢ Collateral

- ❑ Business assets
- ❑ Acquisition cost or replacement cost
- ❑ Liquidation value of assets

➢ Proposed loan

- ❑ Amount required
- ❑ Loan period
- ❑ Interest terms
- ❑ Identification of guarantors
- ❑ Collateral to be pledged

A proposal containing these items gives the banker everything he needs to evaluate your loan. You've anticipated his questions. More importantly, he knows he's dealing with a pro, which immediately gives him confidence in you and your deal. Have your accountant prepare the financial information, or take him to the bank with you. A banker will feel more comfortable if he knows an accountant is navigating you.

E-Z TIP: A well-structured loan proposal will tell the banker more than what's in the proposal. It will reveal that you're a pro.

Be certain the numbers work. If your loan requires a $2,000-per- month payment, you're going to fail if your cash-flow statement shows the availability of only $1,000 per month. Be prepared to defend your proposal if your banker asks probing questions. He/she may want answers or may be testing to find out how much you really know about the business.

What to do if the bank says "no"

Don't let failure discourage you. You may wander from bank to bank failing each and every time, but if you're smart you'll want to find out why. Once you detect the flaw in your proposal you can correct it. Your first loan proposal should give you a message. The banker saw a weakness you overlooked. If it was significant enough to turn you down, then other bankers will spot the same problem. Don't be fooled into thinking bankers are the world's best businessmen, but they can bring to your deal a certain objectivity that can put you on the right track and perhaps even save you from disaster. I knew a retired schoolteacher who wanted to borrow $400,000 to buy a nursery school. Bank after bank turned her down. Finally, one banker pointed out that the school never had a sufficient enrollment to pay the loan. But the teacher ignored the warning signals, borrowed $400,000 from the SBA and went bust just 18 months later.

Sometimes banks say "no" when they really mean "yes," but to a different arrangement. You may have been rejected for a $190,000 loan, but prod further; they may have been willing to go for $75,000. Perhaps your request for interest at 19 percent was below their current rate of 21 percent. It may be that a little more collateral would do the trick. In any event don't take "no" for an answer. There's always more to it than that.

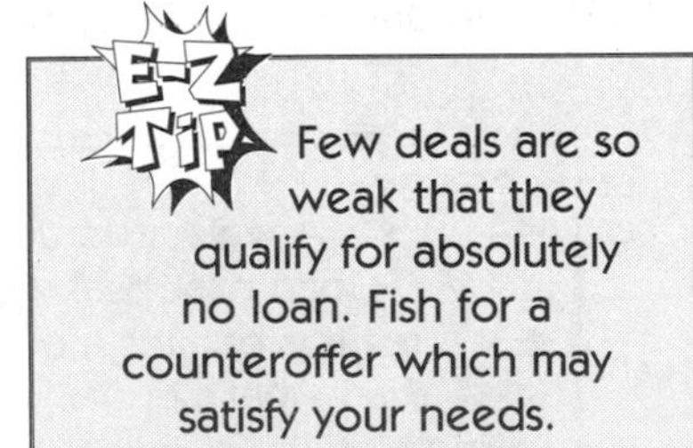

E-Z TIP
Few deals are so weak that they qualify for absolutely no loan. Fish for a counteroffer which may satisfy your needs.

Negotiate the loan to your benefit

There's a right way and wrong way to structure a loan. These rules of thumb can save you money and make the difference between success and failure:

- Do negotiate interest. Like any other business deal, loans are subject to bargaining. Banks can drop the interest rate by a point or two if they think the plan is strong enough

- Do demand the longest loan period possible, thus lowering monthly payments and conserving cash flow,

- Do pledge the business assets as collateral, protecting your personal assets in the event of default. Auction proceeds may satisfy the bank so it won't go after you personally if you signed a personal guarantee.

- Don't give additional collateral, such as a house mortgage, without a fight. Banks will ask for it but that doesn't necessarily mean you have to give it. Confine the collateral to the business (except for your personal guarantee, which will be required) and nothing more.

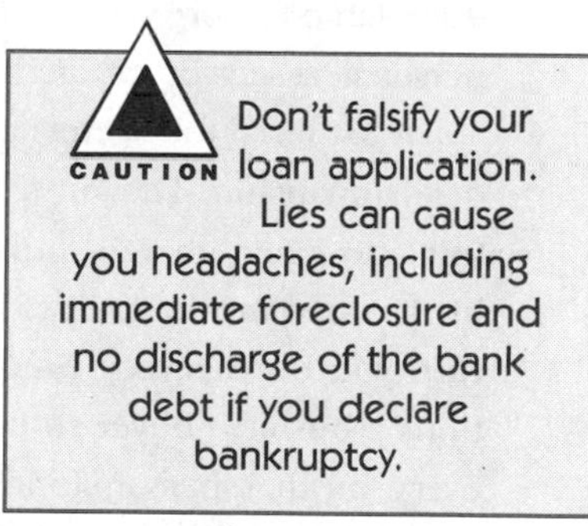

CAUTION
Don't falsify your loan application. Lies can cause you headaches, including immediate foreclosure and no discharge of the bank debt if you declare bankruptcy.

- Don't borrow directly. The corporation should borrow the money. If you personally borrow the money, the bank cannot grab business assets in the event of default, and you will personally have to repay the loan. Your attorney can structure the loan to provide you maximum protection.

- Don't settle for the first loan offer. Banks sit on every corner. Shop around. You may get a better deal next door.

How to borrow a down payment from a bank

Borrowing a down payment from a bank requires a different strategy than you'd use to obtain a long-term loan for most of the purchase price.

- A down payment loan represents a relatively small amount (10 to 20 percent of the purchase price).
- The down payment loan spans a short term (one year or less).
- A bank can't consider business assets as collateral for a down payment loan if such assets are mortgaged by the seller or other lenders who have advanced most of the purchase price.

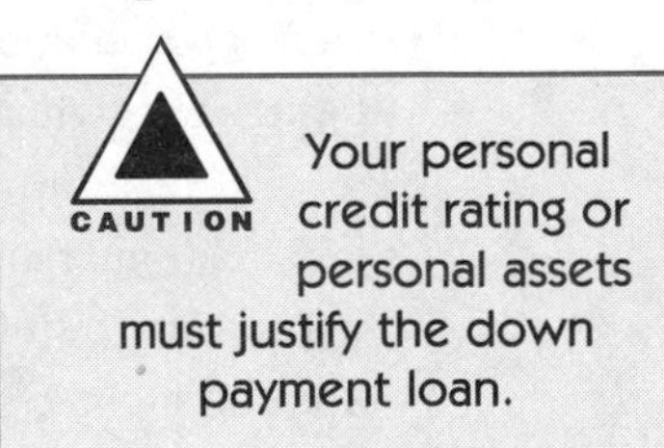

CAUTION
Your personal credit rating or personal assets must justify the down payment loan.

You're after a short-term, unsecured (no collateral) loan which is available to borrowers with minimal personal assets or credit history, but you must learn the secrets of this type of loanmanship. The most important thing to remember is never tell the bank you want the loan to finance the down payment on a business. They'll turn you down every time. Why? Because banks are ultraconservative and think a business buyer should possess 40 to 50 percent of the selling price. If every businessperson followed such advice, businesses such as Monsanto, which started with only $5,090, would never have gotten off the ground.

Banks do understand these needs, however:

- you need cash to remodel your house
- your wife needs plastic surgery
- you're going back to school to get your master's degree in neo-classic literature.

That's right. Millions are available for "sensible" uses for a loan, but not a dime goes to the daring entrepreneur with no cash to put down.

If you need $10,000 to $20,000 for a down payment, you can get it from a bank if you know how to maximize your personal borrowing power. Consider the following:

- The multiple loan. Simultaneously borrow small amounts from several banks (see detailed explanation in Chapter 9).
- Pledge some personal assets. Stocks, life insurance, automobiles, and bank books can be collateral.
- If your credit doesn't warrant the loan, have a friend or relative cosign. It's easier to persuade friends or relatives to guarantee a loan than to make it themselves.

Be careful. If you borrow $10,000 to $20,000 for a down payment, loan it to your business. Repay yourself and pay off the bank as quickly as possible. Once the business repays your loan you're back to a no-cash-down deal. Once you've recouped your investment you have eliminated your investment risk, freed up whatever collateral you pledged, and increased your credit rating through the accelerated payback to the bank.

I call 30-day down payment loans "bridge financing." Watch how Charlie S. did it. He wanted to buy an auto parts store for $120,000, with $30,000 down.

Try as he might, Charlie couldn't get the seller to reduce the down payment. However Charlie knew three ways the business could generate that necessary $30,000. After he persuaded his father to cosign a bank note, he borrowed $30,000, bought the business, and went to work.

First, he sold excess parts for $12,000. Then he reaped $14,000 from daily sales, finally deferring his own salary for the final $4,000. He paid off the bank in less than a month. After he raised a few additional dollars, he sent his father to Hawaii to show his gratitude for the loan guarantee.

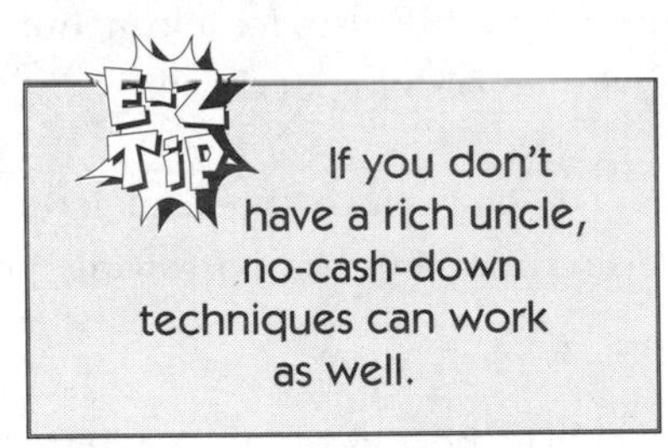

E-Z TIP
If you don't have a rich uncle, no-cash-down techniques can work as well.

When I studied for my MBA degree, my finance professor started the course by saying, "To finance a small business you need to know only one number . . . a wealthy relative's telephone number."

How to borrow 100% or more of the purchase price from a bank

Although a bank usually won't lend more than 50 to 60 percent of the purchase price of a business, the true value of a business may be substantially more than you agreed to pay for it. Every business has a subjective value. How does one determine the true value of a bakery or a flower shop?

> **HOT spot** Unlike real estate, which lends itself to comparative values and accurate appraisals, no business has a quickly determinable or accurate true value.

With a little sleight-of-hand you can increase the contract price of the business for the purpose of obtaining a loan, then you can reduce the actual price to equal the amount borrowed. A perfectly legal approach, you can "finance out" if you use your imagination. Suppose you want to buy Acme Supply and agree on a $60,000 price. In addition the seller wants $40,000 over five years for an agreement whereby he/she agrees not to compete with you. If you went into a bank, it would lend you $36,000, or 60 percent of the $60,000 price. But you word the contract so the price is $100,000 and the cost of the non-compete agreement from the seller is $1. Now when you go into a bank, with a contract showing you're paying $100,000, it might lend you $60,000. Once you obtain the $60,000 loan, you and the seller simply amend the agreement to its original terms with the seller getting $60,000 for the business with the $40,000 for the non-compete agreement payable over five years.

Pyramid your credit into a down payment

Name the type of business you want. How much cash would you need for a down payment? How much of that could you borrow from a bank on your signature alone? If you need $15,000 but your present borrowing power is only $3,000, you might benefit from the pyramid scheme. In three months your signature alone can get you $15,000 if you know how to pyramid your credit rating. It's easy.

- Go to Bank X and apply for a $3,000 loan payable in 30 days.
- Take the loan proceeds and put it into a high-interest account at another bank.
- In 25 days withdraw the $3,066 and pay off your loan.
- Now you're ready to start pyramiding. A couple of weeks later return to Bank X and apply for a $6,066 loan. You'll probably get it because you have proven your reliability. Invest the $6,660 and pay back the loan in 25 days.

- In the third month repeat the process with a $10,000 loan. After you pay it off ahead of schedule Bank X will be delighted to lend you $15,000. Each loan fortifies your credit rating, and your borrowing power grows.

What will it cost you to increase your borrowing power five-fold? In terms of effort, all it costs is three trips to Bank X and the next nearest bank. You'll pay a few dollars difference between interest earned (on the savings) and interest charged (on the loans). In the above example, the actual interest differential would be $200, but that could be the wisest $200 investment you'll ever make, for it will give you the borrowing power you need—when you need it—to land a business of your own that over the years can increase your earnings by hundreds of thousands of dollars.

note
No credit history, like a bad credit history, means no loan.

Many people don't have borrowing power because they haven't developed it. The majority of small unsecured loans are not turned down because the borrower *isn't* creditworthy, but because he hasn't proven himself creditworthy.

SBA loans—a necessary evil

Many entrepreneurs mistakenly believe the shortest path to small business financing is to stroll into the nearest Small Business Administration office.

The SBA can give you all the details, but you should see the big picture. What you see may have you running not walking, in the opposite direction.

Here's why SBA loans (and most other types of government handouts) are low on my list of sources of funds:

- The SBA will consider you for a loan only if you cannot get a loan from a bank. That may sound like a big plus, but think for a moment. If your deal is logical you'd get a bank loan and wouldn't need the SBA. Through the process of elimination the SBA involves itself in the illogical deals.

- The SBA has put more people into bankruptcy than into business. This is the end result of financing deals that had no possibility of making it in the first place. When the SBA loses, they lose only a few tax dollars; you lose everything.

- The SBA can be even more collateral-hungry than banks. If you own a home, be prepared to have an SBA mortgage on it. With banks you have a fighting chance of avoiding a pledge of personal assets, but not with the SBA.

note

SBA loans strongly favor minority groups. Unless you're in a minority group you'll have an uphill fight getting your loan approved.

- The SBA invented red tape. It can take six months to put an SBA loan through. Will your seller sit still while your loan application is buried on some bureaucrat's desk?

- The SBA will want you to match revenues, so you'll have to put up 50 percent of the purchase price yourself. Unlike banks, they drown on secondary sources of financing.

Despite these shortcomings the SBA does offer a few positive points:

- Their loans can extend over ten years, compared with a bank's five to seven, thus enhancing cash flow.

- The SBA will lend for businesses in distressed areas.

- It does not demand a strong credit rating, because the SBA is supposed to start where the banks stop.

note

The SBA offers two major types of loan arrangements—a direct loan and a participating loan with a bank. With the bank participation arrangement, the bank lends you the money, but the SBA guarantees 90 percent of it. If you were to borrow $100,000 and immediately default, the bank would absorb a $10,000 loss; the SBA, $90,000. Most SBA loans are participatory, but you should get a direct loan if possible, because if you have a participation loan you'll deal directly with a bank. If you default payments, the bank is on your neck in short order.

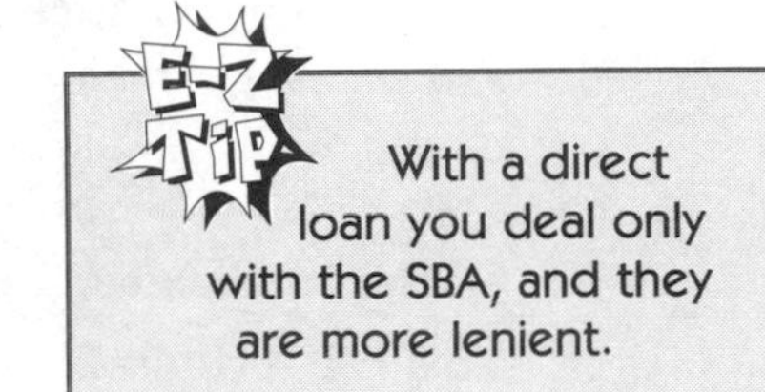

E-Z TIP
With a direct loan you deal only with the SBA, and they are more lenient.

The government has set up more than 1,000 loan and handout programs, many of which are designed to finance specialized types of businesses. Inquire at the SBA office. If they can't help you, they will tell you what governmental program can.

Shoe leather and perseverance

Old Casey Stengel was a perennial optimist. When his New York Yankees returned from a disastrous road trip he simply announced, "You can't win them all."

That message should ring loud and clear in this chapter. You may not find the cash on your first try. You may have to beat the pavement and accept terms that will make life somewhat harder. But regardless of how you borrow, the loan will be paid off someday. Then you'll own the business and it will be all yours—free and clear. And it may have all started with no cash down.

Key points to remember

- Seller financing beats bank financing. Don't think "bank" until you get the final "no" from the seller.

- Banks are like snowflakes; no two are alike. Match your deal to the right bank.

- Know what the bank will look for. Remember the three Cs— credit, cash flow, and collateral.

- There's a right way and wrong way to borrow. Negotiate and structure the loan for your benefit,

- You can borrow 100 percent of the purchase price by manipulating the numbers.

  You're worth more than you think. Your signature alone can get you the down payment—and you can increase that borrowing power by pyramiding.

11

Partners for profit: Your brains, their cash

Chapter 11

Partners for profit: Your brains, their cash

What you'll find in this chapter:

- Deciding whether to choose a partner
- Structuring a realistic and fair deal
- Protecting yourself
- Analyzing a partner's strengths
- Packaging your proposal

You've lined up your dream deal but need $50,000 to close it and another $50,000 to invest in inventory and fixtures. Your cash flow projections verify that the business will make you wealthy if only you can get your hands on the necessary $100,000. Should you sell a piece of the action to an investor, who then becomes a silent or not-so-silent partner? Surely lots of investors would cheerfully spend $100,000 for a piece of the pie. But will your partnership become paradise or purgatory?

Do you really want a partner?

By legal definition a *partner* is anyone who invests money in, and shares the profits or losses of a business venture. An expanded definition would include stockholders in a corporation or beneficiaries of a business or real estate trust. Partners come in all sizes and shapes; they can be Moe and Joe, each putting up $10,000 to open a corner fruit stand, or a sophisticated venture capital firm investing heavily in a business but taking a passive management role. Other partners are the hundreds of stockholders scattered throughout the country, most of whom you will never meet.

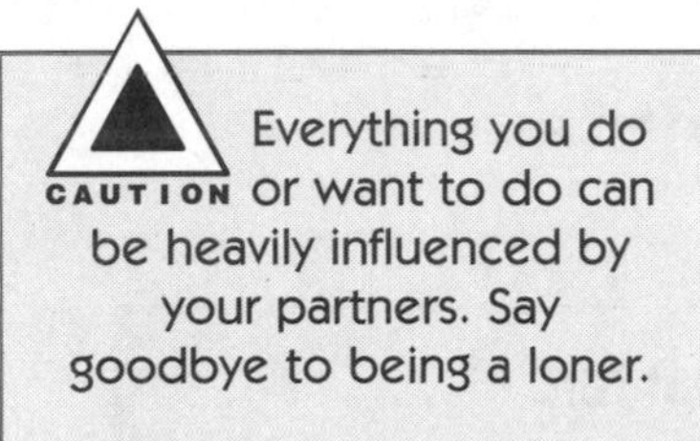

CAUTION
Everything you do or want to do can be heavily influenced by your partners. Say goodbye to being a loner.

Regardless of the number of partners or the amount they invest, they all have one thing in common. Once they're on board, you're accountable to them. You no longer work just for yourself.

Examine yourself. Are you the type who wants to share responsibility or would you prefer total control?

Three classic situations make partners attractive:

1) You need money to buy or capitalize a business, and you can't get it any other way.

2) You need management skills to augment your own.

3) You are simply afraid to go into business on your own. A working partner can provide psychological as well as financial or managerial support.

I heard of a young man who always lacked the self-confidence to go it alone. He became friendly with an equally timid soul with the same business interests, and together they did what neither could do alone. Today they own 17 appliance stores. One of the partners has since branched out and owns several other businesses. Without each having a partner to lean on, our two prosperous businessmen of today might still be clinging to their self-doubts as they continued their lives working for others. If you need partners for money only, move cautiously. Their small investment today could return to them many times that amount over the years. Such money can be the most expensive you'll ever obtain.

Move slowly. Beg or borrow the money from any source you can, and consider partnership funds your last resort. Here's a mathematical example that fortifies the point. If you take in a partner for a $50,000 investment, giving her 50 percent of the company in exchange, she will be a recipient of 50 percent of all future growth, equity buildup, and profits. Grow to a business worth $1 million and your partner is worth $500,000.

Borrow the $50,000 and once it's paid you're through with the lender. But once a partner gives you her cash, she's with you all the way.

Put your partners to the acid test

Act in haste, repent in leisure! Choose a partner without really testing him and you'll learn this lesson the hard way. I have one client, Mr. M., who operates a wholesale bakery business. Over the past two years he has entered three bakery deals with a different partner each time. Unfortunately he did not carefully select his partners. All he demanded was $30,000 to $40,000 and a willingness to spend all day at a baking oven. His first partner physically ousted Mr. M. from the premises and the litigation is still dragging on. His second partner walked away with $36,000 and was last seen heading west, while partner number three spends his days drinking bourbon, his nights at Alcoholics Anonymous meetings. Mr. M. regrets all three ventures.

It wouldn't have taken Mr. M. long to assess his first partner's compatibility, or the gambling or drinking problems of partners number two and three. A prudent businessman would have run a more thorough check when hiring a stock clerk.

What about personal friends? They seem to be a logical choice. What could be more fun than going into business with your bowling buddy or your college sorority sister? Unfortunately, what you prize in a friend is not necessarily what you need in a partner.

E-Z TIP

Friends are social, and partners are business. Don't confuse them.

This is probably the most common error in selecting partners. In my younger days I ventured into a partnership with a close friend. We would spend our social hours planning and conniving. It was a lot of fun. And my partner was a great guy. He just didn't have the business talent to pull his own weight. But my management talent left something to be desired also—after all I picked him as my teammate. Luckily we're still good friends. He's successful at what he does and fortunately I found other fields for myself. It was a bitter lesson to learn that your best friends can be your worst partners.

If your working partner offers full-time management support, you must make certain that you get along with him, because you'll end up spending more time with him than with your spouse. Look for partners whose strengths offset your weaknesses. You may be a super salesman but are bored with production. Perhaps you're good at production but can't stand accounting. Effective management requires a combination of talents.

> E-Z TIP
> Match your partner's skills with your own to cover as many important business areas as possible.

As in selecting your legal and accounting teammates, chemistry between partners is essential. The right partner can create instant synergy, the sum total of the two of you becoming far greater than your individual abilities. On the other hand, the wrong partner can neutralize your skills and cause tremendous emotional strain.

This simple check can help you distinguish the "swans" from the "ugly ducklings":

- Evaluate your potential partner's work history. Does he have a solid record of work experiences? Is he a "doer" or a "drifter"? Does he display the management skills you need? Does he command your confidence? Look for stability.

- What about his personal history? Poor health can pose major problems. What do you know about personal weaknesses, such as gambling or drinking? Check out his criminal record. You'll be surprised at the skeletons lurking in some closets.

- Has he been involved in other business deals? How did they work out? What do prior partners say about him?

- How about his personal lifestyle? You may prefer to live conservatively and plow the profits back into the business, while he may be a high roller living only for today. Such a clash can cause huge partnership woes.

- Do you know your partner's spouse? Most wives and husbands wield great influence on their mates. You may find the perfect partner and still end up broke because of an interfering spouse.

- Does your partner possess the required financial resources? He may be able to match your down payment but can he help you expand a year later? If the business needs another $60,000 you don't want to mortgage your house while your penniless partner whistles Dixie. By the same token, it may not be a good idea to select a partner considerably wealthier than yourself because you may eventually find yourself on the short end of the economic squeeze out.

You may be the brains behind the business but money always wins out. I can give you countless examples of financial backers asserting financial muscle to take over when their financially weaker partners run out of money.

I recently represented one partner in a food processing plant. Each partner owned 50 percent of the company, but suddenly they found that the firm needed an additional $100,000 in working capital. My client had already borrowed against everything he owned to buy into the business. The other partner went into his gyrations and eventually bought my client out for very few dollars.

E-Z TIP
Partnerships ae like a poker game. Make certain your chips match those of your opponents.

Most importantly, are his business ideas compatible with yours? Does he agree with you on important issues such as growth, operation, responsibility, and financial philosophy? That blending of ideas is the key to every successful partnership.

"Have I got a deal for you!"

Let's return to the beginning of this chapter. You lined up a pizza parlor and only need $100,000 for a combination of down payment and working capital. Since you can't swing any more loans, you approach your old school chum who made it big in plastics, saying, "Have I got a deal for you!" For a mere $100,000 investment, what does your buddy get? A percentage of the business? But what is fair—20 percent? 30 percent? Possibly he'll ask for 50 percent based on his money and your labor or "sweat equity." Maybe your well-heeled college pal will decide that for his $100,000 he should have a controlling interest, or 51 percent of the company.

A clever partner might invest $20,000 for 30 percent of the company and loan the company the other $80,000 at 18 percent interest over five years, demanding the right to convert outstanding debt to shares in the firm. If the company succeeds he can cancel the remaining debt and pick up a large percentage of the business. Is that a fair deal? He might even offer to divide his $80,000 "loan" into a $40,000 secured note and a subordinated $40,000 debenture coupled with a warrant for an additional 10 percent share. As Plasticman mixes his next martini he says his lawyers will insist on simultaneous registration of stock so he can sell if you go public.

By now your head is spinning. All you wanted was your friend's $100,000 so you could open "Happy Harry's Pizza Emporium." You knew you'd have to sacrifice a piece of the action, but you don't understand the financial mumble-jumble.

Leave the financial rhetoric to your accountant and lawyer to decipher for you. The question remains: Is the deal fair? There's no easy answer. The *fair deal* is the best deal you can get from potential partners. No magic formula exists. No computer can spill out the right numbers. Your potential partner will fight for as much as he can get, while you will struggle to give up as little as you can.

Happy Harry has nothing but unbridled enthusiasm for his pizza shop, envisioning enormous profits and an ultimate coast-to-coast chain. If he's right why shouldn't his partner accept a smattering of shares for such a ground-floor opportunity?

However, Harry's college friend has other thoughts. What do I risk? How soon can I cash out? How does my investment evolve over time? What are the chances for a public stock issue and substantial capital gains? What tax write-offs apply if the deal goes sour? How can I increase my benefit and reduce my risk? What will Happy Harry really give up? To whom else can he turn?

There are so many variables that all you can do is shop around, negotiating the best deal you can.

Many start-up entrepreneurs offer an exciting concept but ignore the rocks on the road to success. One leading capital source firm reports that only one or two out of a hundred entrepreneurs develop a business proposal that makes sense to the financial community. The other 98 percent spin their wheels with nonsensical ideas, poor packaging of their plans, or bad timing.

E-Z TIP
If you encounter problems with prospective partners' offers, ask yourself "What am I really selling?"

What will excite an investor about Happy Harry's Pizza Emporium? If the investor gets 50 percent of the company for $100,000 but the business only generates a $20,000 profit, the investor earns only 10 percent on his investment. His money would earn more and be safer in the bank.

How can you sweeten that deal? Show the investor that Happy Harry's Pizza Emporium's product is superior or that the enterprise holds a competitive advantage over existing pizza parlors. Get him to visualize another Pizza Hut chain.

> **E-Z TIP**
>
> Since investors want their money to grow into a fortune, you have to demonstrate how that's possible not just for them, but for yourself as well.

Is Happy Harry out of luck if his Pizza Emporium does not mushroom into a national chain? No. All Harry has to do is restructure his deal so it makes sense based on the true situation rather than on a dream. In that case an investor might give Harry the $100,000, but not just for an equity or ownership interest. If someone loaned the business $80,000 (secured by assets) to be repaid over five years with 16 percent interest, and received 50 percent ownership for the other $20,000, the deal would be attractive. The $80,000 is secure and earning interest. The $20,000 equity investment will earn the projected $10,000 profit, creating a 50 percent return. Package your proposal to sell. It must contain:

- Background of the company: Present its history, organization, financial statements to date, and legal structure.

- Management: Identify management people, their backgrounds and accomplishments. Show that the company has or will obtain an effective management team. To investors management is as important as the product.

- Competitive advantages: Outline why your company, product, or service is unique. What advantages would convince a seller that it can grow beyond projections?

- Competition: Analyze your competitors. How do their products compare with yours?
- Marketing: Describe advertising and promotion and sales costs. Detail distribution channels. Identify your market segment.
- Financial information: Project financial statements for several years. Justify your numbers.
- Investment: Show how you will use the money you seek. Will additional funds be needed? From what source? How will you raise money for expansion?
- The deal: Sell the investment plan in terms of safety, return on investment, and growth potential.

Review your proposal. Can you back it up with hard data? In an effort to discover how much you know about your business, investors will try to pick your plan apart. Unless you can convince them that you know it well, they won't open their wallets.

Where the money lurks

A good business will attract potential investors like bears to honey. Would you believe more people are looking for good investments than there are good opportunities? However, you must learn where to look for them.

> **E-Z TIP** If you require less than $100,000, approach private investors, prosperous relatives, acquaintances, or your physician or lawyer neighbor.

Those earning $50,000 or more a year are your best bet, because they can spare investment dollars, want a hedge against inflation, and won't pass up an opportunity for gains conventional investments might not offer.

If the deal collapses, they can deduct their losses from income, and if they're in the 50 percent tax bracket the IRS will share their losses. If your deal involves real estate or equipment that can be depreciated, these investors may be stimulated by its tax shelter aspects. Oftentimes tax implications will sell the deal.

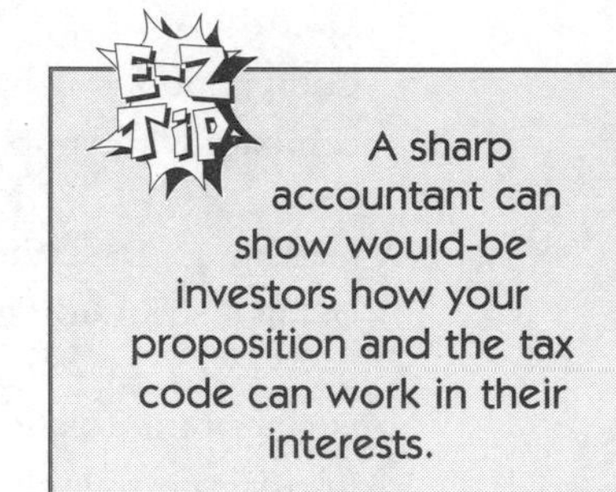

E-Z
TIP
A sharp accountant can show would-be investors how your proposition and the tax code can work in their interests.

Here are a few tips for capital seekers:

- Put your accountant, banker and lawyer to work: They have clients who may be likely investment candidates.

- Advertise: Place a simple ad in the classified section of your local paper, describing your deal and the amount of cash needed. The *New York Times* prints an entire column of "Capital Needed" listings. So will your local newspaper.

- Promote your deal: Mention it to your barber and you may end up with his brother-in-law for a partner. Many marriages come about through word of mouth.

Beware of "little old ladies in tennis shoes"; they may be delightful at tea, but they can spoil business deals. Your "darling" company may excite them more than clipping AT&T dividend coupons, but rarely do their investment objectives or expectations match those of an entrepreneur.

- Avoid close relatives: Business is business. It's hard for relatives to say no, and they seldom bring objectivity to the deal. Lose $100,000 for a stranger, and you lost an investor. Lose it for your mother, and you become the black sheep of the family. Don't risk family relationships over money. The same goes for close personal friends and anyone else whose relationship means more to you than dollars.

Money is a peculiar commodity. I have seen it turn brother against brother and transform parent and child into vicious litigants. I have one acquaintance who tells a sad story. He wanted to buy a carpet showroom for $75,000. For the down payment his mother mortgaged her house, on the promise that she would receive 40 percent of the company, and the company would pay back her loan. Within six months the carpet store failed. Without the business paying off the house mortgage, that loan became in default and the house was foreclosed on. He is too ashamed to visit his mother and is ostracized by his brothers and sisters. This is the most costly money you can find.

- Run away from cry-babies: Unless your business becomes another Xerox, they'll nip at your heels every step of the way. Lose a few dollars for them and they'll mutiny.

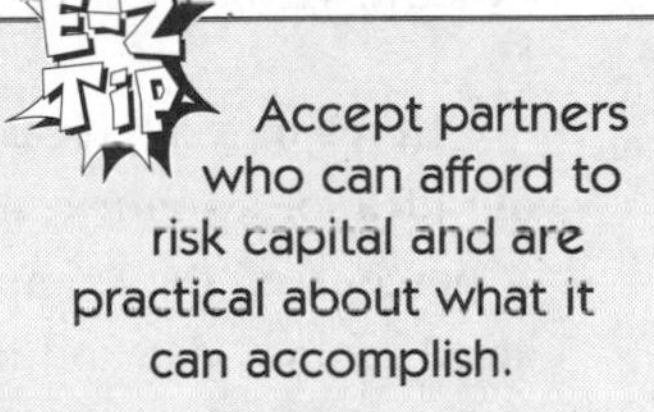

E-Z TIP
Accept partners who can afford to risk capital and are practical about what it can accomplish.

Big money for small businesses

If your capital needs exceed $100,000, you cross the threshold for venture capital and Small Business Investment Companies (SBICS). Venture capital groups take partnership positions in businesses they think will reap vast potential. Historically they go for high technology companies and other "glamour" situations, like bioengineering, but in recent years, they have diversified into more traditional operations.

SBICS are like venture capital groups. They are private organizations (often bank-sponsored) who obtain loans from the Small Business Administration. SBICS invest in equity positions in young start-up companies. Whereas the SBA and banks can loan only money, SBICS can provide capital on a partnership basis.

Money-finders or capital search firms can put you in touch with appropriate venture or SBIC groups, helping you package your proposal, disseminate it, and negotiate the deal. In turn they'll probably want a nonrefundable retainer and a percentage of the capital proceeds you receive. Move cautiously. Deal with capital search firms with respected reputations. Many live off the nonrefundable retainers and rarely win significant capital placement. Massachusetts has a north to south artery called Route 128. The only scenery along it is hundreds of budding "hi-tech" industries, most of which were started with nothing more than an idea and venture capital funds. Many of the founders are now worth millions, and they started with no money of their own.

Here's how a typical venture capital or SBIC deal may work. Once sold on your idea for a venture, the money men advance you $300,000—$100,000 for 40 percent of the company's shares and $200,000 as a loan. The venture capitalists may demand the option to convert the loan into additional shares and may bargain for an option to buy further shares at a nominal price. If the company issues 100,000 shares, the owner holds 60,000 and the capitalists 40,000. At $100,000 they have paid $2.50 per share for their 40,000 shares. The company succeeds. Sales skyrocket to $20 million a year with consistent 15 percent profits. You decide to go public, so the company issues and sells another 100,000 shares at $20 per share. You quickly raise an additional $2 million to help finance future growth, while your venture capital people find that their 40,000 shares are now worth $800,000. An 800 percent gain in a few years is not a bad return!

Venture capitalists look for a company that eventually can go public. Their money starts it and finances it until it does, at which point the shares they purchased for a few dollars become worth considerably more and can be readily sold to the public. You didn't do poorly either. Your 60,000 shares that cost you several hundred

HOT spot If you think your business has the potential for venture capital funds, develop a detailed proposal and shop around.

dollars are now worth $1,200,000. To secure venture capital funds an idea alone may suffice, in which case I call it *ad*venture capital. A few years from now you may be another Polaroid or Apple Computer, both of which started with venture capital funds.

Whatever happened to going public?

Should you take your "hot" idea public and offer people stock? Will that bring you a barrelful of money? Probably not. The public won't buy shares of stock based on an idea alone. Since the late '60s and early '70s investors have been wary of such offerings. The concept worked beautifully in the 1920s before the Great Depression and again in the 1960s, but when the dust settled many found that "too good to be true" deals were just that. In the 1960s all you needed was a catchy name, a crazy idea, and a desk for the investing public to come running. Ever hear of Heimberg Zippers, Inc.? In 1967, Heimberg and his two sons eked out a living making zippers for clothing manufacturers. Occupying 600 square feet of loft space, their enterprise generated sales of $400,000 a year. Wild about going public, they went to the underwriters who suggested sprucing up the company's image prior to the public stock issue.

Since Heimberg's Zippers, Inc. didn't stimulate the imagination, they changed the name to "Great American Techtronics." A bunch of business theorists sporting degrees from Harvard and Wharton joined old man Heimberg and his two sons on the board of directors. By reading the prospectus, no one would guess they were buying into a zipper factory, especially when it said the company "engages in innovative and advanced technology in protective hardware and fabrications." The public bought it and shelled out $1,000,000 for 40 percent of Great American Techtronics; for which they eventually got old man Heimberg and his two sons making pants zippers in a walk-up loft. Heimberg could do it in the '60s but you can't do it in today's times.

> **note** Today, going public for the young start-up company can work if you have a predetermined market of buyers for your shares.

Let's assume you have an idea for a new business—a laundry service for nursing homes in your area which will benefit from one centralized laundry specializing in their type of work. Even at lower prices you will benefit from having a built-in list of customers. After some quick calculations you find you need $200,000 to get the operation rolling. Let's assume that 50 nursing homes are interested in capitalizing the company, each investing $4,000.

First you set up the corporation with 2,000 shares of stock, 1,000 shares for $1,000 for you, the other 1,000 shares for the 50 stockholders who'll pay $200,000 for them. It's illegal to sell shares to more than 25 investors without going through a cumbersome and expensive registration procedure. But in this case you know your shares will sell because you have the buyers lined up. In such situations going public can be the perfect way to get into business with no cash down!

> **HOT spot** The Securities and Exchange Commission and the "Blue Sky" laws will require you to register your issue with them so that investors will have adequate information about your company.

More is not always better

If you *must* go into business with partners, keep the number as low as possible. Finding two people who think alike and get along is no mean feat, and problems can increase proportionally to the number of partners.

Susan H. renovated old homes and sold them for fabulous profits. She contracted to buy ten houses with ten partners, each investing $40,000 for a total capitalization of $400,000. Susan H. contributed "sweat equity" for 50 percent and the partners got a total of 50 percent for their $400,000. A fair deal? Sure, but two months after the business started it disbanded, and all the partners are suing each other. What went wrong? One partner constantly interfered with the manner in which the development work was carried out. Another criticized "overspending." A third and fourth joined forces to "scare off" the other partners so they could buy them out cheaply. Two more partners wanted the first five houses sold before the second five were started, squabbling with two others who wanted all ten renovated simultaneously. Everyone wanted to call the shots, then tried "shooting" the others. In the meantime, Susan spent all her time soothing ruffled feathers instead of developing the properties.

> **E-Z TIP** Follow the axiom that the "best things come in small packages."

Susan learned her lesson. So did I. We set up our next project completely differently. For each house she accepted only one partner. If she had ten houses under renovation, she had ten separate partnerships. She can easily handle any one-on-one situation.

Guard your flanks

Strive for the best but prepare for the worst. If "divorce fever" sets in, it may be too late. You must set up the deal so you control it at all times and always maintain the upper hand. Otherwise you may find yourself on the outside looking in as your partner walks away with the business. Here are a few tricks you can use:

- Don't overestimate potential profits. If you sell an investor on a projected $50,000 profit, you will face a lot of explaining when they come in at $6,000. Always underestimate the good and overestimate the bad to look like a genius.

- Emphasize every risk aspect of the venture. If you fail to disclose substantial problems you can incur liability.

- Demand at least 51 percent ownership. This gives you voting control. If your partner insists on a 50-50 split, at least obtain majority voting rights by having him assign proxy rights to you for whatever percentage of his shares will give you voting control.

- Don't rely on standard corporate books and bylaws to document your deal. Supplement it with a written agreement on all major points, including salaries, bonuses, expenses, and division of responsibility.

- Watch out for secret deals or conflict of interest situations. If you have a side deal or hidden profit coming from the business, bring it out into the open. Be honest.

- Don't let minor feuds mushroom into major battles. Discuss areas of disagreement the minute they pop up.

> **HOT spot** With a good partner and a sound agreement, partnership can provide the path to wealth.

- Create a formula for buying out your partner in the event of a disagreement. This buyout provision should be part of any business agreement.

Minority interests are for dreamers

Kevin had a problem. Several years ago he bought a small chain of fabric stores. Since he had no money of his own, he formed a partnership with two financial backers who advanced $200,000 toward the purchase price of $400,000. They carved a deal whereby Kevin received one-third of the shares of the corporation and they received two-thirds. Kevin was supposed to provide all the management or "sweat equity" in return for his one-third interest. And Kevin certainly did sweat. For two years he averaged 50 hours a week and doubled the size of the chain, generating substantial profits to boot. Everything looked rosy until Kevin proposed to his partners that his salary rise from $60,000 to $100,000 a year. They refused, and a big argument broke out. One word led to another and concluded in "divorce."

Since his partners controlled two-thirds of the corporation, they voted Kevin out as president of the firm and hired a new man at an appreciably lower salary. Kevin fell victim to the "squeeze play." Any partner owning less than 50 percent is vulnerable to it. Of course, Kevin still held a piece of paper showing that he owned a one-third interest, but what did that do for him? He would be entitled to one-third of dividends due stockholders, but dividends in a small corporation are microscopic. He would be entitled to one-third of the proceeds of the business if it were sold or liquidated, but that might not occur within his lifetime. He'll always be outnumbered on any vote affecting the company, and now he cannot even collect a paycheck. Being a minority stockholder secures no employment rights. If you're in doubt, buy a few shares of General Motors, then show up at their employment office. Don't delude yourself—unless you own at least 50 percent of a company you have little more than a job. But you don't want a job; you want a business of your own. Does all this sound like paranoid pessimism on partnerships? I hope not. I do believe that partnerships are a major source of business troubles and I do believe that if your only motive for bringing in partners is their money, then it should be your last resort. But if you must go the partnership route you must know the pitfalls as well as the opportunities.

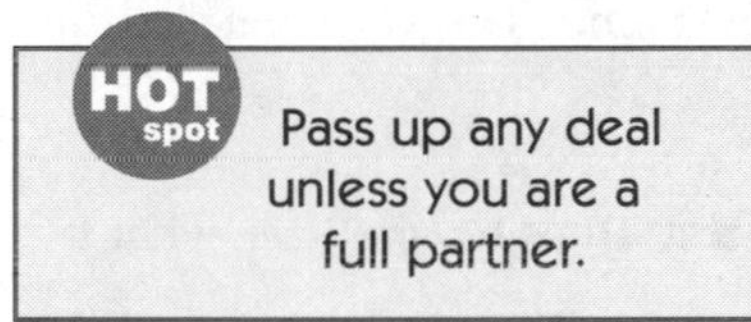

HOT
spot
Pass up any deal unless you are a full partner.

If you choose wisely and for the right reasons, partners can even be the best way to go. I do have my share of partnership success stories. Wiley's example can show you the true potential with a sound partnership.

Wiley himself was a cracker jack landscaper. He could make anything grow—anywhere, anytime. Anything, that is, except money. Wiley was also the world's worst businessman. Although professionally satisfied, Wiley was frustrated over his low-paying job as groundsman for a large museum.

Finally Wiley found the perfect opportunity. A nearby florist and greenhouse was for sale for $300,000.

Wiley could raise $40,000, but that wouldn't swing the deal. Financing might have been available but Wiley knew his limitations. He needed more than capital; he needed management. He found a working partner who invested $100,000 for a 50 percent interest. Wiley handles the horticulture and his partner handles the money—a winning combination that generates $3 million annually in sales. About 40 percent of all small businesses have partners. For many that formula spelled success. Others regret the day they took on a partner. So generalizations are out. But you do have to think very carefully before you decide on a partnership. It's a marriage in the truest sense, and you want to reach your golden anniversary—not the divorce courts.

Key points to remember

- Partnerships are not for everyone. Do you really want to be accountable to others?
- Put your partner to the acid test: Does he/she have what it takes to help the business succeed?
- Be realistic about your deal and the money it can make.
- A "fair" partnership deal is the best deal you can drive. Forget magic formulas; they don't exist.
- Package your proposal so it makes sense. No one will invest if he can't see the benefits of your deal.
- Structure the deal to protect yourself. Guard your flanks; never accept less than 50 percent.
- A partnership is only another form of marriage. It can work if you know what you're getting into.

12 Starting from scratch

Chapter 12

Starting from scratch

What you'll find in this chapter:

- Starting your own business with no cash
- Watching the pennies
- Buying "good will" is not always worth it
- Financing everything—learn the secrets
- Hustling and asking for what you want

Name your business

Whether it's a sporting goods store or a health spa, you could buy one. But you could also start your own. If you start your own from scratch you can bypass inheriting somebody else's headaches, and you can do it with no cash down—but you must know the tricks.

Which is better—to buy or to create a business? There's no right answer. It depends on many factors. But, if you think about it, any business you might consider buying was originally started from scratch.

Approximately two million brand-new businesses spring up in America each year. Many will close within the first five years, but others will not only prosper but may serve as the foundation for a future giant industry, chain, or conglomerate.

New ideas mean new businesses

> **HOT spot** If you think the days of starting from scratch are over, you're wrong.

Statistics show that the number of new businesses increases each year. Clearly, new technology, expanding markets, and new consumer trends and interests lead to startups because all too often existing businesses can't or won't respond to new needs. Besides, it may actually be quicker and less expensive to start from scratch than to change an existing business.

Peruse your local yellow pages. How many businesses appear that were not in last year's edition? Drive down any boulevard. You'll see new businesses popping up everywhere in response to new opportunities. Take any industry. What new fads or business methods suggest startups?

A large shopping mall sits near my office and sports a number of shops unheard of only a few years ago:

- A designer jeans shop. In fact there are two of them. Remember when dungarees occupied one aisle in a discount store? Now they're the latest rage.

- A running shoe store and a tennis shop. Everybody's exercising these days. Ten years ago all sneakers were basically the same; now there are hundreds of models to choose from.

- A weight reducing salon. Along with increasing our exercise, we Americans have become a weight-conscious society. Could you have lost weight in a shopping mall before the 1970s?

- A furniture store specializing in Scandinavian designs. People seem more conscious than ever of "designer" labels.

- A croissant bakery and donut shop. I didn't even know what a croissant was until this place opened, but it's doing land-office business selling 36 types of pastries.

We could go on, but you see the point. Why buy a coffee shop or bakery if you can open "Emily's Famous Croissant and Coffee Shop"? Why pay someone for good will you can't utilize in a new type of service or store?

Are you a jogger? Would you buy a traditional shoe store and convert it to an entirely different line? Probably not. In such cases it makes sense to start from scratch and mold the business the way you want it. Avoid paying somebody else for a business you will have to completely restructure.

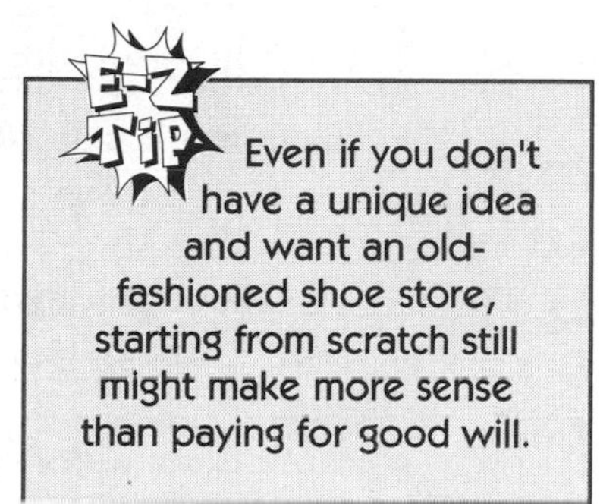

E-Z TIP
Even if you don't have a unique idea and want an old-fashioned shoe store, starting from scratch still might make more sense than paying for good will.

Hard cash for thin air

One reason many entrepreneurs engage in the long, hard work of building a business from nothing is that they don't want to pay for good will, which is as invisible and hard to quantify as thin air. Still, good will dramatically affects a seller's asking price. Everybody knows what good will means but nobody can precisely define it. Fewer still can evaluate it and put a realistic price tag on it.

Wouldn't it be nice if you could walk into your target shoe store and say, "Mr. Seller, I'll buy your business; I'll pay $34,000 for your inventory because that's what it cost, and $20,000 for your fixtures and equipment, since that's their replacement value." That may sound reasonable to you, but the seller will laugh you out of the store, if he doesn't throw you out. No seller is going to part with a business for the price of the tangible assets alone. You also have to pay for the intangible assets of the business. If the business has operated for many years, intangibles—such as always showing a profit, and its customers, employees, and suppliers all being in place—can be worth a lot. What should you pay for these things? Maybe the lease provides a "dynamic location" you might not be able to get starting out on your own. Wrap all the intangibles in a neat package and stick it on the balance sheet under "good will." But what is that good will worth?

Here are just a few ideas of what sellers think it's worth. I plucked them at random from a *Boston Globe*, but you'll find similar examples in your own local paper.

- A convenience store with sales of $100,000 a year and average profits of $260,000—$140,000 of which represents good will.

- A beauty parlor with equipment worth $30,000 sports a $130,000 price tag.

- A marina grossing $600,000 annually. The seller wants $900,000 for good will alone.

- A pizza shop with an asking price of $100,000 based on $65,000 for good will.

- An auto repair shop for sale for $200,000. The seller feels justified in demanding $150,000 for good will. Good will can escalate prices out of sight.

Is it worth it, or is good will really nothing more than thin air? Before you answer you may want to consider what good will can mean to you.

- Reduce Risk. Because you can only guess what sales and profits will be, a startup is a gamble. An operating business's track record provides some predictability and safety.

- No start-up problems. It can take a lot of work and right moves before a new business gets off the ground.

- Valuable intangible assets. What price tag can you put on a top-notch management team's exclusive contacts, established routes, and even the reputation their name represents? I could duplicate the physical plant of a McDonald's for one-third the price of a franchise, but I wouldn't be able to use their name or benefit from their national advertising.

On the other hand, what the seller calls "good will" may be thin air, and it can be really stale. Here's a case in point. What is the good will worth in a card and gift shop with annual sales of $120,000? To Marilyn W. it was more than a rhetorical question, for she agreed to buy the business for $110,000, including $60,000 for good will, since the inventory and fixtures were worth only $50,000.

The card shop never earned its owner more than a moderate salary and it never showed a profit. If stagnant sales continued, the future of this business looked bleak.

However I couldn't persuade Marilyn to walk away from the deal. It made no sense to pay $60,000 for nonexistent good will. Marilyn could have put her $110,000 to better use, as she found out just one year later when a new shopping mall opened near her home. Wanting a second shop, she signed a lease and set up the business. With a total out-of-pocket investment of only $5,400 coupled with creditor financing, she opened her doors, and her second shop grosses twice as much as the $110,000 white elephant she bought a year earlier. It can pay to pass up those thin-air deals!

Make the numbers work

Business is always a matter of shuffling numbers to determine a course of action that will put the maximum number of dollars in your pocket.

Whether to buy or create is just one more such exercise. Unless the seller will hand you the keys for the value of the inventory and equipment alone, you have to give the proposition the acid test. It's easy to do. If you subscribe to the theory that buying good will is nothing more than paying extra to obtain a profitable business, what is the proper ratio between price and profits? Never pay more than $5 for every dollar in annual profits.

HOT spot

In other words, if the business can't pay for the good will in five years or less it's overpriced. If you can't find a business that meets this criterion, open your own.

Buying only looks easier

Let me tell you about Hy W. For ten years Hy wanted to own his own business. He hated his job, but he couldn't quite bring himself to take the plunge. He looked, calculated, and investigated, until I almost thought he was a professional "looker." What was he looking for? Nothing exotic, only a small coffee shop or luncheonette. But he kept looking. To Hy every deal was overpriced. Ninety percent of the time I agreed with him, but one day he surprised me and signed the papers for a luncheonette grossing $360,000 a year. Hy overpaid by $20,000 to $30,000, but it was his only alternative because he just didn't think he was the type to start from scratch.

note

There are lots of people like Hy. They think it's too hard to create a business, and their lack of self-confidence limits them to buying. Whenever I come across a Hy, I know better than to try to change his basic nature, but for every Hy there are two Kirks. Kirk represents an altogether different breed. When he was nine he opened his first lemonade stand, and he's been running businesses ever since. He has opened no fewer than 14 different businesses since his lemon-squeezing days, building everything from scratch: a small restaurant, three bakeries, and even an amusement park. Kirk was a creator. He enjoyed innovating, designing, planning, and even squabbling with the tradespeople he hired to give his ideas life. Kirk would never dream of buying somebody else out. There is no fun in that! Are you a Hy or a Kirk? That important question is a major component of "knowing thyself." The answer can dictate whether you buy or start from scratch.

Now let's pretend you've made up your mind. All signals point to your starting your own business from scratch without any money of your own. Sound impossible? Just watch.

Everything but money

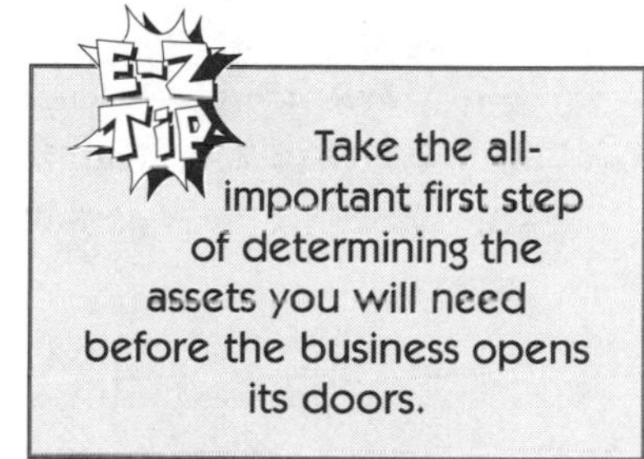

E-Z TIP
Take the all-important first step of determining the assets you will need before the business opens its doors.

Since more than 80 percent of all startups are retail firms rather than manufacturing or wholesaling concerns, let's study a retail drugstore. I once started one with my partner, Frank. A few years ago Frank and I decided that a nearby town needed a drugstore and we knew just the spot—a six-store shopping center that was just opening with a large supermarket and five smaller spaces. We had our eyes on a 3,000-square-foot space next to the supermarket and were all set to go except for a few incidentals like inventory, fixtures, equipment, and working capital. But we were budding entrepreneurs, so we couldn't let such details stand in our way.

After considerable study, we figured that it would take the following to open the doors: $100,000 for inventory, $30,000 for fixtures, and $10,000 for working capital.

We had the money but we opted for a no-cash-down approach. First we tackled the fixtures. Since most fixture companies wanted a 25 to 30 percent down payment, we leased the fixtures for $800 a month with the option to buy at the end of the lease for a mere $200. The fixture company wanted the first month's rent in advance, but we persuaded them to wait until the business was running. Next we needed an advertising sign. The low bid was $4,000, but we rejected it and accepted one from another company for $4,400. Why pay $400 more? For better terms. The second sign man told us he'd bill us after installation in 12 monthly installments. Since you can't have a first-class pharmacy without soft carpeting, we leased first-class carpeting for $100 per month, which included a full-service maintenance policy. We paid the first $160 after we rang up over $150,000 in sales.

To transform a cinder-block store into an attractive drugstore we required a few special lights, plumbing for the pharmacy department, and rich paneling for the cosmetics area. Because tradespeople have a nasty habit of demanding payment when they complete the work, and since the work would cost only a couple of thousand dollars, we asked the landlord to make the improvements and add it to the rent. Since it was his property being improved, he readily agreed.

You can't do business from an empty wagon, so we needed inventory to put on our shelves. We visited a drug wholesaler and used the arguments that usually work on a supplier. Since the wholesaler could expect us to buy about $400,000 in stock a year, and since drug wholesalers build in 16 percent for themselves, we represented a $64,000 annual profit to our supplier. We agreed to secure the wholesaler with a mortgage on the inventory. If we failed, the wholesaler would have first claim on all the inventory, and we agreed to keep it at not less than a $80,000 level so he would be certain his investment was always protected. Within days, trucks loaded with inventory pulled up to our door.

We continued to stock our shelves with creative supplier financing. A tobacco jobber agreed to give us $10,000 credit, so we soon had plenty of cigarettes to sell. Three candy companies were willing to ship without payment in advance, and several greeting card companies tripped over each other for our account, all willing to wait for their money. We selected the card company that agreed to wait one year for payment if they agreed to throw in

some special lighting for the card department to clinch the deal. They didn't think twice. Down the list of suppliers we went until before we knew it, we had $100,000 in inventory without having opened our checkbook once. If one supplier turned us down we'd go to the next on our list until we connected with no cash down.

Opening day! The doors swung wide open and the ringing of our registers was music to our entrepreneurial ears.

Here's what we actually paid out of our own pockets to make it happen:

$1,600	For the first month's rent (we had a tough landlord).
100	To the Board of Pharmacy for permits (government doesn't extend credit).
620	For casual labor to help us set up (we couldn't deprive a high school boy of his day's pay).
$2,320	Total disbursements.

Our thriving business had $130,000 to $140,000 in assets working to make money for us, and our total contribution was only $2,260. It turned out we didn't need $10,000 working capital. But we did contribute imagination, a smattering of know-how, and a lot of nerve. If I had to do it today I could get away without spending a dime.

There's a postscript to the story. We sold the business a few years later for a small profit. The creditors were all paid down so we were able to pocket some cash for our efforts. But that profit was insignificant compared to what I learned.

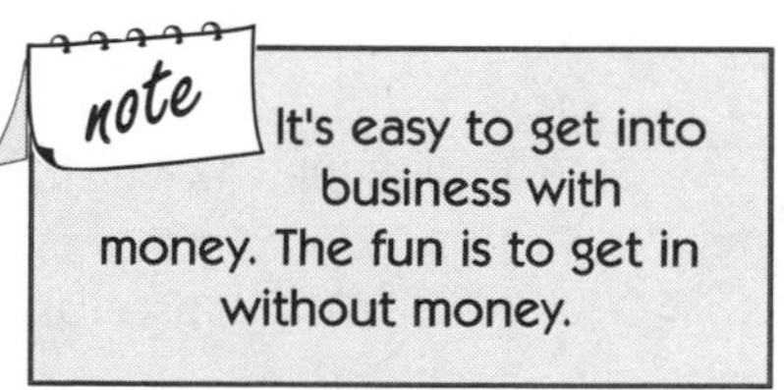

note
It's easy to get into business with money. The fun is to get in without money.

Play it again Sam

I love start-ups; particularly when we try it without the proverbial "shoestring." One of my first no-cash-down clients, Tim P., wanted to open an ice-cream shop across from a local high school. Normally it would take $40,000, mostly for equipment, with about 50 percent down, but Tim didn't have $20,000 to invest. We heard about a restaurant supply house in New York City with a warehouse full of used equipment. A phone call confirmed they had everything we needed, and six hours later Tim was loading his U-Haul with used soda fountains, ice-cream chests, booths, tables and other paraphernalia. The used stuff cost $12,000, compared to $32,000 for new equipment. Since the supplier agreed to finance it for three years with 18 percent interest, secured by a mortgage on the equipment, Tim bought it with no cash down. With a little elbow grease the equipment looked as good as new and was built better than newer models.

Inventory posed no problem. A mountain of ice cream can be bought for $4,000, and several ice-cream companies were eager to extend credit.

Today Tim's ice-cream shop grosses over $600,000 a year, and nets Tim $100,000.

Consider his out-of-pocket startup costs:

$ 600	Advance rent
400	Moving expenses on equipment
800	Installation and plumbing
270	Miscellaneous supplies and labor
$2,170	Total start-up costs

Because Tim didn't even have the $2,170, I loaned him $1,000 and his father gave him the other $1,200. That was one loan neither of us ever regretted.

How would you like to start with no money and end up with a business and $10,000 in cash even before you ring up your first sale? Bryan did it. He was master of the shoestring operation and he ended up with tons of shoestrings!

Boston, the home of Bill Rodgers and the Boston Marathon, is full of joggers. Bryan worked as a shipper at a local factory, but everywhere he went he saw people of all sizes and shapes huffing and puffing as they ran up and down the streets in their sweatsuits and running shoes.

Imaginative Bryan found that jogging could do more than put his body in shape—it could also put his bankbook in shape. He decided to sell jogging supplies.

An idea was born. Bryan not only sold jogging shoes, he started a local jogger's association, which proved a super way to reach customers.

Bryan rented an inexpensive loft for $325 a month and negotiated exclusive New England retailing rights from a Montreal running shoe manufacturer. Here's the deal he assembled:

- The manufacturer agreed to provide $100,000 worth of shoes on credit.

- The manufacturer imprinted on each pair of shoes "The Official Shoe of The Jogger's Association."

- Bryan would make a gross profit of 50 percent on the shoes.

- The shoe manufacturer guaranteed a $100,000 line of credit with a sweatsuit manufacturer. Bryan could offer a complete jogger's outfit endorsed by his own association.

Bryan was in business. And he's still in business, although he moved out of his $325 loft long ago because he couldn't do $3 million a year in sales from cramped quarters. I estimate Bryan pockets at least $10,000 a week in profits. Money pours in from every direction. He operates the association profitably and sponsors jogging classes every night at $20 a head. Most of his students naturally buy merchandise bearing the "Jogger's Association" label.

Where did he get the spare $10,000 cash? Easy. He charged advance membership fees in the association.

There are lots of Bryans who can spot a better way to do business and get into that business—without money.

Bigger deals are only bigger numbers

Most no-cash startups do begin on a small scale, and grow through the subsequent buildup of profits. But there are plenty of no-cash beginnings that started on a grandiose scale. The concepts are the same. It's only a matter of playing for larger stakes with larger numbers.

How would you like to start a "Farmer's Market" grossing $10 million annually, and spend nary a penny of your own in the process? Irving did it. He found a large abandoned mill on a well traveled highway in Georgia. There it was, a prime location just sitting idle. Irv's plan was to set up a shopping bazaar selling everything from meats and fruits to discount clothing. Name it and you'll find it at the Crossroads Farmer's Market. Of course, Irving had no intention of owning all the individual stores and sales booths. He would be the landlord extraordinaire and master promoter. His tenants would pay rent for their concession space and it would all be orchestrated by Irving himself.

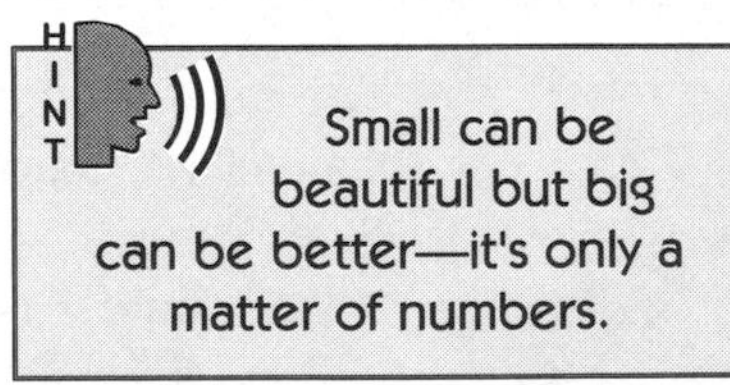

HINT
Small can be beautiful but big can be better—it's only a matter of numbers.

There was only one problem—Irving had no money of his own. This didn't slow him up one bit, however. He projected startup, renovation, and promotional costs of $100,000; and he knew just where to get it from—the boys at the poker club. Irving would sell off 50 percent of the deal in units of 5 percent for $10,000. The numbers defied a turndown. Every $10,000 invested promised a return of $16,000 a year plus tremendous tax write-off advantages. So Irving had his ten partners and his $100,000. He also had his 50 percent ownership interest and the promise of a handsome salary and bonuses.

One year later the Farmer's Market opened with more than 100 tenants hawking their wares. Business is great—Irving nets over $75,000 a year as his share of the profits and $100,000 in salary and bonuses. Irving also owns the popcorn concession right in the center of the complex. He laughs as he tells how he set up the popcorn stand for only $500; it nets him an additional $40,000 in pocket money.

Step carefully—it may be your last one

Starting up without cash can provide the same exhilarating experience as walking across Niagara Falls on a tightrope. One wrong move and the act is over. Unless you have a bankroll in reserve to bail you out you have no margin for error.

What can go wrong? Anything and everything. I've shown you a few successful swimmers, but one short story will show you just how cold the water can be.

It all started with an idea for a catering service. You know the type, *hors d'oeuvres* and roast beef for weddings and parties. Two young ambitious young ladies, Anne and June, with plenty of talent but little luck, found some used kitchen equipment which they set up in one of their garages. Things looked great. Advance orders poured in until one day problems started to rain in.

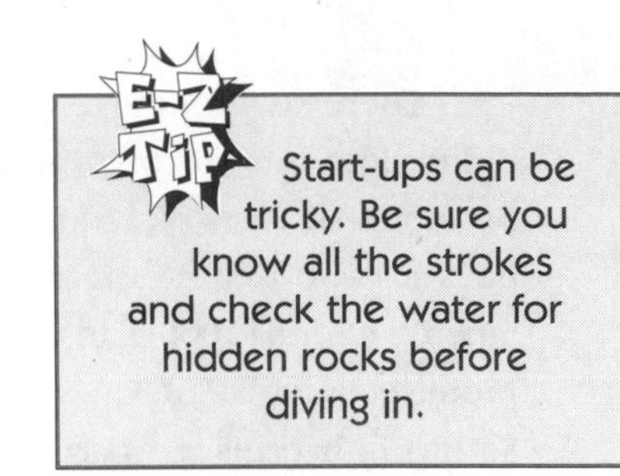

E-Z Tip
Start-ups can be tricky. Be sure you know all the strokes and check the water for hidden rocks before diving in.

The first sign of a storm was a phone call from the hostess of one of their affairs. All her guests had visited the hospital to have tainted potato salad pumped from their stomachs. The newspapers picked it up and before long all their clients canceled their orders. The inevitable lawsuit made Anne and June wished they had bought insurance and wondered where they'd get $8,000 to retain a lawyer to defend them.

Then lightning struck. The health inspector got wind of the situation and cited them for violating health and zoning codes. In two days they moved to "acceptable quarters," but their old ovens burned out while cooking the first dish. Business began to evaporate. Anne and June couldn't pay their suppliers, and three weeks later not only were they broke and out of business, but they still faced heavy legal expenses.

Watch your pennies—you'll need them

note

The one big mistake all too many entrepreneurs make: They forget to save.

You can't have it both ways. You *can* start your own business without capital if you know how to scrimp, scrape, and scramble to put together the assets you need. But once you're in, that's the time you really have to start an austerity program to keep preserving and accumulating every dime of profits and working capital the business can muster.

Stuart could have been the king of the $9.95 portable radio purveyors. His idea was solid enough. He was able to start small and line up import rights for an inexpensive Japanese pocket radio. All he had to do was the final

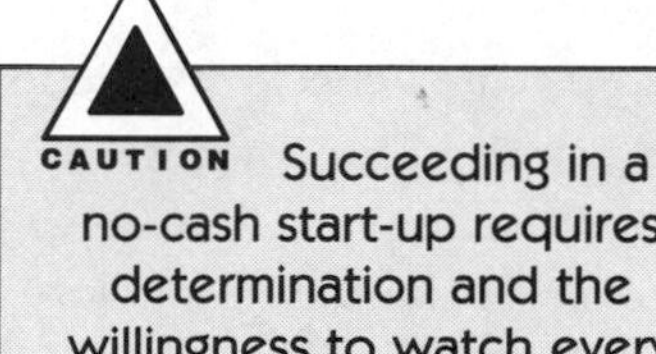

Succeeding in a no-cash start-up requires determination and the willingness to watch every penny. If you can't do it when planning the deal, you'd certainly be the one to throw away those valuable pennies once you get it rolling.

assembly work and then sell them. He started in the basement of his home with his wife and kids spending their waking hours with screwdrivers in hand while he was out peddling. Then the business began to take off. Sales zoomed to $100,000 within the first three months and by the year's end he was grossing $10,000 a week.

Then Stu stumbled. Flushed with success, he moved his operation to expensive facilities. He spent his days in his ultra-plush office and traveled around in his company-bought Cadillac. Every dime in profits was eaten up by needlessly high overhead. Finally the tide turned. One of his major discount store accounts went bankrupt, leaving him holding the bag with an uncollectable receivable of $91,000. Even with this loss Stu could have survived had he been smart enough to conserve profits until he had the solvency to withstand any contingency, but some think the sun will shine every day.

I can usually tell how successful a start-up will be even before the doors are open. The "high flyer" who'll go for any deal as long as he/she can pay it out is a prime candidate for failure because he/she has already shown her stripes.

Buy today—pay tomorrow

You can reduce the risk of failure and increase your chances for success if you know the secrets of buying assets at rock-bottom prices and deferring payments until your cash starts flowing. Study these typical start-up costs to see how you can reduce or avoid them:

- Rent deposits: Landlords usually want the first month's rent and one month's security deposit in advance. Try to defer the security deposit by giving the landlord a postdated check payable five days after your business opens. Then cash flow can cover the check.

- Leasehold improvements: Negotiate to have the landlord install special fronts, lights, plumbing, wall coverings, and air conditioning. The cost could be added to your rent, and it would avoid your own cash outlay.

- New equipment: Don't buy new if you can pick up good used equipment for much less. Sometimes you can finance used equipment more easily than you can new.

- Leases: Nowadays you can lease almost anything—store fixtures, cash registers, computers, carpets, and motor vehicles. Try to obtain an option to buy the equipment at a later date. A lease can get you in with little or no initial money

- Inventory: Scatter your shots. Wring a little credit from a large number of suppliers.

- The best price: It may be better to buy time by paying slightly more for your business. Don't drain your working capital.

God bless sales managers

Your strongest allies in your no-cash-down start-up may be the sales managers for your various suppliers. Their goal is to generate sales, and you are a potential sale even with no-cash-down terms. Sales managers tend not to care when you pay. That's for the credit managers to worry about.

Business is often a tug-of-war. Sales managers try to make sales to anybody who'll buy, and good credit managers will try to nix sales not accompanied by a certified check.

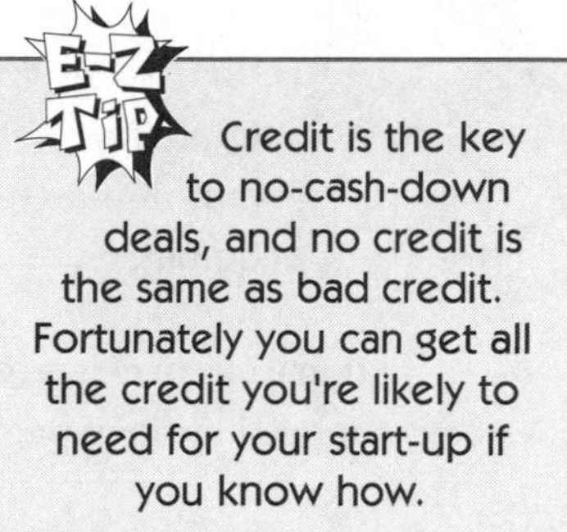

Credit is the key to no-cash-down deals, and no credit is the same as bad credit. Fortunately you can get all the credit you're likely to need for your start-up if you know how.

If the sales manager is on your side, how do you get around the credit manager who dislikes would-be businesses with no sales, profits, credit history, or cash register?

Credit managers are paid to be skeptics. Somebody is always trying to beat them, and if they get beaten often enough, they'll be looking for a new job. The following approach can give you the credibility you need to win credit:

- Deal in person. If it's a large order, the credit manager will want to meet you face to face, and want to size you up in person, which gives you a chance to sell yourself.

- Review your plans with him/her. Tell him/her what they want to know about your business. Become more than a name and address. If your ideas are solid and your projections realistic the credit manager will have confidence in your ability to pay.

- Use your personal credit rating. Your business may not have a rating, but you do. Even though you won't guarantee the debts of your business, it's logical that if you honor your personal obligations you'll do the same in your business. Offer a few credit references to prove you're no deadbeat.

- Control the terms. Let her know how and when she'll be paid. Back up your terms with solid projections. Once you're sure your numbers are right, don't back down and agree to her terms.

- Consider her profits. She may be the credit manager, but she still works for the company. Project purchases so she'll see the profits.

- Offer security. Equipment suppliers will probably want a mortgage on the equipment.

N
W
E
STRATEGY
Offer inventory suppliers a mortgage only if they're your principal suppliers.

It may seem elementary, but even experienced businesspeople often overlook the common-sense approaches to success.

Nice guys do finish last

There can be a big advantage in being financed up to the hilt by benevolent suppliers and creditors who have worked so hard to help put you in business.

I call it the *co-conspirator theory.* It does show why the penniless entrepreneur who put together his operation with some bright ideas and a lot of fast talk will always come out ahead of those nice guys who do it by the book.

Mark was fortunate. He had the "co-conspirator theory" working for him. He had a simple ambition: He wanted a full-scale supermarket of his own. Like most of the other players in the book, he didn't have a *peso* to his name, but that couldn't stifle his ambition.

One day he noticed a supermarket being auctioned off under a bankruptcy. He picked up all the fixtures and equipment by talking the creditors into accepting his note for $95,000, which was well in excess of the $15,000 it was expected to yield at auction.

Since shelves without stock can never spell success, Mark jockeyed for some creative supplier financing. Mark found out that one of the principal creditors who lost out on the former supermarket's bankruptcy was a full-line grocery wholesaler who owed $100,000. Mark's deal was a study in simplicity and persuasiveness. If the wholesaler would stock his store with $40,000 in merchandise on full credit, Mark would agree to assume $10,000 in debt owed by the prior supermarket.

Essentially, the wholesaler would get back $50,000 for a new $40,000 line of credit. Mark knew that the wholesaler once burnt would be somewhat gun-shy, so he agreed to all the safeguards that would protect the wholesaler. A security agreement (mortgage) that would secure the inventory, an agreement that inventory would be maintained at $40,000, a restriction on salaries, and even a provision that the wholesaler would be represented on the board of directors of Mark's corporation were written into the loan agreement. The wholesaler was now a "co-conspirator" in the success or failure of Mark's supermarket.

Mark immediately ran into trouble. The store was slow to reach projected sales. Worse, Mark couldn't pay back the $40,000 on schedule.

Do you think our wholesaler friend would be quick to squeeze Mark, or put him out of business? Of course not. Since all the cash in the deal came from the wholesaler, it was in his best interests to keep him alive. Ironically, this same wholesaler was owed only $8,000 by another retail account who started his operation with plenty of owner capital. Once his account was 90 days overdue they padlocked the place.

That's why I say "nice guys finish last." Throw in your own money and it's your own money you can lose. Play with creditors' money and they'll go to the ends of the earth to keep you alive and well.

Keep your checkbook locked up

Opening a business without cash is nothing more than a tug-of-war. You want to grab hold of all the assets you'll need without laying out a dime of your own. Your suppliers, of course, will have different ideas. As good businessmen they'll want you to part with as much money as they can induce you to part with, and as soon as possible. That, too, is business in the real world.

Therefore, to win you have to develop a psychological frame of mind. Pretend, even if it's in your own mind, that your checkbook is locked up. So despite their demands your position is fixed. You won't give up one inch of your cash lifeline.

Go through the stories in this chapter. Doesn't it sound easy? A supplier giving $80,000 in credit with no cash down, a future company providing $20,000 in equipment—all on terms. Of course it sounds easy.

However, that's only the end result. It's not the process. Every supplier or would-be creditor will demand some up-front cash. Expect it and you won't be disappointed. Notice that the winners knew how to say "no" and make it stick. They didn't go running for their checkbook at the first mention of money. They knew the basics from which no-cash start-ups are born, and that simply means not giving them your money.

The meek may inherit the earth but they'll never start up a no-cash operation. That inheritance will go only to the operator that can master the tricks, persuasiveness, and imagination to get the goods without parting with the cash. It's the entrepreneur who can say "no" today who'll have plenty of bucks tomorrow.

Key points to remember

- New business ideas mean new business ventures.
- Be careful about paying for good will; it may be thin air.
- Opening your own isn't as difficult as you think.
- Determine whether you're a buyer or a creator.
- Who needs money? It will only stifle your imagination when you start up.
- You can finance everything from floor to ceiling if you know the secrets.
- You have no margin for error with start-ups—watch your step.
- Make them want to give you credit.
- Don't be meek—get out there and hustle.

13

Pyramid your no-money-down

Chapter 13

Pyramid your no-money-down

What you'll find in this chapter:

- Grow your mini-empire
- Consider franchising
- Plan each step carefully
- Choose the right business expansion
- Use equity from the business

How would you like to start with one wall-furnishing storc grossing $600,000 annually and within three years have a mini-empire of seven stores with a combined volume of $2,800,000? It sounds even more interesting when you find that each of the seven stores was started with no cash down.

> **HOT spot** That's the secret of pyramiding—taking what you have for a business and using it as leverage to put you into bigger deals that can really expand your wealth.

With your first business underway, certain advantages can propel you along. Existing cash flow is available to you. Creditors will readily help you once you are a proven customer. Banks and other lenders know that you're more than an idea person and will listen to you. Prospective partners can examine what you have done and not what you might do. In short, you have momentum. With your first business you've marshaled assets, power, and influence. To multiply your wealth, strike while the iron is hot.

But who needs it?

That's more than a rhetorical question. Ray Kroc, the founder of McDonald's hamburger chain, is delighted every time they change the signs to announce still another billion sold—not because of the money involved, but because of the tremendous satisfaction in having built something really big. But I doubt that Ray Kroc's lifestyle would change much if McDonald's was one-tenth its present size.

My neighbor Walter is a miniature Ray Kroc. He doesn't deal in hamburgers, but at last count he had 15 businesses, ranging from a car dealership to restaurants and a bicycle rental shop in a local resort town. I'm not privy to Walter's bank account, but I'm sure he has surpassed the point at which more money would change his lifestyle. Does that slow Walter down? No. He keeps going after more and more. Recently he confided that he's negotiating to buy a large motel that would add $60,000 to $80,000 to his six-figure income.

You may not have met Ray Kroc, but you certainly know other Walters. They're easy to spot; their life is wheeling and dealing, collecting businesses like squirrels collect nuts. Ask any "Walter" what makes him run. The surprising answer is that money almost never motivates them. Money's just the yardstick by which they measure success. It's success—the joy of having achieved a major goal—that counts.

Some Walters are driven by ego, the need for personal satisfaction, power, or perhaps the thrill of helping something grow. Such people are rare; 99 percent of us fall into the "who needs it" category shortly after we carve our economic niche. You've heard the rationalizations: "A Chevrolet will go anywhere a Mercedes can." "How many steaks a day can you eat?" "Why kill yourself?" "You only live once." "Besides, I'd rather play poker with the boys than take on more business headaches."

I do not preach giving up your Saturday golf game to go after another deal, but in this chapter I will show the willing how to expand their success, even if it's just for the sheer joy of it.

Bigger can be better

There are good reasons for setting your sights on a bigger operation and expanding from your existing base. Such expansion does not have to change your lifestyle or turn you into a workaholic, nor does it require a wheeler-dealer mentality. The fact is, bigger can not only be better, it can even be easier.

Consider what additional businesses can do for you:

- Increased security through diversification. Why put all your eggs in one basket? Your business gives you your paycheck, but what happens if it suddenly stops? It happens all the time. Fire, flood, unexpected competition, new technology, or a fatal labor strike could happen at any time. An owner of a small business has security as long as he/she is in business, but with thousands of companies failing every year for one reason or another, it isn't all that much protection.

> **HOT spot** Multiply your businesses and spread your risk.

- Improved profits with leverage. Your existing business can benefit financially from expansion. Think of the added purchasing power which can translate into lower prices, higher volume, and greater profits. Such a strategy can help you compete with large chains. Many businesses expand just to survive in the competitive jungle.

- Strengthened management. Regardless of your business, you'll need people who are expert in all areas of management. Modem management and the attack of big business on small mom and pop stores have all but killed the one-man show. A small business cannot afford the overhead of a diverse number of highly skilled specialists on a payroll, but a big business can.

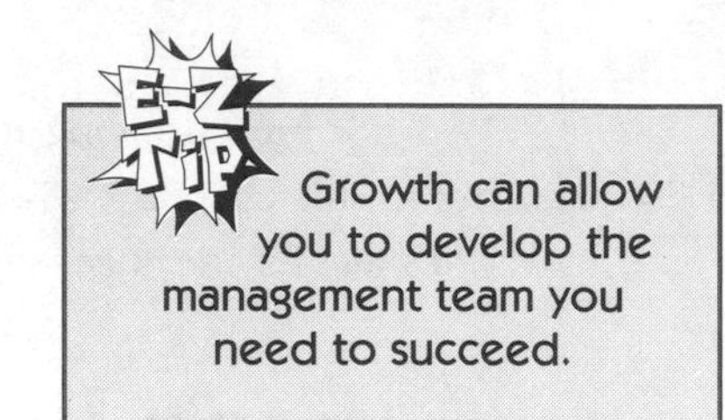

E-Z TIP
Growth can allow you to develop the management team you need to succeed.

- Reduced pressure on you. This may be the number-one reason to expand. Contrary to what you might think, bigger does not necessarily mean more work or more pressure. A larger endeavor doesn't necessarily require that you work harder, just that you be smarter. With strong subordinates to help manage your business you will probably find that you can take even more time off and stop being married to your one-man show.

Lincoln freed the slaves, but a friend of mine, Joe P., evidently didn't realize this. About 15 years ago he bought a small insurance agency. Joe reported to work every day and couldn't bring himself to take a vacation. Even a week away for needed surgery was out of the question. The proverbial one-man show, Joe was the "indispensable man" without whose constant presence the business would immediately fall apart. Or so he thought.

I asked Joe over the years why he didn't expand and build a staff that would allow him to relax a little. He always offered the same excuse. "Who needs more headaches?" Joe clung to the myth that bigger means more problems, never considering that just the opposite could be true.

Quite by accident, however, Joe picked up a combination insurance agency and real estate office in an adjacent town. The owner, who was a friend of his, suddenly died and his widow handed Joe the keys to the business. Joe immediately hired a bright college graduate to oversee both operations. This woman not only relieved Joe of many of the tedious day-to-day matters that kept him chained to his desk, she even improved both businesses by bringing to them fresh ideas and the objectivity of a newcomer.

Joe was thrilled. For the first time in 52 years he took a vacation for more than a few days and began to enjoy life. Today he owns five insurance agencies and has numerous other business interests. He developed a first-class management staff that can run everything efficiently in his absence. When he does work, he does so as a decision-maker, using his head instead of his arms and legs. Joe now enjoys the lifestyle everybody dreams about but few achieve. It all became possible because expansion gave Joe the people he needed to do what he always thought he had to do himself.

Where do you go from here?

Suppose you've dived into the water with a business of your own. The hard part was the cold water of doubt about your management capability and relinquishing the security of a steady paycheck. If you haven't drowned, expansion should be easy. Why not? You not only have your feet wet, you're already swimming. All you have to do is add a few strokes to your repertory.

But before you enter deeper water you have to know where you are and where you want to go. A word of caution: Even the most carefully planned courses are full of interesting detours that can provide opportunities. Who knows where any given business will end up years from now? No crystal ball will give you the answer. That's one of the things that makes business so exciting.

I wonder if Ray Kroc really visualized the present McDonald's empire when he set up his first stand. Did you ever hear of Radio Shack, part of the Tandy Corporation, with over 5,000 stores? Thirty years ago they opened their first hi-fi shop in a crowded little store in downtown Boston. One of their first employees was a radio buff, a high school classmate of mine who in later years told me that when they started the business they foresaw only three or four stores in the Boston area.

Don't waste much time looking ahead five, ten, or 15 years. Long-range planning can provide rough guidelines, but things rarely turn out the way you planned. Take one stroke at a time. You'll recognize the next right move when the time comes.

Always multiply a winner

Ten years ago the Clausons opened their first Quick Stop automotive tune-up center. Despite heavy competition, sales were brisk. The operation required start-up capital of over $200,000 (borrowed from banks, a couple of relatives, and a select partner), and the Clausons opened the doors with nary a penny of their own. They quickly repaid their debts and found that their business was soon worth $400,000 on the open market.

The Clausons drew a respectable $75,000 a year salary each, but they wanted more, so they chose "horizontal" expansion and opened more of the same type of stores. With their equity and track record they were able to borrow $350,000 from a local bank to open a second new unit and convert a defunct gas station into a third unit. With three operations they built sales and profits into even more equity. Today the Clausons have 15 automotive centers and are happy millionaires.

> **HOT spot**
> Observe the pyramid pattern. Borrow against equity; open more units with the borrowed funds; and pay off the loans with increased cash flow, thus amassing additional equity for future expansion.

On my way to my law office in the morning I often stop at a local luncheonette for a cup of coffee. Carl, the owner, has operated his luncheonette for about ten years. It's fully paid for, and he runs it so well that he could sell it tomorrow for $100,000. Sitting on $100,000 in equity, Carl slaved day in and day out behind the counter exactly as he had for the past ten years, and all he had to look forward to was ten more years of the same.

But Carl finally saw the light. His coffee shop provided a decent income, but by tapping his $100,000 equity he made a down payment on a much larger restaurant that not only threw off large profits, but allowed him to build up even more equity. Carl tripled his income and looks forward to a substantial net worth in a few years. That's called *trading up.*

For Carl, trading up to a much larger operation in the same business was a perfect strategy. Unlike the Clausons, who developed a business with a system that lent itself to horizontal expansion, Carl couldn't open a string of run-of-the-mill coffee shops. Diversifying into a nonfood business wasn't for Carl either, so he stuck to what he knew and liked by doing it on a bigger scale.

David, on the other hand, employed "vertical" expansion. This type of expansion plugs you into every inch of the distribution channel.

David entered the business world after working for years as a sales representative for a business forms distributor. The owner was approaching retirement age and agreed to a gradual takeover by David with the purchase price coming from David's sales commissions. Finally, after three years, David owned the company outright. Sales leaped under his management to $2 million a year. That's when he decided to vertically expand. He purchased a printing company so he could print his own forms for the distributing company. After two years elapsed David found a small paper supply firm for sale. A logical acquisition, the paper company could sell to his printing firm, and the printing firm in turn could print the forms for the distributing company. David now owns three companies at different points in the distribution channel. He always drew on the equity in his existing business, borrowing a small amount on a short-term basis to finance the down payment, while the seller provided the bulk of the financing. Each business paid back its own purchase price from profits.

Imagine starting your day by visiting your appliance stores, journeying to your car dealership for lunch, and stopping at the headquarters of your sporting goods chain in mid-afternoon. Before heading home you check your

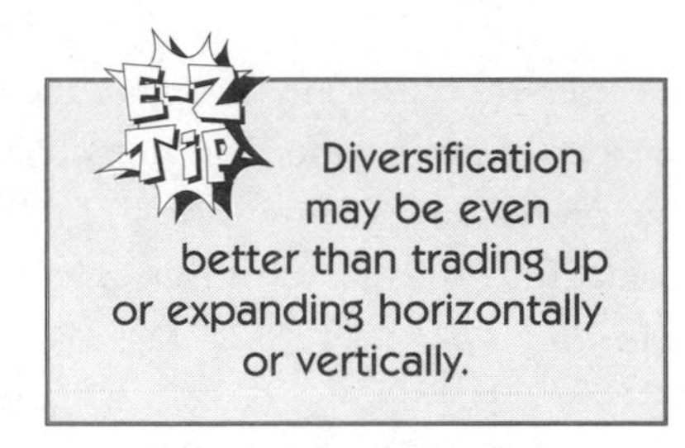

E-Z TiP
Diversification may be even better than trading up or expanding horizontally or vertically.

movie theatre to see that everything is ship-shape. Sound like a hectic schedule and more than you'd like to handle? Not if you're like Ken W. Business is his thing. He would die of boredom if he had to spend his days overseeing just one business or even several businesses in the same line. To Ken, different challenges, problems, and opportunities offer the spicy mix that promises success.

Ken remembers growing up poor and watching his father wiped out when his chain of jewelry stores failed during the depression. Ken learned from his father's experience and would never rely on just one type of business for security.

What makes Ken's story even more exciting is that he did it all without a dime of his own. Here's how he parlayed his way up the ladder.

- His first business, a small appliance store, was taken over for its debts only. Ken bailed it out by settling with creditors for 30 cents on the dollar. Then, with some imaginative marketing, he built it to a $1 million-a-year moneymaker.

- His second appliance store was plenty solvent but Ken still waltzed in with no cash down. He borrowed $20,000 from the available cash of his first store and coupled it with seller financing of $120,000 and the assumption of some existing debts to make up the price of $200,000.

- The car dealership came even easier. The seller turned it over to him with 100 percent financing based on his financial strength alone.

- The movie theatre was a high flyer. It was available for $90,000 but Ken scooped it up for $75,000 plus a good job for the previous owner.

Ken didn't need cash. He now had credit, borrowing power, and a signature on a note that meant something. All he had to do was find businesses in which the seller didn't need money up front, but needed only the security that the buyer was strong enough to justify 100 percent financing. The seller of the movie theatre fell into that category. The theatre did over $3 million a year in sales, and Ken got it going and kept it going without spending another cent of his own.

Pyramid equity into wealth

What is your present business worth? Surprisingly few businesspersons carefully analyze their business's net worth and fewer still understand how to parlay the net worth into bigger business. Before you launch more no-cash-down adventures, add up your business assets. What are they worth on the open market? Remember that good will may be your most valuable asset. Now subtract all your business liabilities from your total assets to find your net worth or equity. This represents your real investment in the business. This hard cash should be working for you. The balance sheet that your accountant gives you at the end of the year does not accurately reflect equity because it includes equipment and fixtures at their depreciated value rather than their market value, and disregards good will and other valuable but intangible assets.

Assume for the moment that you calculate a net worth of $100,000. Ask yourself two questions:

1) Is that $100,000 working for you? What does it return to you? Is it building wealth?

2) What could $100,000 do for you if you invested it elsewhere? Many small businesspersons are unaccustomed to thinking in that way. Periodically I conduct management seminars for businesspersons at local colleges. At the last seminar I asked the participants to bring in their financial statements. One woman, Selma V., owned a large

fabric store with a net worth of over $100,000. We put her business to the acid test. Selma volunteered that all she could take out of the business was $15,000 in salary and $5,000 in net profits. Nevertheless, she was content. To her, $20,000 was a satisfactory return on a $100,000 investment. I hated to disillusion her, but if Selma got a job in another fabric shop, she would still receive a $15,000 salary, so her $100,000 investment was really earning only a $5,000 profit or a 5 percent return on her investment. I explained that she could sell out, take the $100,000 and stick it in a money market account and watch it earn $15,000 to $17,000 without lifting a finger and with no risk. Selma was overwhelmed. Once we'd identified her problem, I asked her what she intended to do about it. "Gee," she replied. "What can I do? I don't want to sell out. I enjoy working for myself. What can I do to earn more money and stay in my business?"

The answer was easy.

1) She reduced inventory in her fabric shop from $80,000 to $50,000. Sales and profits remained at the same level without the unnecessary inventory. Now she had $30,000 in cash for further investment.

2) The fabric shop always paid C.O.D. for merchandise. Changing this policy, she now buys on 30-day terms, so her average trade payables of $20,000 can work for her without cutting into operating profits.

3) With $50,000 in her hands she was still showing a $5,000 profit, but had enough capital to open a second shop in a large mall. She invested $10,000 of the $50,000 in a small down payment for fixtures, rent, and working capital. Her suppliers agreed to stock the store with $40,000 in inventory with a long-term, low-interest payback. This second store promises to show at least a $15,000 profit.

4) Eventually Selma opened two more stores in other mall locations using the same technique and investing $10,000 in cash. Stores three and four will generate a combined profit of $25,000.

5) With the remaining $20,000 of her original $50,000 she diversified. With $5,000 she purchased a 50 percent interest in her son's new ice-cream shop. This will net her $5,000 a year in profits. She spent her $15,000 setting up a small distributorship for a line of imported fabrics for which she obtained exclusive New England rights. This proved a smart move because the distributing company earns a pretax profit of $20,000 on sales of $600,000.

Remember the $5,000 profit that Selma earned on her $100,000?

Look at her pyramid game scorecard.

Store #	Profit
1	$ 5,000
2	15,000
3	15,000
4	10,000
5 (ice-cream shop)	5,000
6 (distributorship)	20,000
	$70,000

What a turnaround! Selma went from profits of $5,000 a year to $70,000.

Of course Selma works harder than ever, and she will continue to do so for the next couple of years, but she doesn't mind. Buoyed by the $70,000 annual profits, she knows she can eventually sell her six businesses for considerable wealth. She's having the time of her life.

Expand through trade credit

Selma raised $20,000 by running up just one month's trade credit. I want to highlight that maneuver because it is probably the quickest, easiest, and least expensive way to raise expansion capital. It's also the most common way. You already understand supplier financing, discussed in Chapter 6.

E-Z TIP
Properly handled, trade credit can allow you to expand without investing any of your own cash.

Many years ago a client of mine, Roy S., proposed that we start a chain of retail pharmacies. Since he had a proven track record in his own pharmacy, I knew he had what it takes to make money. For starters, we scraped together $30,000 and purchased our first pharmacy for $85,000 with the seller financing $55,000. Knowing what I know today I would have kept our $30,000 in the bank and applied no-cash-down techniques.

Once we had our first operation, we decided to exploit trade payables. A safe rule of thumb in the drug business is to operate with 30 days trade credit on the books. Since we purchased $360,000 a year, we could build liabilities to $30,000 and still be financially strong. In a few weeks we had $30,000 in our pockets, rather than in our suppliers' cash registers.

We immediately purchased a second store for $36,000 with $12,000 down, again with the seller financing the balance. Since this new operation purchased $240,000 a year, we tapped it for $20,000 for further expansion. Now we had the $18,000 balance from the first store and $20,000 from the second.

We quickly invested this money in two more pharmacies. Our objective was always the same.

- Use surplus cash flow from prior acquisitions to finance the down payment on new ones.

- Make certain the down payment is less than the amount of cash you can pull out of the business by safely building up liabilities.

- Have the seller finance the balance of the purchase price. With this technique we ended up with eleven stores generating over $2.5 million per year ($5 million in today's dollars). We did it with $30,000, but we could have done it with nothing down.

When Roy's wife wanted him to cut back on his work, we sold off the stores, but from our experience I learned a valuable lesson: Once you have a business with available trade credit you can use it for your next deal and let it take you as far as your management skills and ambition allow.

Building a mini-conglomerate

When American Express or IT&T find a business they want to take over, they usually just swap pieces of paper, exchanging shares of stock and other securities. But what's OK for IT&T doesn't necessarily apply to Dan's Donut Shops. That is, not unless you're Dan W., who found plenty of takers and used them to expand his business. In just over two years he built one small donut shop into a thriving chain of 23. Dan inherited his first donut shop from his father, and soon saw an opportunity to buy another one a few miles away. The seller wanted $20,000 down and would finance the $50,000 balance. Only Dan didn't have the $20,000, so he proposed an interesting deal. He would set up a corporation called Dan's Donut Shops, Inc., a holding company which would own all the shares of both Dan's and the seller's shops. Dan in turn would own 90 percent of the shares of the holding corporation and the seller would receive 10 percent of the shares, in lieu of the $20,000 down payment. The seller would still receive the $50,000 balance over time. Dan convinced the seller that he knew what he was doing and persuaded him to accept the 10 percent stock interest instead of the $20,000 in view of the huge potential payoff. Dan was soon on his way to owning a mini-conglomerate.

Next, he bargained 8 percent of the holding company for the down payment on a $100,000 coffee shop in a downtown office building. As he expanded, his approach was always the same: Exchange a small percentage of the holding company for the down payment on a new acquisition with the balance of the price paid from future profits from the acquisition.

Today Dan owns 52 percent of the shares of the parent company, while the sellers who sold out to him own the other 48 percent. Dan reports corporate net worth of over $1,500,000 which translates into a $750,000 personal net worth for Dan. And he was the guy two years ago who couldn't even raise $20,000 for a down payment! You don't have to play in the big leagues to build your own mini-conglomerate; just follow Dan's method.

- Create a holding company. This is nothing more than a corporation that owns the shares of the individual operating corporations.

- Transfer your stock ownership in your existing business to the holding company in exchange for the shares of the holding company.

- Find other businesses where the seller may be willing to substitute a down payment for a few shares of your holding company. Your selling point is always the same. You have what it takes to make the holding company grow and grow. The few shares the seller accepts may soon grew to a value well in excess of what would have been a down payment.

- Pay the balance of the purchase price on each acquisition from its own profits. Be careful; don't borrow from one company to pay for another. That can create a domino effect if you pick up a loser. Each subsidiary business has to stand on its own.

- Always hold on to at least 51 percent of the shares. You started out as the boss and that's what you want to stay!

Does all of this sound too difficult? It's deceiving, for it is one of the simplest concepts for expansion. And it's not "pie-in-the-sky," it's done all the time. You just may not know about all those little pieces of paper changing hands.

Turn a name into a money-making franchise system

You may be a capable businessperson but still oppose expansion because you don't want the headaches (real or imagined) that come from managing a large number of businesses. If that is so, but you still want the wealth that bigness can bring, franchising may be your answer.

Before you can consider franchising you need one indispensable ingredient—a business with a name, reputation, or approach that lifts it out of the competitive crowd. Franchising presents many advantages:

- Properly handled, you can establish a large network without any investment on your part.
- You don't have the headaches of managing a large number of company-owned operations. Your efforts are confined to selling franchises and providing general business policy and supervision.
- Your income is assured because it comes directly from the sales of the franchisees. You take your cut off the top.

Earlier in this chapter I mentioned Ray Kroc and the McDonald's franchise empire. Not long ago the only McDonald's was a solitary hamburger stand in San Bernardino, California. Colonel Sanders started his "Finger Lickin'" franchise chain when he was in his 60s.

You've heard the expression, "Those who can make money, do it—those who can't, write about it." I always thought that applied only to teachers, but I remembered those words when I started this book, because with a few words I once blew $1 million.

Back in 1967 I delivered a lecture on the "Impact of Franchising on the Retail Drug Industry" before the American Pharmaceutical Association. When 1 finished my talk two men approached me and invited me to dinner. It turned out that they owned two prescription drug centers in the Midwest. They were proud of the fact that they had convinced several major labor unions to promote their pharmacies to their members. The pharmacies gave special discounts to union members but made it up with higher volume.

What prompted the dinner invitation was their need for help to determine the best way to expand. They envisioned hundreds of prescription centers throughout the Midwest to handle the voluminous prescription business from tens of thousands of union members. The two men posed the question: "Do we open more stores owned by ourselves, or do we sell franchises?" After sifting through the pros and cons of each approach, we chose franchising. Expansion would be faster and no cash would be required. They formed a corporation to own the trademark name and to develop, sell, and administer the franchises. The system soared! Within three years they had 115 franchised pharmacies, while the parent company collected $7,500 in franchise fees from each plus 4 percent of gross sales. Since the average franchise generated $300,000 annually, they took in average annual fees of $12,000 from each. Calculate the income—almost $1,500,000 a year in franchise fees alone.

My clients prospered, but I made a big mistake. After dinner they asked me to act as consultant on developing the franchise system. They proposed a $10,000 a year consulting fee or 25 percent interest in the parent company. I opted for the $10,000. A few years later my clients sold out, and my 25 percent interest would have been worth an even $1 million. *C'est la vie!* Even my trusty "crystal ball" can cloud up at precisely the wrong time.

Look around. Observe the number of small regional franchise networks springing up in virtually every type of business. If your business is unique, highly profitable, and has a good track record, why not duplicate it in other locations? Better yet, why not have others capitalize it, manage it, and still pay you for it? You may not be another Ray Kroc, but franchising can give you a no-cash-down empire.

Ten mistakes to avoid

Before you leap into an expansion program, take a hard look at some of the most common mistakes that can bring your venture tumbling down around your ears.

1) Evaluate your own strengths. Do you have what it takes to manage multiple operations? This requires the ability to delegate and motivate. You must be able to work through other people.

2) Watch cash flow. Every acquisition has to stand on its own feet without draining cash from existing operations.

3) Don't build on quicksand. Make certain your existing operations are solid, smooth-running, and in good financial health before you expand.

4) Develop a management team. You can't be everywhere at once. A capable management team will help you manage when you're no longer a one-man show.

5) Limit overhead. Forget fancy offices and big expense accounts. Don't let your ego dim your judgment. Watch every dime, even when you're worth millions.

6) Protect yourself. Set up each business as a separate corporation. If one goes sour it won't bankrupt you.

7) Consider logistics. Confine yourself at first to one geographic area. Forget businesses in distant towns where you cannot adequately supervise them.

8) Use leverage. Being bigger means more advertising and buying clout, which can put more dollars in your pocket.

9) Don't let growth problems discourage you. Growing pains are natural; every business suffers from them, but be prepared for them.

10) Grow with no-cash-down. You can expand quickly with little or no cash if you master the techniques. What money you may need can come from the existing business. Don't dig into your own pocket.

Key points to remember

- It's easier to expand on no-cash-down terms than it is to start from scratch.
- Running ten businesses does not have to be harder than operating one—but it can be more profitable.
- Plan each step carefully. Long-term road maps are only guidelines, not magic formulas.
- Expansion takes many forms. Choose the one that's best for you.
- Unleash the equity in your business. It can be the springboard to an empire.
- A dollar in trade credit is a dollar toward your next down payment.
- Shares of stock are more than pieces of paper. Consider setting up your own mini-conglomerate to put you on the fast growth track.
- Franchising can give you your own chain—with no cash down.
- To play in the big leagues you must play like a pro. Avoid mistakes that can stunt your growth.

Booby traps

Chapter 14

Booby traps

What you'll find in this chapter:

- Examine the options carefully
- Don't let emotions rule
- Calculate benefit/risk ratios
- Beware of "fake rabbits"
- Know when to abandon a plan

The woods are full of traps, and the smart buyer must learn to avoid the snares. Dishonest sellers, deal-killing attorneys and advisers, businesses too far gone to save, and other booby traps can turn your dream into a nightmare. An emphatic "no" can often save you time, effort, and money. You don't want a booby trap deal at any price, on any terms, including no cash down! Sellers peddling booby traps will offer you practically anything to get you on the hook, and paint pretty pictures to reel you in. Remember P.T. Barnum's famous saying, "There's a sucker born every minute." Don't be that sucker.

You'll encounter your share of booby trap deals. Announce that you're in the market for a business and sellers will waltz out of the woodwork, proclaiming, "Have I got deal for you." No one can protect the gullible from their own foolish fantasies.

Some people need a guardian angel more than a lawyer. Never learning from previous lessons, their lives seem to consist of nothing more than stumbling from one booby trap to another. These people suffer from:

The rose-colored glasses syndrome

What an expensive disease! Those afflicted suffer from chronic symptoms of seeing what they want to see (even if it's not there) and not seeing what they should.

Any deal can appear attractive if you view it through rose-colored glasses.

Take Jack M. He fantasized about a business of his own. He decided to pursue a health club for which the seller wanted $200,000. Unfortunately Jack ignored a whopping 80,000 a year rent. Since the business only grossed $1600,000 a year and had little prospect for more members, $80,000 represented an astronomical expenditure. In fact, the health club had lost $40,000 during its first year of operation and promised even greater losses in its second. The seller was so desperate to get out, he would have snapped up a no-cash-down offer. Ignoring the facts and figures Jack walked right into the trap. I remember his customized T-shirt emblazoned with the words "Jack's Health Club" on the front and "Have a new body overnight" on the back. No one who joined on the promise of that ad could say it was misleading, because that's all the time he had to develop that new body.

The jaws of the trap have sprung shut on Jack, who went broke in two months. He's still ducking the seller, to whom he owes $200,000. The wounds on his ankles had barely healed when Jack fell into the books-by-mail business. It was a simple proposition. He could buy $40,000 worth of how-to-do-it books for $2.0,000 and nothing down—all he had to do was mortgage his house to secure the payment. The seller convinced Jack that all he had to do was advertise his books in leading journals and the money would roll in. But if this was such a super moneymaker, why didn't the seller place his own ads and rake in the money himself? Jack's enthusiasm prevented him from seeing the gaping hole at his feet. All he wanted was to be a "publisher." You can guess the result. Two months later Jack lay in the bottom of a pit under 95 percent of the books.

It's no sin to try and then fail. Everyone makes mistakes and will make more as time goes on. Even giant corporations can fall into traps. Remember how 200 MBAs at Ford Motor Company decided every American would want an Edsel in the garage?

But Jack wasn't a victim of the backfiring educated guess. No, he was a victim of his rosy outlook, which blinded him to obvious facts. Don't allow your eagerness to be your own boss blind you. Emotion can obscure all logic.

> E-Z TIP
> Remove your rose-colored glasses and whip out your magnifying glass. Know what you're getting yourself into and give the deal the acid test.

Calculating the benefit/risk ratio

Here's a simple proposition: Every business decision you will ever make should depend on the benefits outweighing the risk. When you picked up this book at the bookstore you noticed the price. Didn't you immediately quantify the risk in terms of the price? You glanced through the book to see what you might learn, how it might benefit you. Once your calculations indicated that the benefit would exceed the risk, you decided to buy.

What if the book had been on sale for half-price? The benefit to the reader would remain constant, but the risk would be cut by 50 percent. How many more books would people buy? Of course, this calculation propelled publishing into the current paperback boom. Suppose I offer to sell you a perfectly legitimate business which will earn for you $60,000 a year, year in and year out, and you need no investment or down payment. You will incur no personal liability, notes, or other obligations. Further, you don't even have to visit the business for it to hum along making money. Interested? Of course you'd be interested. You see the $60,000 a year benefit with no risk. How can you lose?

> **HOT spot** If you ever encounter an all benefit/no risk deal, stick it under your microscope. Chances are you'll spot a booby trap.

The answer is easy. You couldn't lose. Unfortunately, such deals don't exist in the real world. "There's no such thing as a free lunch" may strike you as being a trite phrase, but everything has its price. In the real world every deal will offer benefits and risks. All you have to do is calculate that the potential benefit exceeds the risk by a comfortable margin.

You cannot easily define "benefit." If you make $40,000 a year at your present job but see that a prospective business will give you $60,000 in income for the same amount of work, you might define "benefit" as $20,000 for each year these numbers hold true—a reasonably precise benefit. But suppose you would build the business and sell out in ten years with a $200,000 profit. By then you would have reaped a $400,000 benefit: $20,000 increased income for ten years plus the $200,000 profit. Regardless of the mathematical probability, however, not everything in life reduces to dollars and cents—not even in business.

I learned that lesson from a young client with a constant smile and easygoing manner. For several years Paul worked for a high-powered Madison Avenue advertising agency, earning $100,000 and the prospect of greater financial rewards. I helped him purchase an art gallery on Cape Cod, though I could not understand why he'd abandon a $100,000 position for a business that would generate an income of only $40,000 to $50,000.

Two years later I got the answer. He was happy being his own boss. He loved art and had turned an avocation into a vocation. Although he knew he'd earn less, the satisfaction and reduced stress of doing what he was doing benefited him sufficiently. Paul's story isn't unique. Go to the small villages of any state and you'll find shop-keepers, artisans, teachers, and writers who have chosen an alternative lifestyle. They do not measure benefit solely in monetary terms; money represents only a fraction of their equation.

Maybe you're the opposite of Paul. Perhaps the challenge of seeing a business grow spurs you on, not solely for the sake of money—but because the hustle and bustle of succeeding makes you happy. For such people, money becomes the yardstick for measuring success, but success is still the real goal.

> **note** You can't value subjective monetary considerations in terms of dollars.

Add up the benefits. What will your business realistically provide in monetary and non-monetary terms? Underline realistically. When evaluating financial factors, be conservative. Don't overestimate a business that historically gave its owner $60,000 a year. It won't generate $180,000 for you unless you've got a track record for tripling businesses.

What about "risk"? Risk can assume one or more of these forms:

- cash investment
- personal debts and obligations
- lost time and effort, including lost alternative opportunities

Evaluate each of these risk factors.

- Cash investment

If you adhere to the methods in this book you can ignore this factor, because you intend to take over your business with no cash down.

- Personal debts and obligations

Be a pessimist. What if the business fails? Eighty percent do fail within the first five years. What liabilities will you face if the business assets cannot surpass obligations? Quite often you can reduce this risk to numerical terms. If you find a no-cash-down deal for $100,000 and you give the seller your personal note for the $100,000, your potential loss on the obligation is $100,000. If the seller holds a mortgage on the assets of the business or otherwise realizes $40,000 on the liquidation of the business you still have a $60,000 remaining liability. For your risk to be minimal or nonexistent you must have confidence that the business assets can cover the obligations on which you are personally indebted. Now come the crucial questions. Can the risk be reduced? Can you readily absorb the loss? What are the chances of failure? In a typical no-cash-down deal, personal liability is the only financial risk, but it can be considerable. Know what you're getting into and add any potential loss to your calculated risk.

HOT spot: Remember, start-ups are considerably riskier than taking over existing businesses.

- Lost time and effort

If you're sitting home day after day, time and effort present no risk. But if you sacrifice a $80,000 a year position hoping to make $100,000 in your business, but wind up earning only $60,000 a year, then you have "lost" $20,000 per year. As straight-forward as that may appear, some people have trouble seeing it. Carl, for example, operated a toy store for three years. All he could afford to pay himself was $400 a week, although any other employer would have paid him $800 a week. Since his business showed a $2,000 a year marginal profit, he was satisfied. But in reality, his business had lost $20,000 a year because Carl has subsidized it with an inadequate salary. Carl could not understand that he had unwittingly invested $60,000 in his toy

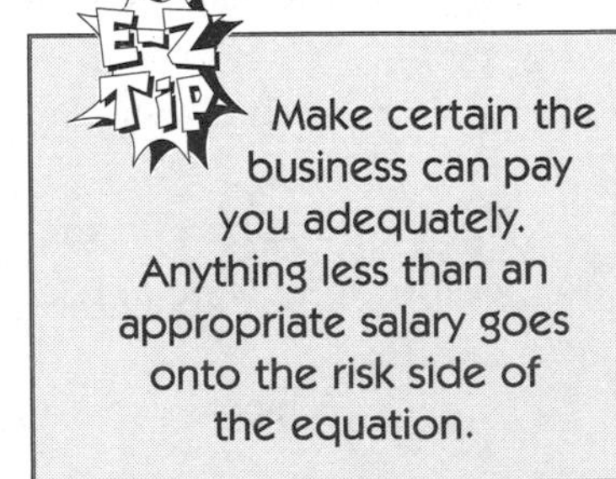
E-Z TIP
Make certain the business can pay you adequately. Anything less than an appropriate salary goes onto the risk side of the equation.

store over three years and would never recover it. Time and effort can spell high risk, for time is money. Analyze that benefit/risk ratio. Be conservative in what you have to gain and pessimistic about potential loss. Weigh one against the other. Are the odds in your favor? If not pass the deal up—even if you can get no cash down. Don't forget, that's only one small part of the total equation.

Three deals you don't want at any price

In my travels I've observed thousands of deals. From this experience, I've learned to avoid certain types of deals because they produce nothing but headaches.

1) *The high risk-low benefit deal*

You can't afford to gamble on deals that expose you to risks greater than their potential benefit.

2) *The no-profit business*

Whatever business you enter, it must eventually show a profit. If it can't, ignore it. Even if you think no risk exists, avoid the temptation to overlook profits, or you'll make a big mistake. If you cannot develop a credible plan for producing profits, your business will monopolize your time and energy, sidetracking you from deals that can produce a profit. Don't forget that profit is what the game of business is all about.

3) *The negative-cash-flow business*

There are thousands of businesses that do or can generate a profit and present a favorable benefit/risk ratio, but they contain another trap. If money goes out faster than it comes in, you face inevitable insolvency despite

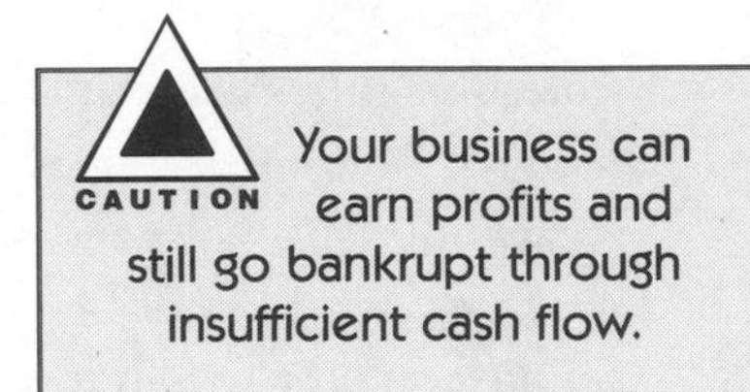

CAUTION
Your business can earn profits and still go bankrupt through insufficient cash flow.

continued profits. Here's why cash flow analysis is so important: If a business has a $10,000 annual profit it cannot pay $30,000 a year on a purchase money note. The $30,000 note payment is not reflected in the profit and loss statement. The net consequence would be that the business would be forced to pay $20,000 a year more than it earns. After a period of time that $20,000 cash drain will take its toll. You may be draining inventory or building up unpaid bills, but eventually it will kill you. This problem can be particularly troublesome on no-cash-down deals. The seller probably can survive on modest profits, as he may not have big notes to pay. But you will have such payments. Make certain the cash will be there when you need it. If you cannot handle the financing package from positive cash flow, either restructure the payback on the debt or leave the deal behind.

> **HOT spot**
> Getting into business with no cash down is only the first move in the game. To win the game, you must stay in business and make money.

More "fake rabbits" that can stick to you

In a popular children's fable, a fox catches a rabbit by building a fake baby rabbit out of tar. When the rabbit comes hopping along, he takes the cute baby in his arms and soon finds himself so stuck to the goo he cannot flee. Instant supper for the fox! Some deals are "fake rabbits."

1) Absentee ownership

I have never seen absentee ownership succeed. I'm sorry to say I should have followed this advice myself years ago. I held an interest in a small drug chain but my partners and I did not take time to personally oversee the operation. Employee theft, absenteeism, and uncontrolled expenses forced us to sell out before there was nothing left to sell. I learned a bitter lesson: If you don't watch your business yourself, your employees will be happy to watch it for you—at your expense. If you depend on employees to protect your business you have adopted your first "fake rabbit."

> **HOT spot** If you can't devote sufficient personal supervision to your business, stay away from it.

2) Government-regulated businesses

Shun any business that's tied to government. Red tape, arbitrary rulings, audits, and cost limitations can destroy you. Government has ruined more businesses than it has helped. Of the ten most recent business bankruptcies handled by our firm, five were caused in large measure by governmental interference or bureaucratic red tape. Here are just a few examples of how "big brother" travels like a tornado, chewing up small businesses that have the unfortunate distinction of being involved with it:

- A small aerospace instrumentation firm depended on Uncle Sam for 80 percent of its business. The contract was suddenly switched to a California firm, and that was the end of one more company.

- A nursing home was cut off from most of its operating revenue when Massachusetts ran out of Medicaid funds for nursing home patients. Since the home didn't have staying power, it went into receivership.

- Then there's the story of a pencil factory that closed down because an OSHA inspector arbitrarily decided that a $400,000 air filtration system had to be installed. Since the company earned an annual profit of only $40,000, this demand spelled doom.

- Next we come to a construction company doing a massive job for a firm dependent on SBA funds. The SBA misplaced its paperwork and the cash flow to fund the project came to a standstill. After ten weeks without SBA promised funds, the construction company was disbanded.

- And our final story. A local township overspent its budget and couldn't pay a school bus company that was under contract to transport 3,000 children daily. With four months remaining on the contract, the bus company had to file bankruptcy. It's tough to fight City Hall. To them you're only another statistic. Depend on government and you can look forward to eventual trouble.

3) *Personal good-will deals*

Some businesses prosper because of personal relationships established between owner and customer. When a new owner takes the keys, the customers vanish. If the owner has a personal following, make certain you can transfer their loyalty to you after the seller leaves. I have seen businesses in this category experience as much as a 75 percent decline in sales after the new owner took over.

Ask Cami—she was a victim. She purchased a local dry cleaning and dye house doing $600,000 a year. Had she checked she would have found out that most of this volume came from several nearby motels, a major-league baseball team, and a large restaurant chain. The prior owner developed these accounts over 30 years of business and even had a strong social relationship with their owners. Their allegiances left with the seller. Within a week of takeover these accounts defected, leaving Camie with $150,000 in annual sales. If you are counting on existing sales volumes to make the deal fly, ask yourself the question "Will the customers stay with me?" There are almost as many "fake rabbits" as there are deals. In Chapter 3 we underscored the need to investigate, investigate, investigate.

HINT

Use your common sense. Ask questions. Talk to employees. Interview customers and suppliers. Check around the industry. Have your accountant scrutinize the numbers with a microscope. Make certain your attorney has done everything possible to reduce your legal risk. But in the final analysis you and you alone can give a deal the red or green light.

note

Minimizing risk makes it easier for you to flash the green light. Only then can you confidently apply no-cash-down techniques.

Although Black's law dictionary defines a guarantor as "one who obligates himself to pay the debts of another," I call a guarantor "an idiot with a fountain pen." Leave your pen at home. Refuse to personally guarantee payments on any debt.

Watch how Frank W. handled it. After several months of negotiation, Frank had almost landed his auto parts store for $150,000. Only one stumbling block remained. The seller was willing to accept Frank's $100,000 note if Frank assumed $50,000 in liabilities. Not unexpectedly, the seller wanted Frank to personally guarantee the corporate note. If the business failed, Frank would be personally liable for $80,000, since the seller couldn't anticipate more than $20,000 from proceeds of an auction. How could Frank satisfy the seller that his note was secure, and at the same time limit his own liability?

E-Z TIP
Skillful negotiating can free you from personal risk.

Frank presented some interesting alternatives. First, he proposed that the seller secure the note with a mortgage on the assets of the business. If the business failed, the seller would be entitled to all the auction proceeds up to the remaining balance. In the event of bankruptcy the seller would enjoy an advantage over other creditors because the seller would get his money first. Using this common legal technique, Frank could reduce his personal exposure considerably. Since Frank had to convince the seller he would have adequate protection even without Frank's personal guarantee, he offered to pledge his shares in the corporation to the seller. In the event of default in making the note payments, the seller could assume immediate ownership of and continue to operate the business, thus eliminating the need to foreclose.

Finally, Frank issued his most convincing commitment. Emphasizing the benefit/risk ratio to the seller, Frank argued that if the business did fail, the seller really had little to lose. If the seller foreclosed on the mortgage, he could bid for the assets at auction. Since the seller would be entitled to all the proceeds, he could reclaim the assets of the business without spending a dime. The seller would be back in his old business but could ditch the $50,000 liabilities which foreclosure would eliminate. The risk side of the equation was negligible.

Frank next presented the very small benefit the guarantee represented. Frank was honest and straightforward as he told the seller that his only personal asset was a half-interest in the home he shared with his wife, which was worth $100,000. The house was mortgaged for $80,000, bringing Frank's share of equity to only $10,000. Therefore Frank's personal guarantee would net only $10,000. Frank said, "If I guarantee the note and subsequently default I'll have to file bankruptcy. That won't enable you to get more than $10,000, and probably less." Frank cemented the deal with a simple proposition:

"As I've explained, my guarantee is only worth $10,000. Since I don't want you to think I'm insincere about my responsibility on your note, I'll give you a $10,000 limited guarantee securing it with a mortgage on my interest on my house. You know I'll find some way to pay $10,000 to save my house. My bankruptcy wouldn't do either of us any good." Study Frank's approach. He appealed to the seller's logic by calculating the benefit/risk ratio for the seller. He convinced the seller of his sincerity and honesty, structuring the deal to give the seller every possible benefit while sharply reducing his own potential risk.

Follow the steps Frank used to protect himself:

- Offer the seller a mortgage on the business assets plus any other form of business security that will maximize his return if you default.

- Show the seller how small his risk is if you default.

- Disclose your personal assets (if nominal) to prove your personal guarantee "won't put money in his pocket."

- If necessary, offer the seller a limited guarantee equal to whatever amount you're willing to forfeit if you default. Sellers usually ask for a personal guarantee because they believe the guarantee automatically insures their getting paid off. In reality all they can hope to get are your personal assets—which may be negligible. Each situation will dictate how much you can reasonably expose yourself to personal liability.

I'm working on a deal as I write this chapter. My client developed a laser light show system for movie theatres. A week ago Roger found a movie theatre for sale. It was owned by an industrious middle-aged woman who would rather spend her time developing real estate.

Roger set up an appointment to see what we would negotiate. Marilyn, a ball of fire, was ready to wheel and deal. She began perfectly. "Dr. Goldstein, I know you're looking for a no-cash-down deal for your client, so let's not waste time. No cash down is OK with me, but I want something in return. The theatre is for sale for $320,000 cash, but since I don't need the money right now, I'm happy to let it grow over the long term. I'll sell to your client for $400,000 at 10 percent interest payable over 20 years. The added $80,000 on the price is fair considering the very low interest rate and the fact that your client can walk in without a penny of his own." It was refreshing to hear Marilyn talk candidly without the blue smoke and mirrors we usually suffer before we reach the same point. I hoped to make this the shortest negotiation since the Dutch bought Manhattan from the Indians.

I accepted her terms, provided the following terms were met:

- The note must contain a prepayment bonus. If the buyer paid off the note early, the seller would deduct 8 percent from the balance (the difference between the 18 percent she could get reinvesting the money elsewhere and the 10 percent due under the note).

- Roger would not give a personal guarantee on the note. If he defaulted, Marilyn could foreclose on the mortgage, taking back her movie theatre. The buyer would lose whatever payments he had made but would otherwise avoid personal risk.

Marilyn readily agreed. She asked me to draft a simple letter of intent to show her attorney. You can guess what happened then. Two days later I received a phone call from her deal-killing lawyer. I'd heard it before. He told me everything looked fine, except the lack of any personal guarantee. I stifled my sigh and reminded him that:

- The seller agreed to $400,000 instead of $320,000 to compensate for no guarantee.

- The seller wanted to unload the theatre so she could pursue other interests.

- Since Roger had a novel idea, he couldn't be sure it would work, but if it did, everyone would win.

- The seller incurred no risk. Either she got her $400,000 or her theatre back.

- A personal guarantee transferred all the risk to the buyer. If Roger defaulted Marilyn could buy back the foreclosed theatre at a nominal price and sue Roger for the difference.

- Roger's personal guarantee was practically worthless. If he defaulted he would be stuck in bankruptcy, and the seller would receive nothing.

At this moment the ball is in the seller's court; Marilyn must make up her mind. But you play the negotiating game like chess—anticipating your opponent's next moves so you can prepare for them, Luckily Marilyn will have decided before this book is published, so I'm not tipping her off to my strategy. Here's what I intend to do to cement the deal.

If Marilyn's attorney insists on a guarantee, I'll offer to lease the theatre for one year with an option to buy. We'll sign a guarantee because Roger will know by then whether his laser light show will succeed, and we'll have succeeded in reducing his risk. Now at this point you may say that if you had sizeable personal assets you wouldn't be reading books on no-cash-down business deals. Without personal assets, what do you really have to risk with a personal guarantee? The answer simply is that you'll avoid bankruptcy and be able to preserve your credit rating for the next deal. So don't be too quick with the fountain pen. It can cost you even if you don't write out a check.

Bail out—the graceful retreat

note
Businesses don't come with money-back guarantees.

No matter how carefully you search for hidden booby traps before you buy, they can snare you long after you buy your business. When this happens, it's time to bail out.

The bail-out is a two-step process. First, turn valuable assets into a benefit. Second, extricate yourself from remaining liability. With a little one-upmanship you can convert even a full-blown disaster into a learning experience. With some luck you can even walk away with some money in your pocket.

My favorite bail-out story involved a large drugstore located in a shopping center south of Boston. The owner had a severe problem because the center's largest tenant, a discount store, went bankrupt and the landlord couldn't find a replacement. Without the "anchor" tenant the shopping center was a desert. Sales for the smaller shops, like Lou's drugstore, dropped 50 percent. To make things worse, Lou owed the bank $120,000 secured by a mortgage on his house, and he had personally guaranteed the store's lease. Unfortunately, he owed $36,000 in back rent and was falling further behind each month. After deliberating our strategy, we learned the landlord owned a local supermarket chain. That saved us.

First we organized a tenants' association whose members agreed to abandon the shopping center if Lou's drugstore closed. No one could survive a further reduction in traffic. I approached the landlord with this heavy ammunition.

I couched the proposition in the landlord's terms—but to Lou's benefit.

- If the drugstore vacated, the landlord would lose five or six other tenants, leaving the shopping center vacant.
- The landlord could buy the drugstore to stabilize the shopping center.
- The insolvent drugstore could be liquidated for only $60,000 despite an $160,000 inventory. If the landlord bid $120,000 for the assets Lou could pay off the bank, but the landlord had to agree to bid the $120,000. The landlord would also discharge the lease guarantee as part of the deal.
- The landlord would acquire $160,000 in assets for only $120,000. The clincher—since rival supermarket chains were expanding into the drug field this was a golden opportunity for the landlord to experiment himself at bargain basement prices.

- The shopping center would survive.

The landlord eventually accepted the proposition, but the story doesn't end there. He was sufficiently sold to agree to pay Lou $50,000 over three years in return for his agreement not to compete in the drug business within the town for that period. Lou leaped from certain bankruptcy to $50,000 in his pocket in one bound! The landlord also won. Going into the drug business was such a good idea that his supermarket chain opened five additional pharmacies last year.

Chrysler can run to Washington for help when things get rough, but you're left to your own wits. Once you find your foot in the booby trap, your wits are the only thing that will get it out.

Key points to remember

- Watch out for booby traps; they're everywhere!
- Remove your rose-colored glasses; use a microscope.
- Don't let emotion blind you.
- Always calculate benefit/risk ratios.
- Don't fall for "fake rabbits."
- Reduce risk but give the seller what he wants.
- If disaster strikes, bail out. Design a graceful retreat.

15

Sell for no-cash-down and reap the rewards

Chapter 15

Sell for no-cash-down and reap the rewards

What you'll find in this chapter:

- How no-cash-down can benefit the seller
- Be willing to negotiate the down payment
- Reinvest the down payment
- Don't limit your options—be flexible
- Obtain the best price over the long term

I'd never sell a business to a buyer with a down payment. In fact, if I were looking to sell I'd probably work even harder than the buyer to find a way to have him take over my business with absolutely no investment on his part. And my motivation isn't for charitable purposes—unless I could be considered the charity. Does that sound illogical? I don't think so. In fact, selling a business for no cash down can be the most logical way to sell a business if you're a seller who wants to go contrary to convention and put plenty more dollars in your pocket in the process. In this chapter I'll show you how you can do just that.

So far I have aimed everything in this book at buyers. Every case illustrated yet another method by which a successful buyer can get into business without cash of his or her own. Now I'll show you—if you're that smart seller—why you should help him reach his objective. In Chapter 2 you learned that in the game of business buying, both sellers and buyers can win. Here you will see where both will win.

Imagine yourself ready to sell that prosperous business you have spent years building. Now it's time to cash in your chips. I suggest that you have only two basic objectives:

1) Sell as quickly as possible.

2) Sell for as much money as possible.

The simple truth is that the best way to satisfy both of these objectives is to sell for no cash down.

Cash demands bring slow sales

Time and time again a perfectly saleable business with a fair price tag sits on the market without moving. Chances are it's a typical listing with a high down payment demand. The truth is, most businesses either don't sell, or they sell fast enough to satisfy sellers because they narrowed the number of possible buyers to a precious few by demanding a high down payment. But what if one of those precious few who do have the money decides not to buy? To stimulate a fast sale you can expand the market dramatically by including those who don't have substantial cash. Obviously many more people could buy without cash than with it. That's the thought process that makes quick sales!

My client Cal S. had a superette for sale for over a year and just couldn't consummate a deal. The business grossed $500,000 annually and always showed a respectable net profit. Cal was asking $150,000 with $50,000 down. Business brokers and others within the industry insisted the price was consistent with prices for comparable stores. Cal couldn't dig up a buyer, even though he advertised every week in the "opportunity" section of the *Boston Globe*, and exhausted the efforts of seven local business brokers.

There was sufficient buyer interest, with Cal receiving inquiries from 30 people, but the story was always the same. The down payment threw up a big stumbling block. Not one of the 30 would-be buyers wanted to invest $50,000.

At this point I offered to put a no-cash-down ad in the *Globe*: Superette, NO CASH DOWN. Sales $500,000. Price only $200,000 on good terms to responsible buyer.

That $17 ad prompted over 400 phone calls. Notice we didn't offer the business for $150,000 but for $200,000. Why not? If the number-one concern of buyers is the down payment, the price becomes secondary if the business can comfortably pay it off. We screened the phone calls, setting up appointments for the 12 buyers who displayed the strongest backgrounds.

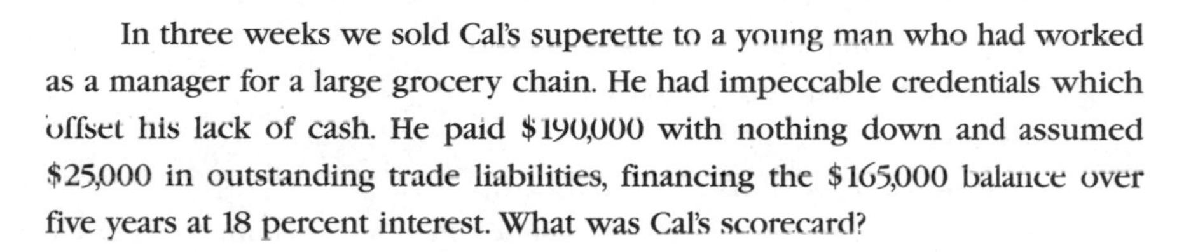

In three weeks we sold Cal's superette to a young man who had worked as a manager for a large grocery chain. He had impeccable credentials which offset his lack of cash. He paid $190,000 with nothing down and assumed $25,000 in outstanding trade liabilities, financing the $165,000 balance over five years at 18 percent interest. What was Cal's scorecard?

Cal sacrificed a $50,000 down payment with which he would have paid off the liabilities—walking away with only $95,000 in his own pocket. But don't feel bad for Cal. He originally was willing to take back a $100,000 note for five years at 12 percent interest. Instead, he'll receive $165,000 at 18 percent. Here's how it breaks down in real numbers:

Original deal

Cash to Seller:	
Net cash to seller on down payment	$ 25,000
Interest on $25,000 at 14%, if invested	15,500
Total payback: $100,000 X 12% X 5 years =	146,670
Total cash to seller:	$187,170

Actual deal	
Down payment:	0
Total payback: $165,000 X 18% X 5 years =	243,780
Total cash to seller:	$243,780

Cal came out ahead by a whopping $56,610! Equally important, he now enjoys his retirement playing golf every day at his Arizona country club. He says, "It sure beats putting cans of peas on the shelf and hoping somebody will walk in and write a $50,000 check."

note
There aren't many buyers who can raise $20,000 to $50,000 for a down payment—especially wage earners buying their first small business.

The problem grows more acute if the business doesn't appeal to masses of buyers. A superette would attract the largest number of buyers, regardless of the terms, because it falls within that broad range of businesses that almost anyone can operate without special training, experience, or education. It's appropriate for either men or women. Despite all those plusses, Cal still couldn't find a buyer with $50,000 in a city with over 1 million people. What would the odds be in Horseshoe, Wyoming?

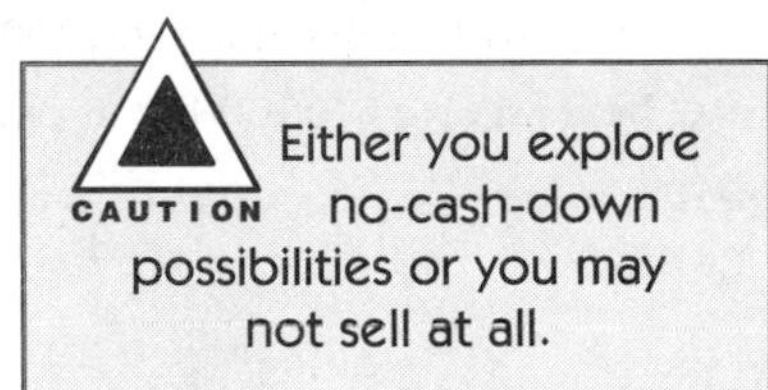

CAUTION
Either you explore no-cash-down possibilities or you may not sell at all.

Consider a business requiring a specialized background. What if Cal were selling a pharmacy? At any given time there aren't more than 15 to 20 young pharmacists in Boston capable of taking over a drugstore.

Less now—for more later

Cal's story showed you how no cash down can get you on the golf course sooner, but it offers a second message: Take less now in exchange for more later.

note

Buyers will pay a premium for no-cash-down terms. When I represent a no-cash-down buyer I expect the seller to make up for it on the other end, whether through a higher price, higher interest rates, or some other concession. An astute buyer will realize he'll have to give up points for no cash down, but he/she will try to sacrifice as few as possible. The seller, on the other hand, will want to strike a bonanza for his generosity, and you can strike a bonanza if you play it right. As with every deal, playing it right depends on knowing your adversary—and a few tricks.

Most buyers will buy any business on any terms at almost any price if they can get in with little or no money of their own. Even unprofitable businesses are grabbed up by no-cash-down buyers, and I have seen sellers forgo a small down payment for a selling price triple the original asking price!

Why? Buyers are down-payment conscious because the down payment presents the most immediate concern and an overwhelming stumbling block if they have no money. In contrast, they often view price as only so many dollars a month they must pay the seller. Once the buyer is satisfied the business can make those payments and return a healthy income to boot, price is no object.

What about interest rates? If the sharp buyer with money in his/her pocket will zero in on interest rates as a key bargaining item, the no-cash-down buyer will consider them nothing more than an extension of price.

HOT spot

Remember, the buyer's objective is to eliminate his stumbling block, the down payment, while the seller's chief concern is to sell on terms that will ultimately put the largest amount of dollars in his pocket. The two objectives can co-exist.

I know from experience that a "cash" buyer can bargain very low interest rates on the seller's part of the financing, and these hard-bargain rates can be as low as one-half of bank rates. But can you see a buyer without a penny in his pocket driving a hard bargain to save a few points on interest?

Cal understood the psychology of no-cash-down buyers. So did Fillmore, a "horse trader" who started out in real estate. He bought older homes at low prices, paying quick cash to desperate sellers, then he put the house right back on the market for 30 to 50 percent more. When he sold, however, he focused on no-cash-down terms. By age 35 Fillmore had earned profits of $1 million, represented by mortgages on the homes he sold. At 18 percent interest on this profit, he figured he could afford to wait for his fortune to roll in. Theorizing that this approach could work on business deals, "no-cash-down Fillmore" set out to make his second fortune. On his first deal he picked up a small general store in town. The seller's husband had just died and she was desperate to get out as quickly as possible with ready cash. The store was for sale for $80,000, but Fillmore didn't care what they asked. He pulled the "suitcase full of money" stunt. When he met the bereaved widow, he said he "might" be interested but he'd only pay $50,000. Opening his suitcase loaded with $100 bills, he offered it to her. The widow snapped it up.

With his millions, Fillmore had no intention of operating a little general store. A week after he bought it, he placed an ad in the newspaper.

General store owner must sell — $100,000, $10,000 down.

Buyers flocked to the deal. Most didn't have $10,000, but those were exactly the ones Fillmore wanted. To the lucky successful buyer, he said, "Young man, if you can't come up with $10,000 I can't sell to you." He stuffed his pipe with fresh tobacco, looked up and continued. "However, since I think you would do a good job, I'll tell you what I'll do. Make the price $114,000 and pay it off over five years at current bank rates and it's yours." The ecstatic buyer signed a binder, ran to the phone and shouted, "Hey Ma! I'm in business."

> **HOT spot** This could be the most important lesson in your life: You can sell a business for huge dollars if you'll forget the small dollars up front.

Fillmore bought a business on Tuesday for $50,000 cash and sold it the following Monday for a $64,000 profit. The buyer didn't fare badly either. The store was the starting point of a successful career that made him wealthy. So what if he paid a few more dollars for his first business? Over a period of years it made him rich.

The best investment you'll ever make

note

What constitutes a fair return on an investment? Considering such factors as liquidity, safety, and taxes depends on the nature of the investment. Suppose you invest in the business you're selling. What return will now satisfy you?

Having sold over 40 businesses for no cash down, Fillmore contends a good return is 300 percent, excluding interest. Here's how he explains it.

"If I have a business that would typically sell for $100,000 with $20,000 down, I figure I can boost the price to $140,000 and peddle it any day of the week with no down payment. Since I'm lending the buyer $20,000, and since it's the only way he can get the business, he'll agree to a 40 percent higher price. I not only get back my $20,000, I receive another $40,000 in the process, The buyer's interest payments on the entire $140,000 gives me a healthy bonus!" Intrigued with Fillmore's ideas, I tried my hand at it when I came across a drugstore for sale.

It was a perfect setup. The seller was anxious to sell for only $30,000 cash. I signed a contract to buy, but before I took title to it I sold it after one phone call to an old college classmate looking for his own drugstore. I went into my spiel. "I have a super drugstore for sale for only $60,000 with no cash down." In two days my classmate was in business and I was back at my desk with his $60,000 secured note at 16 percent interest.

Was my drugstore beginner's luck? I don't think so. I may not do as well on every deal, but it beats almost any other investment I have ever made. I have done many such deals since, picking up a business for a few dollars and selling it for a giant profit on paper. Many clients trying to figure out the best way to sell have followed in my path. Next week I'm going to close a small deal for a client just learning no-cash-down lessons. Just three months ago he bought a run-down cheese and fruit shop for only $6,000. It was a tiny store with hardly any stock, but my client did absolutely nothing to improve it. How is he selling it? For $30,000 payable over three years—a five-fold return on his investment! The best part is he never spent $6,000 to buy it in the first place because he assumed $3,000 in payables. His new buyer agreed to assume the same trade payables, giving my client a $30,000 profit without a dime invested. Could he have done as well had he looked for a buyer with a large down payment? I doubt it.

What are you really giving away?

Big no-cash-down dividends are only half the equation. The average business sale requires a 25 percent down payment. On a $200,000 deal with a $50,000 down payment you stuff only $20,000 into your wallet after paying off hypothetical liabilities of $30,000.

Unless you're desperate for $20,000 cash, latch onto a buyer with no cash, sell him/her the business for $250,000, and have the buyer assume the liabilities. That would give you a $50,000 bonus later instead of $20,000 today.

But I need cash now!

If that's your predicament, then it's easily solved. You can walk away from a no-cash-down sale with as much money as you would get from a sale requiring a hefty down payment, and that can be plenty of cash! Just don't expect it to come out of the buyer's pocket. Remember Fillmore and his $114,000 general store? True, Fillmore walked away from that deal with nothing but $114,000 worth of paper, plus future interest, but he could have exercised other options that could have given him immediate cash. He could have proposed that the buyer obtain a $60,000 loan on the business from a bank, with Fillmore accepting a second mortgage for $54,000. If the buyer didn't have an adequate credit rating to swing the $60,000 loan, Fillmore could have guaranteed it. Would it have mattered to the buyer? Of course not. He would still be paying $114,000 on the same terms, but he would just break it into two separate loans. The point is that Fillmore could have had $60,000 cash plus a $54,000 note.

Or consider the business selling for $200,000 with $50,000 down. Assume you agreed to hold a note for the $150,000 balance and could look forward to a $20,000 balance from the down payment after paying off creditors. Why not urge the buyer to borrow $100,000 against the business with you accepting a note for the balance? On the original deal you would have sold for a net price of $170,000 based on $200,000 less $30,000 in payables. The $170,000 is in the form of $20,000 in cash from the balance of the down payment and $150,000 in notes.

Using this method you'd probably be able to sell for $125,000 financed by:

$ 100,000	Mortgage from bank
120,000	Note to you
30,000	Liabilities to be assumed
$250,000	Purchase Price

You actually increased your walk-away money from $20,000 to $100,000, and you made an extra $50,000 with the increased price. The buyer still gets your business without spending a dime of his own.

HINT
Use your imagination. Don't be a psychological slave to a few dollars down.

A promise is not a payment

How can you sell a business for no cash down without knowing for certain you will get paid?

Many sellers quote a down payment requirement because they think a buyer's $25,000 down proves he's a person of substance, reducing his risk on the balance.

Others say, "I need a down payment to cover the value of the inventory." It all comes out to the same thing: The seller wants security.

You can't blame sellers for this attitude. A promise is not a payment, and the woods are full of birds who'll promise anything to get their hands on your business then let you whistle for a check to arrive in the mail.

If Fillmore had bargained for a $20,000 down payment, to what extent would that have given him added security on the $94,000 balance? Not much.

What could go wrong? Everything. The buyer could back up a truck, move the inventory and futures out, and take off for Wyoming. Where is Fillmore's security then?

Maybe the buyer is not a crook, but belongs to the fraternity of "Lousy Business people," who are as common as sparrows in springtime. Then you may see the inventory slowly but surely dwindle as losses cut into credit and cash flow. Good will vanishes as customers patronize competitors. Finally the business folds with Fillmore holding his $94,000 note.

Unfortunately, unless you sell your business for cash, you always incur a risk of not collecting the balance. If security is your number-one concern, perhaps you should consider an all-cash sale, but unless you have an unusual deal you'll pay a price for

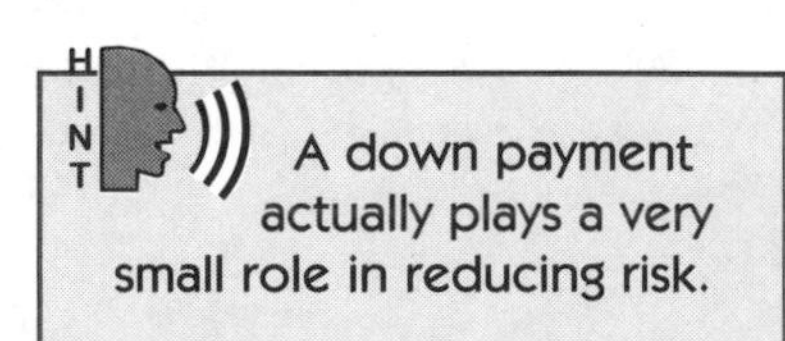

HINT
A down payment actually plays a very small role in reducing risk.

escaping risk. You'll get a much lower selling price and face considerable difficulty finding a buyer with so much cash.

The risk/benefit ratio for sellers

I asked no-cash-down Fillmore about the risk involved in turning keys over without cash in return.

Fillmore offered a simple philosophy. He answered, "Son, when I sell a business for paper, one of two things happens. Either the buyer fulfills his obligations and makes all the payments, or I foreclose, taking back the business and selling it again. Of course, I keep all the payments he made in the meantime. Sometimes I get an even better price the second time around."

That sounded reasonable, but I had other concerns. What if the buyer starts with $100,000 in inventory and it's down to $50,000 by the time you foreclose? Isn't the business worth $50,000 less?" That question required yet another pipeful of tobacco. "Sure, but it never happens to me. I tie up the buyer so I can foreclose even if he looks at me the wrong way, let alone drains my inventory or otherwise reduces the value of the collateral. It's all in the paperwork and how well you screen and monitor the buyer. That, not the down payment, guarantees you'll get paid one way or the other."

E-Z TIP

Set up your deal so you can't lose. Either you get your payments or you get the business back with the collateral intact. That's the only way to operate if you're financing any part of the purchase price.

Formulas for airtight deals

I promised to stay away from legal jargon that your lawyer will handle, but a businessperson must know a little about law for self protection.

Examine these methods for securing your note. Fillmore calls them the "can't-lose formulas."

- Secure the buyer's note with a mortgage (security agreement) on the business's assets. In the event the buyer defaults, you can foreclose and take over the assets without assuming the buyer's outstanding liabilities. This is so elementary, few attorneys will overlook it, but other methods are less well- known.

- Require the buyer to maintain inventory at required levels. As Fillmore explains, "It's no good if I give the buyer $50,000 in inventory and he runs it down to $25,000. I stick a clause in my mortgages that forces the buyer to maintain a specific level of inventory. If it dips below that level I can foreclose." Standard mortgage forms do not contain this vital safeguard. Tell your lawyer about it, and he'll agree that it makes sense.

- Take an "assignment of lease" as further collateral. This can be the most important weapon in your self-protection arsenal—an agreement between landlord, seller, and buyer that lets the seller step in and take over the buyer's lease if the buyer defaults on his note to the seller. If location is an asset, Fillmore always demands it. He puts it into perspective in this discussion about his $114,000 general store. "Let's suppose the buyer defaults. With my security agreement (mortgage) I can foreclose and take over the inventory and fixtures and sell them to someone else. But what are they worth if I can't give the new buyer a lease? When selling the business again I want a viable ongoing business. I don't want to auction it off. Otherwise, I can't get top dollar to recoup what's owed to me." Good ol' Fillmore with his fourth-grade education should be teaching law at Harvard.

- The instant-default clause is also a favorite of people like Fillmore. The standard note provides that the seller cannot foreclose or take back the business as long as payments come on time. Fillmore told me of one experience that forced him to invent the "instant default" clause. He sold a hobby shop for $150,000 (after buying it for $84,000 one month earlier). Since it was a no-cash sale Fillmore accepted a secured note for the full $150,000, a clause requiring the buyer to maintain inventory at $80,000, and an assignment of the lease. When the business was sold it grossed $600,000 a year Unfortunately, the buyer didn't tend to business and sales went downhill. Fillmore watched the business go on the skids, but he could do nothing because the buyer made all his payments on time and maintained a $80,000 inventory. If the buyer eventually went belly-up Fillmore would end up with a ruined business.

Sure enough, two years after Fillmore sold the business the payments stopped. The business was destroyed to the point where Fillmore could get only $80,000 for it, and since he was still owed a balance of $96,000 on his original $150,000 note, he "lost" $16,000 on the deal. Actually, Fillmore didn't lose because his profits on the deal were simply reduced from $66,000 to $50,000 for one month's work. But Fillmore learned a lesson. He now writes into all his notes a provision that allows him to foreclose at any time he deems himself insecure. "Now," says Fillmore, When I see a buyer doing anything that can hurt the business, I can step right in and take it back. That's real protection."

Of course Fillmore doesn't overlook all the other methods for increasing security. He'll try to get a mortgage on the buyer's house or car, and he'll get as many signatures on the note as possible. Fillmore laughs at conventional sellers. "They'll sell a business for $100,000, accept $25,000 down, and think they have it made. But they don't really protect themselves. When the business flops, they pick up a few more dollars but still face a

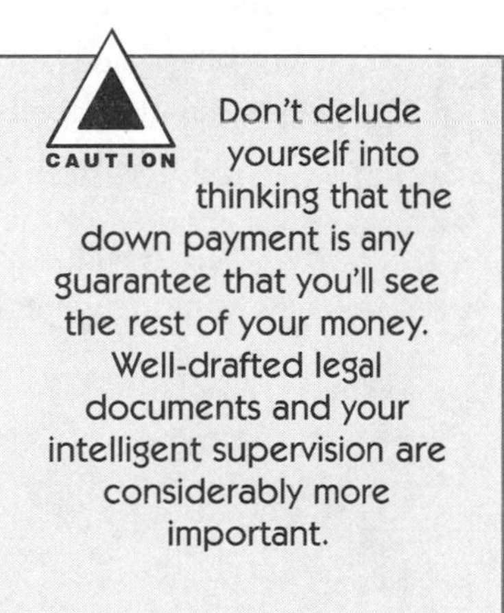

CAUTION
Don't delude yourself into thinking that the down payment is any guarantee that you'll see the rest of your money. Well-drafted legal documents and your intelligent supervision are considerably more important.

whopping loss. Not me. It's not what's up front that counts—it's setting up the deal so you get it all—no matter what happens. I like 'airtight' deals with no leaks." I agree with Fillmore.

Beware the phonies with Rolex watches

I have nothing against Rolex watches. They are among the world's finest timepieces. But they don't really care whose wrists they adorn.

I first met a phony buyer sporting a $10,000 Presidential Rolex ten years ago. He was negotiating to buy my client's moped dealership, and was angling for no-cash-down on a $125,000 purchase price. I was blinded by the glare of this buyer's watch, his Brooks Brothers suit, and Hathaway shirt. His "Mr. Solid" image was fortified by the new Jaguar parked outside my office and his deep tan recently obtained at his Palm Beach villa. Who wouldn't be impressed? He looked impeccable, spoke "money," and oozed success. Anyone should gladly accept his note for any amount with no further questions. We fell for it. Two months after taking over (and ripping off) the moped place, "Mr. Solid" declared personal bankruptcy with liabilities of $2,800,000. His only declared asset was one Rolex watch. I tell this story to underscore a most important point. As a seller you want payment, not promises. When you're gambling that your buyer can make the business work, check him or her out. Probe into the prospective buyer's work record, personal credit, work habits, and lifestyle.

I'd rather go with a hard-working guy without a penny to his name who knows his stuff than a phony flashing a Rolex.

From no cash to comfortable retirement in five years

Get in with no cash and sell on no-cash terms and you could see enough money coming in to keep you in style for a lifetime. That's what Everett did.

He bought a small steak and beer restaurant in 1971 for $150,000 without a dime of his own, using creative financing to get the keys. The seller agreed to finance $100,000 with the remaining $50,000 coming through $20,000 in seller's debts (assumed by Everett), $14,000 from cash flow, and a short-term $16,000 loan from a meat supplier. He expanded the restaurant twice and added an upstairs "function room" for parties. Sales increased from $400,000 to over $1 million by 1976, at which point Everett owned the business free and clear and decided to sell. He figured it was worth $400,000 with a conventional $100,000 to $150,000 down payment,

But Everett decided to make it available to a responsible no-cash-down buyer—his night manager with whom he had worked side by side for years.

Everett structured the deal for his own retirement, selling the restaurant for $550,000—with no cash down—payable over ten years at 18 percent interest. Everett had it made. He would live on the $100,000 a year interest payments and preserve the principal. Everett enjoyed his retirement at the ripe old age of 43. Of course he didn't really retire but began dabbling in other small businesses to keep his entrepreneurial juices flowing. Everett knew how to get started without capital, and he knew how to increase his wealth by selling to somebody else without capital.

As Everett says, "If I didn't have the imagination and courage to find ways to overcome my empty wallet, I'd be a short-order cook working for somebody else for $300 a week."

Key points to remember

- You want to sell as quickly as possible and for as much as possible. No-cash-down deals accomplish both those objectives.

- Don't limit your market. There's no such thing as a buyer "without cash."

- Buyers are down-payment conscious. Give up a few dollars now for a lot more later.

- Reinvest your down payment. It could earn you as much as 300 percent interest.

- You can sell for no cash down and still walk away with plenty of money.

- Sell your business on airtight terms to guarantee your payments.

- Your best security is a no-nonsense buyer.

- Buy for no cash down and sell on the same terms . . . it can make you wealthy.

Resources

Where you'll find these Resources:

••• Online Resources •••

- **America's Business Funding Directory**

  http://www.business finance.com/search.asp

- **AOL.COM Business & Careers**

  http://www.aol.com/webcenters/workplace/home.adp

- **BizMove.com**

  http://www.bizmove.com

- **BusinessTown.Com**

  http://www.businesstown.com

- **EntrepreneurMag.com**

  http://www.entrepreneurmag.com

- **Commercial Law League of America**

  http://www.clla.org

- **Consumer Counseling Centers of America, Inc.**

  http://www.consumercounseling.org/about.html

- **Credit Information Exchange**

  http://www.rmahq.org/ciex/ciex.html

- **Creditworthy, Co.**

  http://www.creditworthy.com

- **Council of Better Business Bureaus, Inc.**

  http://www.bbb.org

- **Dun & Bradstreet, Inc.**

  http://www.dnb.com

- **Education Index, Business Resources**

  http://www.educationindex.com/bus

- **Electric Library® Business Edition**

  http://www.business.elibrary.com

- **National Association of Small Business Investment Companies**

  http://www.nasbic.org

- **National Foundation for Women Business Owners (NFWBO)**

  http://www.nfwbo.org

- **National Small Business Development Center (SBDC) Research Network**

  http://www.smallbiz.suny.edu

- **Small Business Primer**
  http://www.ces.ncsu.edu/depts/fcs/business/welcome.html
- **U.S. Business Advisor**
  http://www.business.gov
- **U.S. Small Business Administration**
  http://www.sbaonline.sba.gov/starting

••• Related Sites •••

- **Equifax, Inc.**
  http://www.equifax.com
- **Experian Information Solutions, Inc.**
  http://www.experian.com
- **Institute of Certified Financial Planners**
  http://www.icfp.org
- **International Association for Financial Planning**
  http://www.iafp.org
- **Mining Company, The**
  Small Business Information
  http://sbinformation.miningco.com/msub2.htm?rf=dp&COB=home
- **National Association of Personal Financial Advisors**
  http://www.napfa.org

- **National Foundation for Consumer Credit (NFCC)**

  http://www.nfcc.org

- **National Technical Information Service Technology Administration**

  U.S. Department of Commerce

  http://www.ntis.gov/

  http://www4.law.cornell.edu/uscode/11

- **Trans Union LLC**

  http://www.transunion.com

- **United States Department of Commerce**

  National Technical Information Service

  FedWorld Information

  http://www.fedworld.gov

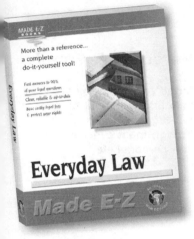

E-Z to load, E-Z to run, E-Z to use!

For our complete list of titles, call 1-800-822-4566
or visit our web site: www.MadeE-Z.com

Legal

Easy to understand text explains how to fill out and file forms to perform all the legal tasks you need to—without all those legal fees!

Financial

Make smart investment decisions to secure your financial future. Expert advice to make more money, and keep and protect more of what you have made.

MADE E-Z™ PRODUCTS

Made E-Z Products, 384 S. Military Trail, Deerfield Beach, FL 33442
(800) 822-4566 • fax: (954) 480-8906
web site: http://www.MadeE-Z.com

ss 2001.r1

	ITEM #	QTY.	PRICE‡	EXTENSION
Made E-Z Software				
E-Z Construction Estimator	SS4300		$24.95	
E-Z Contractors' Forms	SS4301		$24.95	
Contractors' Business Builder Software Bundle	SS4002		$49.95	
Corporate Secretary	SS4003		$24.95	
Asset Protection Made E-Z	SS4304		$24.95	
Corporate Records Made E-Z	SS4305		$24.95	
Vital Records Made E-Z	SS4306		$24.95	
Managing Employees	SS4307		$24.95	
Accounting Made E-Z	SS4308		$24.95	
Limited Liability Companies (LLC)	SS4309		$24.95	
Partnerships	SS4310		$24.95	
Solving IRS Problems	SS4311		$24.95	
Winning In Small Claims Court	SS4312		$24.95	
Collecting Unpaid Bills Made E-Z	SS4313		$24.95	
Selling On The Web (E-Commerce)	SS4314		$24.95	
Your Profitable Home Business Made E-Z	SS4315		$24.95	
Get Out Of Debt Made E-Z	SS4317		$24.95	
E-Z Business Lawyer Library	SS4318		$49.95	
E-Z Estate Planner	SS4319		$49.95	
E-Z Personal Lawyer Library	SS4320		$49.95	
Payroll Made E-Z	SS4321		$24.95	
Personal Legal Forms and Agreements	SS4322		$24.95	
Business Legal Forms and Agreements	SS4323		$24.95	
Employee Policies and Manuals	SS4324		$24.95	
Incorporation Made E-Z	SW1176		$24.95	
Last Wills Made E-Z	SW1177		$24.95	
Everyday Law Made E-Z	SW1185		$24.95	
Everyday Legal Forms & Agreements Made E-Z	SW1186		$24.95	
Business Startups Made E-Z	SW1192		$24.95	
Credit Repair Made E-Z	SW2211		$24.95	
Business Forms Made E-Z	SW2223		$24.95	
Buying and Selling A Business Made E-Z	SW2242		$24.95	
Marketing Your Small Business Made E-Z	SW2245		$24.95	
Get Out Of Debt Made E-Z	SW2246		$24.95	
Winning Business Plans Made E-Z	SW2247		$24.95	
Successful Resumes Made E-Z	SW2248		$24.95	
Solving Business Problems Made E-Z	SW 2249		$24.95	
Profitable Mail Order Made E-Z	SW2250		$24.95	
Deluxe Business Forms	SW2251		$49.95	
E-Z Small Business Library	SW2252		$49.95	
Sub-total for Software				$
Made E-Z Guides				
Bankruptcy Made E-Z	G300		$14.95	
Incorporation Made E-Z	G301		$14.95	
Divorce Made E-Z	G302		$14.95	
Credit Repair Made E-Z	G303		$14.95	
Living Trusts Made E-Z	G305		$14.95	
Living Wills Made E-Z	G306		$14.95	
Last Will & Testament Made E-Z	G307		$14.95	
Buying/Selling Your Home Made E-Z	G311		$14.95	
Employment Law Made E-Z	G312		$14.95	
Collecting Child Support Made E-Z	G315		$14.95	
Limited Liability Companies Made E-Z	G316		$14.95	
Partnerships Made E-Z	G318		$14.95	
Solving IRS Problems Made E-Z	G319		$14.95	
Asset Protection Made E-Z	G320		$14.95	
Buying/Selling A Business Made E-Z	G321		$14.95	
Financing Your Business Made E-Z	G322		$14.95	
Profitable Mail Order Made E-Z	G323		$14.95	
Selling On The Web Made E-Z	G324		$14.95	
SBA Loans Made E-Z	G325		$14.95	
Solving Business Problems Made E-Z	G326		$14.95	
Advertising Your Business Made E-Z	G327		$14.95	
Shoestring Investing Made E-Z	G330		$14.95	
Stock Market Investing Made E-Z	G331		$14.95	
Fund Raising Made E-Z	G332		$14.95	
Money For College Made E-Z	G334		$14.95	
Marketing Your Small Business Made E-Z	G335		$14.95	

‡ Prices are for a single item, and are subject to change without notice.

See an item in this book you would like to order?

1. Photocopy this order form.
2. Complete your order and mail to:

MADE E•Z PRODUCTS

384 S Military Trail
Deerfield Beach, FL 33442
www.MadeE-Z.com

CONTRACTORS' CORNER

...when contractors need it in writing!

All the forms and software for builders, electricians, plumbers, sub-contractors, painters, and other trades.

www.contractorsforms.com

Company Purchase Orders welcome with approved credit.

All orders ship UPS Ground unless otherwise specified.

continued on next page

	ITEM #	QTY.	PRICE‡	EXTENSION
ıg A No-Cash-Down Business Made E-Z	G336		$14.95	
›re Investing Made E-Z	G337		$14.95	
evel Marketing Made E-Z	G338		$14.95	
ıt Of Debt Made E-Z	G340		$14.95	
›rofitable Home Business Made E-Z	G341		$14.95	
ng Business Plans Made E-Z	G342		$14.95	
l Fund Investing Made E-Z	G343		$14.95	
ss Startups Made E-Z	G344		$14.95	
ssful Resumes Made E-Z	G346		$14.95	
tuff For Everyone Made E-Z	G347		$14.95	
Sub-total for Guides				$
ıde E-Z Kits				
uptcy Kit	K300		$24.95	
›oration Kit	K301		$24.95	
e Kit	K302		$24.95	
Repair Kit	K303		$24.95	
Trust Kit	K305		$24.95	
Will Kit	K306		$24.95	
'ill & Testament Kit	K307		$19.95	
; and Selling Your Home Kit	K311		$24.95	
›yment Law Kit	K312		$24.95	
d Liability Company Kit	K316		$24.95	
ess Startups Kit	K320		$24.95	
Business/Home Business Kit	K321		$24.95	
Sub-total for Kits				$
ıde E-Z Books				
lay Legal Forms & Agreements Made E-Z	BK407		$24.95	
ınel Forms Made E-Z	BK408		$24.95	
ting Unpaid Bills Made E-Z	BK409		$24.95	
rate Records Made E-Z	BK410		$24.95	
lay Law Made E-Z	BK411		$24.95	
ecords Made E-Z	BK412		$24.95	
ss Forms Made E-Z	BK414		$24.95	
Sub-total for Books				$
ıbor Law Posters				
eral Labor Law	LP001		$14.95	
Specific Labor Law e state listings below			$39.95	

State	Item#	QTY
AL	83801	
AK	83802	
AZ	83803	
AR	83804	
CA	83805	
CO	83806	
CT	83807	
DE	83808	
DC	83848	
FL	83809	
GA	83810	
HI	83811	
ID	83812	
IL	83813	
IN	83814	
IO	83815	
KS	83816	
KY	83817	
LA	83818	
ME	83819	
MD	83820	
MA	83821	
MI	83822	
MN	83823	
MS	83824	
MO	83825	
MT	83826	
NE	83827	
NV	83828	
NH	83829	
NJ	83830	
NM	83831	
NY	83832	
NC	83833	
ND	83834	
OH	83835	
OK	83836	
OR	83837	
PA	83838	
RI	83839	
SC	83840	
S. Dakota not available		
TN	83842	
TX	83843	
UT	83844	
VT	83845	
VA	83846	
WA	83847	
WV	83849	
WI	83850	
WY	83851	

☆ Required by Federal & State Laws

Sub-total for Posters	$
AL FOR ALL PRODUCTS	$
hipping & Handling for first item, $1.50 for each additional item	$
AL PRODUCTS and S & H	$
da Residents add 6% sales tax	$
AL OF ORDER	$

are for a single item, and are subject to change without notice.

❊ FOR FASTER SERVICE ❊

Order by phone: **(954) 480-8933**

Order by fax: **(954) 480-8906**

r3

Name

Company

Position

Address

City

State Zip

Phone
( )

PAYMENT

❑ check enclosed, payable to:
Made E-Z Products, Inc.
384 S. Military Trail
Deerfield Beach, FL 33442

❑ charge my credit card: ❑ MasterCard ❑ VISA

ACCOUNT NO. EXP. DATE

Signature: (required for credit card purchases)

See an item in this book you would like to order?

1. Photocopy this order form.
2. Complete your order and mail to:

MADE E•Z PRODUCTS

384 S Military Trail
Deerfield Beach, FL 33442
www.MadeE-Z.com

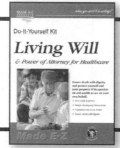

Index

A-D

E-L

M-P

R-W